KU-392-738

The Stalin Affair

Also by Giles Milton

NON-FICTION

The Riddle and the Knight

Nathaniel's Nutmeg

Big Chief Elizabeth

Samurai William

White Gold

Paradise Lost

Wolfram

Russian Roulette

Fascinating Footnotes from History

Churchill's Ministry of Ungentlemanly Warfare

D-Day

Checkmate in Berlin

FICTION

Edward Trencom's Nose

According to Arnold

The Perfect Corpse

The Stalin Affair

The Impossible Alliance that Won the War

GILES MILTON

JOHN MURRAY

First published in Great Britain in 2024 by John Murray (Publishers)

1

A CIP catalogue record for this title is available from the British Library

Hardback ISBN 978-1-529-39851-9
Trade Paperback ISBN 978-1-529-39852-6
ebook ISBN 978-1-529-39853-3

Typeset in Bembo by Hewer Text UK Ltd, Edinburgh
Printed and bound in Great Britain by Clays Ltd, Elcograf S.p.A.

John Murray policy is to use papers that are natural, renewable and recyclable products and made from wood grown in sustainable forests. The logging and manufacturing processes are expected to conform to the environmental regulations of the country of origin.

Carmelite House
50 Victoria Embankment
London EC4Y 0DZ

www.johnmurraypress.co.uk

John Murray Press, part of Hodder & Stoughton Limited
An Hachette UK company

For my late mother, Jo

Contents

Author's Note

This is a true story. Anything enclosed in quotation marks is reported dialogue, any description of daily life is taken from letters, diaries, and memoirs. Many of these accounts were hastily written and never intended for publication. I have standardised spelling and rectified grammar to make them easier to read. References to the original documents can be found in the endnotes.

I have also spelled out most (but not all) acronyms and abbreviations: thus FO becomes Foreign Office and ACK becomes Archibald Clark Kerr. But some, like NKVD (People's Commissariat for Internal Affairs, precursor to the KGB), remain as acronyms. And PM, as most British readers will know, means prime minister. There is little consistency to my method: my objective has been clarity.

Likewise with the transliteration of Russian names: I have used the preferred spelling of the British and Americans living in Moscow during the war and have followed the same rule for place names. Thus Arkhangelsk is Archangel, as it always was in the 1940s.

One of the principal characters in this book, Archibald Clark Kerr, insisted that everyone should call him Archie, a most unusual break from diplomatic convention. I have followed his wish and extended this informality to the other main characters as well. There is good reason for doing so: Kathleen Harriman was known to everyone as Kathy, and her father, Averell Harriman, was always Averell, or Ave.

Stalin, however, must remain as Stalin. He was not amused when told that his nickname was 'Uncle Joe'.

There is only one thing worse than fighting with allies, and that is fighting without them!

Winston Churchill, 1944

Prelude

Midsummer Night, 1941

It was the shortest night of the year.

The sky to the west was still streaked with light, but in the Soviet borderlands, which stretched from the Baltic to the Black Sea, it was finally dark. The waning moon appeared as no more than a faint glance of silver.

Along the entire Soviet frontier, 1,800 miles in length, the greatest army in history was crouched in the shadows. Infantry, gunners, drivers, mechanics; all were watching and waiting. More than three million battle-hardened troops of the German Wehrmacht were on the highest alert, having just received news that Operation Barbarossa was to be launched that very night. The Nazi invasion of the Soviet Union was poised to begin.

Those three million soldiers were in the vanguard of a vast mechanised army that had already steamrollered across Europe. Poland, Norway, Denmark, Belgium, the Low Countries, and France – all had been crushed by the Nazis. Now the Wehrmacht was to take on its most formidable enemy to date, Stalin's Red Army. Hitler and his generals were confident of success, for their invading force included 3,350 tanks, 2,770 aircraft, and 7,184 artillery pieces, as well as 600,000 trucks and 600,000 horses. No fewer than 148 divisions had been assembled into three gigantic army groups designated North, Centre, and South. They were to thrust deep into Soviet territory with the aim of capturing Leningrad, Moscow, and the Soviet Ukraine. Hitler was determined to triumph where Napoleon and his Grande Armée had so spectacularly failed.

In the early hours of Sunday, 22 June 1941, German artillery troops began removing the camouflage netting from their guns and dragging them from their shelters. Soldiers synchronised their watches; whispered last-minute instructions. In Army Group Centre, they checked the waterproof screens on tanks that were to ford the River Bug. It was 2 a.m. German time, and the air was heavy with suspense. Within the hour, the panzers would fire their engines, belching diesel fumes into the night sky.

On the Soviet side of the frontier all was quiet. In scores of villages, farmers, workers, and housewives had long since taken to their beds, unaware that their lives were about to be turned upside down. Similarly unprepared were the Red Army border guards. Most lacked weaponry. All lacked information.

Just a few weeks earlier, Hitler had warned his generals that Operation Barbarossa would require a wholly new form of warfare in which brutality was to be a weapon of war. 'This is a war of extermination,' he said. 'Commanders must be prepared to sacrifice their personal scruples.'[1] Captured Soviet officers, saboteurs, and partisans were to be summarily shot, along with hundreds of thousands of Jews. Entire populations were to be liquidated, in order that Germans could have more 'lebensraum', or living space. No less malign was the Führer's 'Hunger Plan' which would be used to starve to death millions of Soviet citizens.

Hitler was confident of a rapid victory. 'We will only have to kick in the door,' he said, 'and the whole rotten edifice will come crashing down.'[2] He expected triumphant German troops to be parading through Moscow within months, if not weeks.

The Führer had laid the groundwork for victory earlier that spring, luring Bulgaria, Romania, and Yugoslavia into his camp. When the pro-Nazi government of Yugoslavia had been overthrown in a pro-Western military coup – an unexpected setback – Hitler had invaded the country and forced Belgrade's capitulation in just ten days. Now, with Western, Central, and Eastern Europe under his thumb, the path was open for his greatest victory of all. Great Britain alone had the potential to upset his plans, but she was in grave peril that summer. Hitler's U-boats were sinking British ships at a faster rate than they could be replaced.

Two years earlier, in the summer of 1939, Hitler and Stalin had stunned the world by signing a formal treaty of friendship. After much behind-the-scenes negotiation, it was announced that their long-standing enmity had been overcome and the two dictators were now allies. Political leaders in Europe and America waited aghast to see what would happen next.

They didn't have to wait long, for the consequences of the Nazi-Soviet Pact* became apparent within weeks. One of its secret clauses divided Poland into two halves, with the western half to be swallowed by Nazi Germany and the eastern half by the Soviet Union. On 1 September 1939, the Führer had invaded western Poland, leading Britain and France to declare war on Germany. This marked the beginning of the Second World War.

Three weeks later, Stalin had sent his Red Army into eastern Poland, an occupation followed by mass killings of politicians, intellectuals, and army officers. Over the months that followed, once-independent countries were gobbled wholesale by Germany and the Soviet Union.

The Red Army occupied the three Baltic states and attacked Finland; the Wehrmacht swept into Denmark and Norway in April 1940. This was followed by Hitler's blitzkrieg invasion of France, Belgium, and the Low Countries. Throughout these long months, the Führer's alliance with Stalin underpinned his every move.

But by June 1941, the Nazi-Soviet Pact was increasingly fragile, and there were countless signs that Hitler was preparing to betray his erstwhile ally. Stalin refused to believe these signs. He turned a blind eye to Luftwaffe reconnaissance flights over Soviet territory and dismissed intelligence from a Communist sympathiser in the German Air Ministry. 'Tell the source in the staff of the German Air Force to fuck his mother!' was Stalin's response. 'This is no source, but a disinformer.'[3] He even discounted highly accurate intelligence from Richard Sorge, a Soviet agent working inside the German embassy in Tokyo.

When Moscow's British ambassador, Sir Stafford Cripps, issued his own warning – one that came directly from Winston Churchill – Stalin dismissed it as *angliiskaya provokatsiya*. He despised the British

* Officially the 'Treaty of Non-Aggression Between Germany and the USSR' and supplemented by the 'German–Soviet Boundary and Friendship Treaty'.

prime minister and was convinced he was trying to goad the Soviet Union into a war with Hitler.

Stalin's foreign commissar, Vyacheslav Molotov, was sufficiently disquieted by the rumours to summon to the Kremlin the German ambassador, Count Friedrich-Werner von der Schulenburg. He asked Schulenburg if it was true that all the embassy wives had been repatriated to Berlin. 'Not *all* the women,' said the ambassador disingenuously. '*My* wife is still in town.'[4]

The starkest warning came on the eve of the invasion when a German deserter named Arthur Liskov crossed the border and told Soviet border guards that the assault directive had just been issued to his unit. Operation Barbarossa was to begin at 4 a.m. This news was flashed to Stalin, who ordered Liskov to be shot for giving out disinformation. But he was sufficiently alarmed to place his frontier troops on high alert, although this order came with a caveat: 'The task of our forces is to refrain from any kind of provocative action.'[5]

Stalin spent that midsummer evening at his dacha in Kuntsevo, six miles from Moscow, with a small entourage of generals and advisers. At eleven o'clock, they moved to the upstairs dining room. 'Stalin kept reassuring us that Hitler would not begin the war,' recalled one of those present.[6] Even now, the Soviet leader refused to believe the intelligence.

At around two in the morning, his guests returned to their Kremlin apartments. An hour or so later, Stalin himself retired to bed.

At precisely 3.15 that morning, Sunday, 22 June, a thunderous artillery barrage shattered the silence as thousands of German guns opened up along the 1,800-mile front line. A Luftwaffe aerial armada simultaneously passed over the frontier: its mission was to wreak destruction on Soviet airfields and defensive positions.

Over the previous days, German reconnaissance planes had mapped every strategic target, including bridges, command posts, railway junctions, and power plants. Now, with clinical precision, Hitler's pilots rained havoc on the infrastructure below. They undertook their destruction with swagger, dive-bombing Soviet airfields in their nimble Stukas. Five hundred bombers, 270 dive bombers, and 480 fighter aircraft struck sixty-six Soviet bases. Virtually unchallenged, they destroyed more than twelve hundred aircraft. In one stroke, Stalin's air force had been emasculated.

German special forces were also working behind enemy lines. Disguised in Red Army uniforms, they had been parachuted into key areas and were now cutting telephone lines and communications cables. This paralysed Soviet command and control centres, causing organisational chaos.

Operation Barbarossa was the largest land offensive in the history of warfare. German bombers attacked ground targets, clearing the way for a rapid artillery advance.

Once the initial artillery bombardment had come to an end, the forward lines of German infantry began crossing the Soviet frontier. The Führer had hoped to achieve tactical surprise, and he was entirely successful, for the first wave of Wehrmacht troops steamrollered through the flimsy defences.

Hitler had long predicted a quick victory. 'When Barbarossa commences,' he said, 'the world will hold its breath.'[7] More accurately, the world watched in horrified astonishment as the Red Army collapsed in disarray. Soviet border guards emerged bleary-eyed from their barrack beds that dawn, only to find themselves staring into German gun barrels. Most were shot before they realised the enormity of what was taking place.

Stalin was asleep in Kuntsevo when General Georgy Zhukov called the dacha. A nonchalant NKVD general answered the phone.

'Comrade Stalin is sleeping.'

'Wake him immediately!' shouted Zhukov. 'The Germans are bombing our cities.'

A few minutes passed before Stalin himself came to the phone. Zhukov told him the shocking news.

'Did you understand?' he asked.

Silence.

'*Comrade Stalin . . .?*'[8]

Stalin said nothing. Zhukov could hear him breathing heavily at the other end. His words were only slowly sinking in. When Stalin eventually spoke, he dismissed the assault as a limited act of provocation. Hitler, he said, would not break his treaty of friendship. He nevertheless summoned a crisis meeting of the Politburo, and he also ordered his foreign commissar, Vyacheslav Molotov, to contact the German ambassador.

As it transpired, Molotov had no need to contact the ambassador. Dawn had scarcely broken above Moscow when a stony-faced Count von der Schulenburg could be seen making his way to the Kremlin. It was an unusually early hour for a meeting, but the ambassador bore a message of the utmost gravity.

He had received it from Berlin in the small hours of that morning, at the very moment when the first of the Wehrmacht's tanks crossed the Soviet frontier. Written by Germany's Foreign Minister Joachim von Ribbentrop, the telegram was prefaced by an order addressed to Schulenburg himself. 'Please inform Herr Molotov at once that you have an urgent communication to make to him and would therefore like to call on him immediately.'

Ambassador Schulenburg called Molotov's office and said he needed to speak with the foreign commissar. He then headed directly to the Kremlin. Molotov must surely have expected bad news, for he had already received intelligence about disturbances at the frontier. He was nevertheless stunned as Schulenburg read word for word the contents of the Berlin telegram: 'The Soviet Government has broken its treaties with Germany and is about to attack Germany from the rear, in its struggle for life,' said the ambassador. 'The Führer has therefore ordered the German armed forces to oppose this threat with all means at their disposal.'

As Schulenburg knew, the Soviet Government had not broken its treaties with Germany. Nor was it about to attack Germany. These were outlandish lies on the part of Hitler and Ribbentrop. So was the rest of the telegram, which openly accused the Soviets of hostile intent.

Foreign Commissar Molotov was no stranger to duplicity, yet he seemed genuinely shocked by what he was hearing. For a while he sat in silence. Then he turned to Ambassador Schulenburg and said bitterly, 'This is war.'[9]

PART I

Shock Waves

London, Washington, and Moscow
22 June 1941

I

Winston's Broadcast

WINSTON CHURCHILL'S PRIVATE secretary, John 'Jock' Colville, was dozing lightly when his telephone rang at 4 a.m. on Sunday, 22 June. It was the Foreign Office calling with sensational news. Thousands of Wehrmacht soldiers were pouring across the Soviet frontier, a clear sign that Hitler's long-expected invasion of the Soviet Union had begun.

Colville was under strict instructions not to wake the prime minister unless the British Isles itself was under attack. He therefore waited a couple of hours before knocking on Churchill's bedroom door. The PM's first reaction was 'a smile of satisfaction', for this was the best possible news.[1] Hitler was now fighting a war on two fronts. He then took a snap decision. 'Tell the BBC I will broadcast at nine tonight.'[2] Finally, although it was still early, he reached for a celebratory cigar. Life had just changed for the better.

The news grew increasingly dramatic as the morning progressed. A vast wave of German tanks and infantry was advancing eastwards, smashing through Soviet defences. The most urgent question facing Churchill was how to respond.

The answer was not so easy. Many in the prime minister's inner circle felt Joseph Stalin should be abandoned to his fate, arguing that the Soviet dictator was one of the most murderous leaders in history, an absolute ruler with hands drenched in blood. His ruthless economic policies had caused the 1932 famine that left at least five million Ukrainians dead, and he was known to have liquidated many of his loyal commissars in the Great Purge of the late 1930s. Stalin was also a keen supporter of the Comintern, a body established to foment revolution in the Western democracies.

Churchill was sympathetic to the anti-Soviet views of his advisers. He detested the Soviet Union and had spent much of his political career castigating Stalin and his commissars. In one of his more colourful speeches, he described the Soviet regime as 'a league of failures, the criminals, the morbid, the deranged and the distraught'.[3] And it was Churchill who, as minister of war, had sent British troops and munitions to northern Russia in 1919 – his doomed attempt to strangle the Bolshevik regime at birth.

But on that June day, the prime minister had to make a pragmatic calculation. Should Britain watch from the sidelines as Hitler's Wehrmacht smashed through the Soviet defences? Or go to Stalin's rescue in his hour of need? It came down to a simple question: who was worse, Hitler or Stalin?

Churchill had discussed this very dilemma with Jock Colville the previous evening while strolling through the garden at Chequers, the prime ministerial retreat. It had been a swelteringly hot day by English standards, with temperatures in the high seventies, and both men had headed outside to enjoy the first cool of evening. As they walked across to the far side of the lawn, Churchill confessed to Colville that he would 'go all out to help Russia' in the event of a Nazi invasion. Colville was surprised, and asked how he could possibly support Stalin when he had openly opposed the Communist regime for years.

Churchill had a ready answer. 'I have only one purpose,' he said, 'the destruction of Hitler.' Pausing for a moment, he added a characteristically witty afterthought. 'If Hitler invaded Hell, I would make at least a favourable reference to the Devil in the House of Commons.'[4] Colville was so amused that he jotted it down in his diary.

A number of senior officials were staying at Chequers that weekend, including the foreign secretary, Anthony Eden. Joining them for Sunday lunch was Britain's ambassador to the Soviet Union, Sir Stafford Cripps, who happened to be on a rare visit to England. Churchill loathed Ambassador Cripps, who was teetotal, vegetarian, and an evangelical Christian – a trio of unforgiveable vices.

Worse still, from the prime minister's perspective, Cripps was a socialist. Indeed it was his radical political outlook that had led to his appointment to Moscow, in the hope that he might improve relations between Britain and the Soviet Union. But Cripps never got to see

Stalin, nor was he welcome inside the Kremlin. On one occasion, when he repeatedly petitioned to see Foreign Commissar Molotov, he received a terse message from Molotov's secretary: 'Mr Molotov does not *wish* to see the British ambassador.'[5]

Over the previous two years, the Soviet regime had shown no interest in forging closer ties with the British government. It was comprised of hated figures like Winston Churchill, who continually expressed his hostility towards the Soviet Union. Besides, Stalin was assiduously courting Nazi Germany, the dominant power in Europe and the only country that represented a potentially existential threat to the Soviet regime.

When Ambassador Cripps had left Moscow a fortnight earlier, the Soviet regime had expressed its delight at seeing the back of him. The official news agency, TASS, went so far as to declare him persona non grata. Cripps's embassy colleagues assumed he would not be returning.

Now, over Sunday lunch at Chequers, Winston Churchill pressed Cripps for information about Stalin. There was an urgent need to know how the Soviet leader was likely to react to the Nazi invasion. But Cripps knew almost nothing about the Soviet leader, who rarely appeared in public. Stalin held no official post, apart from general secretary of the Communist Party, and never attended state receptions for visiting diplomats. Nor did he receive foreign ambassadors.* Incoming dignitaries presented their credentials to President Mikhail Kalinin, the titular head of state, never to Stalin.

All of Churchill's guests agreed on one thing that weekend: without assistance from the West, Stalin's Red Army would be defeated. And such a defeat would have catastrophic consequences for Great Britain, because Hitler would be able to transfer all his forces from the Eastern Front to the Western, making the future liberation of occupied Europe all but impossible.

Winston Churchill always had a gift of seeing the big picture, and he saw it right now. Both Britain and the Soviet Union had been attacked by Hitler, and this turned them into de facto allies in the

* Anthony Eden had been granted a rare audience in the spring of 1935, when Britain's minister of foreign affairs.

great struggle. To the dismay of many in his inner circle, he told them of his resolve to go to Stalin's aid.

It took him the rest of the day to write the script for his BBC broadcast, aware that he would be selling a tough nut to a sceptical public. 'I had not the slightest doubt where our duty and our policy lay,' he would later write in his memoirs. 'Nor indeed what to say.'[6] But he didn't finish writing his speech until 8.40 p.m., just twenty minutes before it was due to be broadcast from a live microphone installed in Chequers.

Its tone was powerful and grave, with the prime minister's growling delivery giving it extra punch. He spoke artificially slowly and with long pauses, which served to heap significance onto each key phrase.

'Hitler is a monster of wickedness, insatiable in his lust for blood and plunder,' he said. 'Not content with having all Europe under his heel or else terrorised into various forms of abject submission, he must now carry his work of butchery and desolation among the vast multitudes of Russia and of Asia.'

Churchill was brutally honest when admitting he had despised the Soviet regime for his entire political career. 'No one has been a more consistent opponent of Communism than I have for the last twenty-five years. I will un-say no words that I've spoken about it. But all this fades away before the spectacle which is now unfolding.' He disliked Joseph Stalin – intensely – but he detested Adolf Hitler.

'We are resolved to destroy Hitler and every vestige of the Nazi regime . . . Any man or State who fights against Nazism will have our aid.'[7] It was Britain's duty to help the Soviet Union in its hour of desperate need. It was also in Britain's own interest.

Churchill's guests at Chequers began a post-mortem on the speech within minutes of the broadcast. Anthony Eden was concerned that many people would be appalled at the idea of supporting the Soviet Union. In terms of politics, he said, 'Russia was as bad as Germany'.[8] Jock Colville focused more on Churchill's pugnacious delivery. 'Dramatic,' he thought, 'and it gave a clear decision of policy-support for Russia.' Young Mary Churchill, the prime minister's teenage daughter, was even more rapturous. 'Papa broadcast – superb. O darling, I love you so much and admire you more than you will ever know. Pray God you will be spared and supported.'[9]

Churchill detested Stalin, yet he broadcast his support for the Soviet Union within hours of Hitler's invasion. He said that Britain would help any nation fighting against the evils of Nazism.

Churchill had pledged in his broadcast to do everything possible to save the Red Army from battlefield catastrophe, but there were many unanswered questions. *How* was he going to aid Stalin? By what means? Britain was in no position to help the Soviet Union with either armaments or raw materials.

And there were other questions, too. If Stalin was now an ally, then the prime minister would need an acceptable representative in Moscow – someone working alongside the Soviet leader, preferably inside the Kremlin. But who? It was hard to think of a suitable candidate. And that provoked yet another question: would Stalin even accept such a person? Few Westerners, either British or American, had ever penetrated the crenellated walls of the Kremlin and it had been years since partisan journalists like Walter Duranty and Eugene Lyons had secured their interviews with the Soviet leader. Even they had never gained entry to Stalin's private study. The Soviet leader remained a near-total enigma, unknown and possibly unknowable. It was a worrying lacuna, given that he held the fate of the world in his hands.

2

Roosevelt Meets the Press

In distant Washington, President Roosevelt reacted to news of the Nazi invasion with far greater caution than Winston Churchill. He gave no statement on the day of the invasion and declined to hold an emergency press conference. The State Department was equally tight-lipped, releasing a short communiqué saying that Hitler's invasion was 'convincing proof that the Reichsführer Hitler plans to dominate the world'.[1] But when journalists asked if America would supply the Soviet Union with tanks and guns, they were told that Stalin had not requested any weaponry. 'Consequently, any questions regarding Lend-Lease aid need not be discussed at this time.'[2]

There was good reason for avoiding the subject: President Roosevelt's inner circle could not agree on what to do next. Secretary of State Cordell Hull supported supplying Stalin with weaponry, while Secretary of War Henry Stimson was against such a policy.[3] It would be for the president himself to decide.

An additional headache for President Roosevelt was the powerful America First movement, whose leading figure, General Robert Wood, derided those in favour of backing Communist Moscow. 'The war party can hardly ask the American people to take up arms behind the Red flag of Stalin,' he said mockingly.[4]

Influential voices in the Senate agreed. 'Stalin is as bloody-handed as Hitler,' opined one senator. 'I don't think we should help either one.' Senator Harry Truman took a yet more cynical approach: 'If we see that Germany is winning, we ought to help Russia, and if Russia is winning, we ought to help Germany, and that way let them kill as many as possible.'[5] His was by no means a lone voice. When Gallup conducted a poll on Tuesday, 24 June, two days after the invasion, it found that two-thirds of the population were against aiding the Soviet Union.

That same day, at four o'clock, President Roosevelt finally called a press conference in the Oval Office of the White House. The NBC radio journalist Earl Godwin was first into the room, joking with the president about enhanced security. Roosevelt liked Godwin, a veteran radioman, and had nicknamed him God. 'We've been checking up on God for some time,' he joshed as he mock-scrutinised Godwin's press pass.

Journalist May Craig was next through the door: she brought Roosevelt a sprig of forget-me-nots, which she placed on his desk. 'Very nice, very nice,' smiled the president as an increasing number of journalists filtered into his office. 'I don't know why everyone's coming in,' he said with a grin. 'I haven't got any news today.'

The first questions that afternoon were mundane. One reporter asked about Mammoth Cave National Park; another wanted to know about price controls. But it was not long before Godwin quizzed the president about the Soviet Union. He wanted to know whether Roosevelt was going to support Stalin.

The president gave an unequivocal reply. 'Of course we are going to give all the aid that we possibly can to Russia,' he said. But he quickly added that he had not been in contact with Stalin and had no idea what aid he might need. He also told Godwin it would be far from easy to produce the necessary weaponry. 'You can't just go around to Mr Garfinckel's' – a Washington department store – 'and fill the order and take it away with you.'

At this, everyone laughed.

It soon became clear that the President was intending to reveal very little to the assembled journalists.

'What kind of things shall we give them, Mr President?' asked one of the more persistent reporters.

'Oh, socks and shoes and things like that!' joked Roosevelt.

'Have you got a list now?'

'No.'

'Will any priorities on airplanes be assigned to Russia?'

'I don't know,' said Roosevelt. 'I haven't the faintest idea.'

Another journalist asked if weaponry for Stalin would be delivered under the same terms as it was being sent to Great Britain.

'I don't know,' sighed the increasingly exasperated president, before adding, 'I probably know less about the situation on the fighting front in Moscow than the average desk man does at this particular moment.'

Another journalist asked if the defence of Russia was essential to the defence of the United States.

Roosevelt baulked at this. 'Oh, ask me a different question,' he said. 'You know I never answer those.'[6]

It was an uninformative press conference, with the president remaining tight-lipped. But he did tell the reporters that he had ordered the release of frozen Soviet assets and he also suggested that the Neutrality Act, designed to keep America out of foreign conflicts, would not apply to the Soviet-German war. This left open the potential for deliveries of American weaponry to Soviet ports.

Little was made public in the days that followed, to the great frustration of the White House press corps. But behind the scenes there was a great deal of activity, with constant discussions between the State Department and the Soviet Embassy in Washington. Within a fortnight, the Soviet ambassador, Constantine Oumansky, presented American officials with a formal request for two billion dollars' worth of aircraft, guns, and ammunition.

Without it, he said, the Soviet Union faced defeat.

3

Stalin's Crisis

STALIN WAS STUNNED by news of the invasion. He had ignored the warning signs and dismissed the intelligence. Although he had never trusted Nazi Germany, he didn't believe that Hitler would attack the Soviet Union in the foreseeable future. Just a few weeks earlier he had addressed a group of military cadets warning them to be 'prepared for any surprises', but also assuring them that Hitler was fully preoccupied with his attempt to crush Great Britain.[1]

Stalin's initial response to the invasion was to summon an emergency meeting of the Politburo. It was not yet dawn when he was driven to the Kremlin from his dacha at Kuntsevo. The Politburo members met in a second-floor room at 5.45 a.m., little more than an hour after the first German tanks had crossed the Soviet frontier. Among those in attendance were senior figures in Stalin's inner circle, including his foreign commissar, Vyacheslav Molotov, his defence commissar, Semon Timoshenko, and the chief of the General Staff, General Zhukov. Everyone was shocked to see Stalin in such a visible state of disarray: 'His pock-marked face was drawn and haggard,' recalled one of those present, while others would remember him bewildered and speaking in an unusually faltering voice. Stalin was indeed shocked by the enormity of what had happened and was unable to process information coming from the battle-front.

He clung to his earlier contention that the Wehrmacht's attack was a limited act of provocation. But Molotov dismissed this out of hand, reminding him that the German ambassador himself had confirmed that this was a full-scale invasion. This news hit Stalin hard. 'He sank in his chair and was locked in deep thought,' noted Zhukov. There was a long silence as he summoned the strength to speak. 'The enemy will be beaten all along the line,' he said blandly.[2] He then turned to his generals and asked how the military should respond to the German blitzkrieg. Zhukov began explaining the importance of frontier troops holding up the Wehrmacht's advance when he was stopped mid-sentence by an irritable Timoshenko. 'Annihilate,' he interjected. 'Not held up.'[3]

At 7.15 a.m., Stalin issued his first wartime order. Luftwaffe aircraft were to be destroyed; air attacks were to be launched on German territory; and Soviet troops were to 'annihilate' the invading forces. The Politburo members then discussed how best to break the news to the nation. There was widespread agreement that Stalin himself should broadcast the news, but the Soviet leader demurred. 'Let Molotov speak,' he said, reasoning that it was Molotov who had put his signature to the Nazi-Soviet pact.[4]

Molotov managed to control his stammer as he informed the Soviet people of the momentous events that had taken place during the night. 'At four o'clock this morning, without declaration of war, and without any claims being made on the Soviet Union, German troops attacked our country . . . This unheard-of attack is an unparalleled act of perfidy in the history of civilised nations.'

In his customary monotone he told them of Hitler's abject treachery. 'This attack has been made despite the fact that there was a non-aggression pact between the Soviet Union and Germany, a pact the terms of which were scrupulously observed by the Soviet Union.' Molotov also reminded his listeners that Hitler had already ridden roughshod over all the peoples of Central and Western Europe, bringing misery to millions.

He ended his broadcast with a reminder that Russia had been invaded before, in the Great Patriotic War of 1812, and that the people had risen as one to crush Napoleon. The same thing would happen to Hitler. 'Our cause is good,' he said. 'The enemy will be smashed. Victory will be ours.'[5]

Stalin congratulated Molotov on his performance, although he did so with a customary lack of grace. 'Well,' he said, 'you sounded a bit flustered, but the speech went well.'

Muscovites greeted news of the invasion with horrified astonishment. For the previous two years, they had been fed uplifting stories about Stalin's ongoing alliance with Hitler. Now, in a startling volte-face, they were being told their Nazi ally was a treacherous thug.

Stalin's mood darkened that morning as news of enemy successes reached the Kremlin. He was appalled to learn of the destruction of vast numbers of Soviet planes before they had even taken to the skies. 'Surely the German air force didn't manage to reach every single airfield?' he asked, incredulous.[6]

The Wehrmacht swept through the Soviet border defences with astonishing ease, crushing everything in its path. A similar story unfolded on all three fronts: Red Army soldiers were defeated before they even had a chance to fight.

The military situation seemed hopeless. Railway junctions and lines of communication had been destroyed; command posts were in flames; and there was a disastrous shortage of army vehicles in the frontier districts. Most Soviet soldiers had turned and fled, but their hasty flight brought its own problems. 'Bottlenecks were formed by troops, artillery, motor vehicles and field kitchens,' wrote General Ivan Boldin, one of Stalin's front-line commanders, 'and then the Nazi planes had the time of their life . . . Often our troops could not dig in, simply because they did not even have the simplest implements. Occasionally trenches had to be dug with helmets, since there were no spades.'[7]

As the day progressed, Stalin learned that the situation was even worse than he had feared. The Germans were everywhere advancing, with the city of Minsk already in their sights. He fumed at his commissars. 'Lenin founded our state', he said, 'and we've fucked it up.'[8]

A short time afterwards, he shocked his Politburo comrades by issuing a five-word statement of intent. 'Everything's lost,' he told them. 'I give up.' With this phrase ringing in their ears, he left the Kremlin and retreated to his Kuntsevo dacha.

In the days that followed, Stalin was seen by no one. He refused to receive any visitors and wouldn't even answer the phone. Nor did he respond to Winston Churchill's BBC broadcast, in which the prime minister had pledged British support for the Soviet Union. Yet he surely knew what Churchill had said, for transcripts of the PM's speech were already being translated into Russian, Georgian, and

Ukrainian. Before long, hundreds of thousands of copies were rolling off the printing presses.[9]

Those in Stalin's inner circle were horrified to discover that their leader had disappeared without trace, intent on quitting his post. In its hour of desperate need, with the Wehrmacht storming eastwards, the Soviet Union had been left adrift.

Unless Stalin recovered – and fast – defeat seemed a certainty.

PART II

First Alliance

Washington and London
Spring 1941

4

A Man Named Averell

FOUR MONTHS BEFORE Hitler invaded the Soviet Union, Great Britain had herself been under attack. Her cities were being pummelled by the Luftwaffe, her supply lines severed by German U-boats. The country was being steadily strangled.

Winston Churchill had personally begged for help in his first message to President Roosevelt: 'We expect to be attacked here ourselves, both from the air and by parachute and airborne troops, in the near future, and are getting ready for them.' He vowed that the country would fight on until the bitter end, but his defiance came with a caveat. 'I trust you realise, Mr President, that the voice and force of the United States may count for nothing if they are withheld for too long.' Time was of the essence. 'You may have a completely subjugated, Nazified Europe established with astonishing swiftness.'

The world had darkened yet further since Churchill's first appeal. The Low Countries had been ruthlessly conquered and France had been brought to her knees. Large swathes of London and other British cities were being pounded to dust by Nazi bombers. It was imperative for America to come to Britain's aid, argued Churchill, for a Nazi-dominated Britain would leave America itself in grave peril.

By the spring of 1941, Roosevelt was ready to act. On Friday, 7 March, he hosted a luncheon at the White House at which there was only one guest and only one topic of conversation. The guest was a man named Averell Harriman, and the president's discussion with him that afternoon was to mark the beginning of a compelling four-year adventure. More important, it would lay the foundations of a remarkable, if bizarre, three-power wartime alliance.

To his many friends, Averell seemed to belong to a gilded elite. A youthful forty-nine-year-old, he was rich, tall, and amiable, with striking good looks: trim and athletic to boot, he had slicked-back hair and an all-American smile. One acquaintance said he had the features of Gary Cooper and the allure of Ray Milland, thereby linking him to two of the greatest idols of the silver screen.

Known to everyone as Averell or Ave, he was also an expert skier who had perfected his skills at Sun Valley, the glitzy Idaho ski resort that he developed and owned. 'With his head tossed back and wearing sunglasses,' wrote one journalist, 'he exuded the effortless style of an American aristocrat.'[1]

Averell Harriman was rich, athletic, and good-looking. A multi-millionaire tycoon, he was tasked with developing a close personal relationship with both Churchill and Stalin.

Above all else, Averell was mind-blowingly rich. The chairman of the Union Pacific rail empire, he commanded a network that extended across twenty-three states. He had invested in banking, shipping, and mining – activities that had increased his fortune yet further. He also dabbled in art, buying masterpieces by Van Gogh, Renoir, and Picasso. The $70 million fortune amassed by his father grew larger with every passing year. By the spring of 1941, he was the fourth-richest man in America.

Great wealth had brought powerful connections: he had known Franklin and Eleanor Roosevelt since his schooldays at Groton, when he was friends with Eleanor's younger brother. Now he had been invited into the White House, and his luncheon with the president was the opening act in what was to prove a day of big surprises.

The first surprise was the disgusting food. 'An extraordinary meal,' he recorded in his notebook – and extraordinary for all the wrong reasons. '*Spinach soup*' – he was astonished that the White House chefs couldn't cook something more appetising for the most powerful man in the world. 'Looked like hot water poured over chopped-up spinach. White toast and hot rolls.'

The main dish was little better: 'Cheese soufflé *with spinach*!! Dessert – three large fat pancakes, plenty of butter and maple syrup.'[2]

Averell thought it a poor diet for a president recovering from a heavy cold and was bemused to hear Roosevelt talk about Great Britain's urgent need for protein and vitamins. He felt the White House itself needed a dietary makeover.

Only when the two men had finished their grease-slicked pancakes did Roosevelt turn to the matter at hand. Averell had not been invited to the White House for a culinary treat, nor indeed for idle chatter. He was there because the president was poised to make him an extraordinary offer, one that would soon be extended to his twenty-three-year-old daughter, Kathy.

The Harriman family fortune was entirely self-made. Unlike those other titans of the Hudson Valley, the Rockefellers and Vanderbilts, Averell's father had begun life as a penniless messenger boy with a bold outlook and a run of good luck. Displaying a ruthlessness that stunned his contemporaries, he seized control of the bankrupt Union Pacific Railroad and turned it into a highly profitable enterprise.

His ever-growing profits gave young Averell a childhood of opulent luxury. The family's Manhattan home was a cavernous pile of marble on Fifth Avenue, but they spent much of their time at Arden, a sprawling baronial castle some fifty miles up the Hudson. It was outlandishly huge (Averell's wife would later confess to having trouble locating the kitchen), with tennis courts, a polo ground, croquet lawn, and billiard room.

Averell had inherited the unvarnished bluntness of his father, but he could also play the pussycat, especially when his two daughters were around. He adored Mary and Kathy, helping them through school after the untimely death of their mother. He had subsequently remarried a woman named Marie Norton, but his daughters continued to view him as a bachelor father on whom they doted. The doting was mutual. Averell was particularly close to his vivacious younger daughter, Kathy, whom he nicknamed 'Puff'. She called him 'Popsie'.

Kathy realised from an early age that her father was a magnet for desirable women, who invariably found their way into his bed. These included the beautiful Russian costumier Katia Krassin and the vaudeville performer Teddy Gerard. Most recently he had been seduced by Vera Zorina, the film star ballerina married to the choreographer George Balanchine.

Averell's wife, Marie, took such liaisons in her stride, perhaps because she was having an affair with the society musician Eddie Duchin. That, at least, was the gossip of New York society. In the Harrimans' universe, promiscuity was acceptable, as long as it was discreet.

President Roosevelt blew his nose for the umpteenth time that lunchtime; his head was swimming with cold. Averell couldn't help thinking how haggard he looked. 'Foggy . . . obviously tired and mentally stale.'

'I want you to go over to London,' said the president at length, 'and recommend everything that we can do, short of war, to keep the British Isles afloat.'

Here, in a nutshell, was the reason for Averell's invitation to the White House. Britain was sinking fast: short on food, supplies, and weaponry. The country was also under relentless attack from the Luftwaffe. There were real fears it was close to collapse. Averell's mission was to see what could be done to save the beleaguered island.

This had become an imperative for Roosevelt, because a Britain under Nazi control would leave America dangerously exposed. Saving Britain was a route to saving America as well.

The president had already laid the groundwork in the first half of February, when he summoned the White House press corps to a conference. After a rambling monologue about the Great War, he told the assembled journalists that he intended to supply aid to the British Isles regardless of whether or not she could pay. 'What I am trying to do,' he said, 'is eliminate the dollar sign.'

When the reporters asked to know more, the president offered a simple but lucid analogy. 'Suppose my neighbor's home catches fire,' he told them, 'and I have a length of garden hose four or five hundred feet away. If he can take my garden hose and connect it up with his hydrant, I may help him to put out his fire.'[3] He added that he wouldn't ask for payment, nor would he expect it. His only demand was to get back his garden hose once the fire had been extinguished.

Roosevelt would later expand on this theme in one of his 'fireside chats' regularly broadcast to the nation. 'If Britain should go down,' he warned, 'all of us in the Americas would be living at the point of a gun . . . We must produce arms and ships with every energy and resources we can command.'

When reporters asked if the president's new policy had a name, Roosevelt was momentarily caught off-guard. 'Lend-Spend . . .' he said vaguely. 'Lend-Lease . . . whatever you call it.' He was unwilling to take questions and grew irritable when one journalist persisted in asking for more detail. 'I don't know, and I don't give a —— [damn], you know.' His only concern was that Britain should be supported in her struggle.

Now, in the aftermath of that press conference, he was putting flesh onto the bones of Lend-Lease. Averell Harriman was to be sent to London as his official representative. He would answer to the president alone – not to the State Department – and was to deal directly with the prime minister. Roosevelt wanted 'the undiluted words of Churchill'. There was to be no role for bureaucrats, diplomats, or intermediaries.

The White House journalists were surprised that Averell had been chosen for such a prestigious position. He was a business tycoon, after all, not a politician. He knew nothing of keeping a nation supplied with weaponry and food. It was certainly a handsome reward for Averell's long-term loyalty to Roosevelt. It was Averell who had switched his family's long-standing allegiance from Republican to Democrat; Averell who had enthusiastically backed Roosevelt's bid for office in 1932, 1936, and 1940. He had even supported the president's New Deal at a time when many were pointing out its flaws. Now he was getting his payback.

Among the journalists' many questions that day was how they should refer to Averell in their articles. 'Call him an Expediter,' said Roosevelt vaguely. 'There's a new one for you!'

Averell himself was in no doubt as to the importance of the work ahead. His role was to transform Britain into a fighting bastion that would at some future date be able to take on Hitler's war machine. He would be dealing directly with Winston Churchill on a day-to-day basis. And he was being given carte blanche to act as he saw fit. 'An excellent mandate,' he thought, 'in no way tying my hands.' Aware he was being offered the job of a lifetime, he accepted with alacrity. It would place him at the very heart of the war.

Lunch was over and the plates were cleared away. The coffee had gone cold. Averell had never seen Roosevelt as worried as he was that day at the White House. The president was deeply concerned that Lend-Lease would draw America into the war, and this had left him shaken and uncertain. 'All in all, rambling on as he does on many subjects, he was far more humble, less cocksure and more human than in any conversation I had with him since he was President.'

Averell thanked Roosevelt for the pancakes, the job, and the presidential advice. But as he left the White House that day, his overriding impression was that the Lend-Lease programme was too little, too late. 'I left feeling that the President had not faced what I considered to be the realities of the situation: namely, that there was a good chance that Germany' – any day soon – 'could so cripple British shipping as to affect her ability to hold out.'[4]

Averell intended to leave America on Monday, 10 March 1941, giving him just three days to hire a staff, wrap up his business affairs, and bid farewell to his family.

His wife, Marie, declined to accompany him to England. She was suffering from glaucoma and had only recently undergone eye surgery. Specialists counselled against her undergoing a punishing transatlantic flight. She also had the extended Harriman clan to consider, with two offspring apiece from their two marriages. And there was that rumoured affair with Eddie Duchin.

Averell knew exactly who he wanted as his personal assistant. Bob Meiklejohn (pronounced 'Micklejohn') had worked as his secretary at Union Pacific for the previous four years. No one was more diligent and loyal than Meiklejohn. Thirty-two years old, tall, and prematurely balding, he was a shrewd judge of human nature and a dependable right-hand man.

But there was a problem. Meiklejohn's father had just been diagnosed with terminal cancer, causing Meiklejohn to hesitate when offered the job. Not only would he never see his father again, but it would also be hard to stay in touch in a meaningful way. Although he could write letters home, he was warned they would be heavily censored.

His brother, David, contrived a solution. Aware that one of Bob's tasks was to keep an hour-by-hour record of the Harriman Mission, as it was now called, he suggested that he expand this diary to cover everything of interest, from London bombing raids to society gossip. This could then be sent to America by diplomatic bag (thereby avoiding the censors) and smuggled to Meiklejohn senior's sickbed.

'Thus the diary and its editorial policy was born,' wrote Meiklejohn in the introduction to a daily account that would eventually fill two volumes – 841 pages – and weigh fully nine pounds. His modesty led him to downplay the diary's significance, calling it 'a record of trivialities during a time when matters of great moment were taking place'.[5]

Yet he would later concede that it contained 'momentous events that were secret and could not be revealed'. It was to prove a unique record of a tumultuous time, one that has been overlooked for decades in the Manuscript Division of the Library of Congress.

The three days of preparation passed in a flash as Meiklejohn wound up his affairs. Averell, meanwhile, had a flurry of meetings with the most important players in Washington, including Secretary of State Cordell Hull. Hull had little to say about the Harriman Mission itself, which was to act above his authority. His principal concern was that the US Navy was keeping all its major warships in Hawaii, leaving them exposed. One enemy bombing raid could wreak havoc.

'What's the name of that harbor?' he asked Averell, confessing to a momentary lapse of memory.

There was a moment's pause.

'Pearl Harbor.'[6]

'I felt very much the adventurer,' wrote Averell as he boarded a Yankee Clipper flying boat at New York Municipal Airport. It was 9.15 a.m. on Monday, 10 March, and this was the first leg of a flight that would require several stop-overs. He and Bob Meiklejohn were allowed two bags apiece (maximum weight sixty-six pounds) and were travelling on newly issued diplomatic passports.

'Had steak lunch on the plane,' recorded Meiklejohn on the first page of his new diary. 'Arrived in Bermuda after uneventful flight in bright sunshine.' The passengers were ordered to pull down the window shades as they came in to land, for the airstrip was in a prohibited military area of the British-controlled territory. 'Five-hundred-dollar fine for raising the shade.'

Averell and Meiklejohn spent a relaxing evening in the Belmont Manor Hotel. At 4 p.m. the following day, they once again boarded the Clipper for the fourteen-hour passage to the Azores, from where they took another flight to Lisbon.

Here they hit an unforeseen snag. There were no London-bound planes until Saturday, 15 March, necessitating a three-day stop-over until they secured seats aboard a Dutch DC-3 aeroplane. Averell had an 'eerie experience' as he prepared to board, passing a Luftwaffe plane adorned with a large swastika. In neutral Lisbon, the enemy was ever-present.

The flight to England was dangerous and uncomfortable. 'Camouflaged and very dirty and rundown on the outside,' wrote Meiklejohn of the airplane, 'all but ten to eleven seats taken out to reduce weight and passenger load because of the heavy fuel-load needed for the thousand-mile flight to England.'

The final leg of the voyage ended with a terrifying 8,000-foot plunge to ground level to avoid Luftwaffe patrols over the English Channel. Finally, at 3.30 p.m., they touched down in Bristol after a journey that had taken four days and six hours.

Their ordeal was not quite over. Greeted warmly by Commander Tommy Thompson, Winston Churchill's aide-de-camp, they were escorted to the prime minister's twin-engine Flamingo that was to take them to Chequers, Churchill's official residence outside London. They were told there were parachutes in the seat pockets – just in case – and two Hurricane fighters were to accompany them as escorts. It was a sign of the importance attached to their mission.

'A grand view of the country,' wrote Meiklejohn as he stared out of the porthole. 'Two RAF men in the cabin with us pointed out bomb craters.' The late afternoon sun was slumping into the horizon, casting the fields into deep shadow. Not a single light shone from the farmsteads below.

After a flight of just thirty minutes, they landed at a makeshift airfield in Buckinghamshire. Everywhere there were signs of war. 'Saw about a dozen bombers,' wrote Meiklejohn, 'all black, and being prepared for a night flight.'

Averell himself was struck by the enormity of being in a country under siege. Recollecting the event years later, he said: 'I entered a Britain in the shadows.'[7]

5
Meeting Winston

THE LIGHT WAS fast fading by the time Commander Tommy Thompson drove Averell Harriman from the airfield to Chequers. This pocket of Buckinghamshire, all meadows and chalky uplands, had a bucolic beauty that was not lost on Averell. The winding lanes were flanked with gigantic oaks, the oldest dating from Tudor times, and the villages were steeped in the past. The church in Little Hampden was virtually unchanged since the reign of Edward Longshanks.

The car stopped at the wrought-iron gateway so that police officers could conduct a security check. It then swept up the long gravel driveway. The great house loomed large in the gathering twilight, appearing to Averell as a dark grey silhouette. Not an inch of light came from its mullioned windows, for the blackout was as strictly observed in the countryside as it was in London.

Chequers was a gabled Elizabethan mansion, bequeathed to the nation in the early 1920s by the philanthropic politician Sir Arthur Lee. It was an idyllic place, all faux-battlements and pinnacles, with a profusion of red-brick chimneys that poked improbably high above the rooftops. It was smaller than the Harriman mansion at Arden, and a lot draughtier, but it was redolent of Olde England. Yet even here, far from London, there were reminders that Britain was a country at war. Guns had been installed in the grounds, and the place was under heavy guard.

Averell was not accompanied by Bob Meiklejohn on this first visit to the prime minister; his assistant had gone directly to London to establish the head office of the Harriman Mission. But Averell was by no means alone. Churchill had invited his loyal secretary, Brendan Bracken, and America's newly appointed ambassador, Gil

Winant. Also present was Mary Churchill, the prime minister's giddy-headed youngest child. Eighteen years of age and bursting with life, she was keeping an intimate diary of everything she saw and heard.

Averell was relieved to have arrived after such a hellish voyage. Chequers that evening was homely and warm. A wood fire crackled in the Great Hall, while the book-lined Long Gallery was heated by another monumental chimney. Atop the mantelpiece, two of Oliver Cromwell's swords glinted in the candlelight. Churchill liked to refer to Chequers as a 'panelled museum, full of treasures'.[1]

Averell later confessed that it felt almost unreal to be a guest of the British prime minister. 'I was very excited,' he wrote, 'feeling like a country boy plopped into the center of the war.'[2]

Churchill put him at ease, shaking his hand warmly before reminiscing about the two occasions when they had met before, albeit briefly. 'He remembered our first meeting when I called on him at Cannes in 1927 . . . and he talked about our meeting in New York two years later.' This had been at the time of the Wall Street crash, when Churchill had squandered a lot of cash. 'He freely admitted having caught the speculative fever of the time and lost the money he had just received from the publication of a new book.'[3]

Watching wide-eyed from the sidelines and noting everything, Mary was entranced by her father's two American guests. 'Both good-looking,' she confessed to her diary. 'Charming and most inspiring.'[4]

Averell was so swept up in the excitement of the evening that he completely forgot to present the letter he was carrying from President Roosevelt. But he did remember his gift for Churchill's wife, Clementine, who appeared shortly before dinner. 'I was surprised to see how grateful Mrs Churchill was for a small bag of tangerines I had brought her from Lisbon,' wrote Averell, who had possibly hoped to buy clementines for his hostess. 'Her unfeigned delight brought home to me the restrictions of the dreary British wartime diet, imposed by the sharp reduction of imports, even in the Prime Minister's house.'[5] It was his first experience of the desperate situation in which blockaded and starving Britain now found itself.

The serious discussion began after dinner. Churchill took Averell to one side 'and began to describe in considerable detail the problems of the war and what the United States might do to help'. The news was bleak. In the Libyan desert, Hitler's Afrika Korps had inflicted a string of humiliating defeats on the British. On the borders of Yugoslavia and Greece, the Wehrmacht were poised to invade. But the most immediate peril was in the North Atlantic, where German U-boats had sunk half a million tons of shipping over the previous month.

Shipping losses were so colossal that the country was being starved to death. 'The stark facts needed no Churchillian oratory for emphasis,' wrote Averell. 'I immediately realised how close they were to disaster. If the trend were not checked, and eventually reversed, there would be no reason for Hitler to invade the British Isles. By cutting the line of supply, he could strangle them.'[6] It was a simple question of mathematics. The Germans were sinking British vessels two to three times faster than shipyards could build new ones.

Averell told Churchill he had come to help but warned that he would need unrestricted access to the facts. He would require sensitive information; he would need to know state secrets. His usefulness, he said, would 'depend entirely upon the extent of my knowledge and understanding of her [Britain's] position and needs'.

Churchill's reply came from the heart.

'You shall be informed. We accept you as a friend. Nothing will be kept from you.'[7]

As the dinner candles guttered and the brandy fumes swirled, Averell spoke of his private hope that Germany would commit an overt act of war against the United States, thereby forcing President Roosevelt into the conflict. Public opinion could be rapidly shifted if Hitler were to sink an American ship, especially if it involved a large loss of life.

Listening in the shadows was young Mary Churchill. 'The weekend was thrilling,' she wrote in her diary the following Monday. 'Here was the hub of the Universe. For many billions of destinies may perhaps hang on this new axis – this Anglo-American–American-Anglo friendship.'[8]

After ten desperate months, there was a glimmer of hope.

Monday & Tuesday
Work comme toujours
The weekend was thrilling.
Here was the hub of the Universe.
For many billions of destinies
may perhaps hang on this new
axis" – this Anglo-American
American-Anglo friendship
Papa recently recited Arthur
Clough's "Say not the struggle
nought availeth".
I did not know it before – but
I think it is a very beautiful
poem

The PM's daughter, Mary, kept a diary record of Averell's arrival at Chequers. She quickly realised the importance of American support for the British war effort.

Bob Meiklejohn had meanwhile headed to London and checked into Claridge's hotel, where he found himself in a massive bedroom with a bathtub 'deep enough to drown in'. Claridge's was far too expensive for his limited budget – more than a guinea a day – and the dinner so meagre that it left him wanting more. 'Got a piece of butter about the size of a fifty-cent piece, and the same thickness.' Meiklejohn had come to London expecting to see exhilarating dogfights in the skies over the capital. Instead, he was cold and hungry.

As he struggled to sleep in his freezing room, it struck him how little guidance he and Averell had been given by President Roosevelt. 'No instructions, directives or guidelines . . . no arrangements for permanent office space . . . no supplies in a strange country at a time of extreme shortage.' All he had was $75,000 in cash and a gigantic office (the size of six tennis courts) adjoining the American Embassy at No. 1 Grosvenor Square.

The following day was Sunday; Meiklejohn took himself off for a stroll around town. 'Almost every block has a number of buildings blown up,' he wrote, 'and almost all completely eliminated.' Overhead, barrage balloons floated like artificial clouds in the clear sky.

Over the days that followed, Meiklejohn moved to cheaper lodgings, had a gas mask fitted, and took delivery of a £2,000 Bentley – Averell's official car. He also welcomed an influx of experts from Washington and hired a seven-strong team of female stenographers, all security-cleared on account of the 'super-duper secret cables' they had to transmit to Washington. But he found it hard to adapt to wartime London, where even the chophouses were short of food. 'Carrots and brussels sprouts,' he wrote glumly in his diary. 'Everything tastes the same . . . tea strictly rationed.' Among his many grouches were the uniquely awful English fridges. 'They make all the noise like a Model T Ford with the heaves, and run incessantly, never stopping for a rest like an American ice-box does.'[9] The majority of them were not even cold. Meiklejohn began to wonder how on earth the British hoped to win the war, given that they couldn't even produce ice cubes for his evening Scotch.

Averell, whom he had begun referring to as 'his nibs', was rarely at the Harriman Mission headquarters. He spent all his waking hours with Churchill, either at Chequers or at Downing Street. Frustratingly, he wouldn't reveal the slightest detail about his repeated weekends at Chequers. 'So hush-hush', wrote Meiklejohn, 'that he wouldn't even tell me where it was.'

For the next four years, he and Averell were to inhabit a world of secrets.

6

A Deepening Friendship

Averell Harriman spent six of his first seven weekends in England with the prime minister, and the two men formed a bond that delighted young Mary Churchill. After one of Averell's visits to Chequers, she wrote a private note in her diary: 'I think he is so charming. He has the root of the matter in him. He feels and works for us so much.'[1]

Averell was also a regular visitor at 10 Downing Street, dining there with Churchill at least once a week. He attended the War Cabinet, 'an extraordinary privilege for a foreigner', and met all the senior officials in Whitehall. The red carpet was unrolled for him at every ministerial doorway. The prime minister had been true to his word when he'd said that nothing would be withheld. 'Ministers talked freely . . . and gave me the most sensitive information. It was a great deal more than I expected.'[2]

Churchill kept up an optimistic public facade that spring, but he was far bleaker when speaking to Averell. On Saturday, 22 March, their second weekend together, Averell found the PM in a particularly sombre mood. 'He made it plain that they were in a serious position and that he was not sure they could hold out.'[3] In the Middle East, the fate of British troops hung in the balance as they struggled to retain control of the Suez Canal. In Bulgaria and Hungary, the deployment of Wehrmacht forces offered a clear sign that Hitler's invasion of Yugoslavia was imminent. The situation was even more desperate in the North Atlantic, where shipping losses had become so catastrophic that Churchill discontinued the weekly communiqués listing the ships that had been sunk.

Averell listened to the prime minister's woes and acted with haste, pleading with President Roosevelt for more vigorous American intervention. 'England's strength is bleeding,' he wrote. 'In our own interest, I trust that our Navy can be directly employed before our partner is too weak.'[4]

Roosevelt reacted swiftly, announcing that the US Navy would extend its patrols to more than halfway across the Atlantic. Although its ships would not shoot at German vessels – a clear act of war – it would report their whereabouts to the Royal Navy.

Averell also relayed Britain's most urgent material needs to the president, including weaponry, food, and machine tools. Once again, Roosevelt ensured these requests were met. Within weeks, the first shipment of emergency food was crossing the Atlantic: thousands of tons of cheese, canned pork and fish, dried milk, powdered eggs, flour, and dried peas. These provisions were to be followed by aeroplanes, tanks, ships, and heavy machinery.

In private letters to friends, and in confidential conversations with Churchill, Averell shared his hope that America would soon enter the war. 'Every day that we delay direct participation, we are taking an extreme risk,' he wrote.[5] 'The sooner we come in, the shorter the job will be.'[6]

Averell lived at the Dorchester Hotel, in a suite of rooms overlooking Hyde Park. It was one of the safest buildings in central London, a palace-fortress constructed of sufficient steel and concrete to withstand all but the strongest bomb blast. For this reason, it had become the gilded cage for London's aristocrats and super-rich who had shut up their town houses, stood down their servants, and moved into the Dorchester as long-term residents.

'What a mixed brew we were,' recalled the fashion photographer Cecil Beaton. 'Cabinet ministers and their self-consciously respectable wives; hatchet-jawed, iron-grey brigadiers, calf-like airmen off duty, tarts on duty, actresses, déclassé society people, cheap musicians, and motor car agents.'[7] Champagne flowed in the principal dining room and black-tailed waiters served lobster on ice. The war had not yet arrived at the Dorchester.

Averell spent up to sixteen hours a day at the office, astonishing Meiklejohn with his capacity for work. In a letter to his old friend Knight Woolley, Meiklejohn confessed that 'it would be impossible to work any harder'. He was amused to watch Averell at his huge desk, in his huge office, discussing huge quantities of supplies. '[He] achieves a somewhat Mussolini-like effect, not at all to his liking, by reason of his office being a very large room that used to be the living room of a rather elegant flat.'[8]

But Averell was also absent for long periods, accompanying Winston Churchill on impromptu tours of bomb-shattered towns and cities. One such tour took place on the long weekend of 11 April – Easter weekend – when the prime minister invited Averell to join him on a visit to Swansea, Bristol, and Cardiff. All three cities had been heavily bombed by the Luftwaffe.

'Churchill's idea of security was to rely on surprise,' noted Averell. 'He never publicized his plans. He would travel to a bombed city' – often an industrial port – 'and then drive or walk into the dock area.'

Averell was particularly impressed by the warmth of the reception they received on arriving in Swansea. 'Out of their houses they poured – homes with windows broken, slate shingles blown off. Across the street or next door their houses were gone – roofs blown in, walls blown in or nothing left but a pile of debris.' Many families had lost homes, some had lost loved ones. Over the previous four weeks, the Luftwaffe bombers had killed five hundred and wounded a further thousand. Yet still people filled the streets. 'Out they came, women bent and toothless, red-cheeked girls with first babies in their arms, boys pushing their way through the street.'

Churchill savoured the attention. 'Down the street he came in an old Ford car,' wrote Averell, 'smiling, a long cigar stuck deep in his teeth, waving on both sides at once, looking each one in the eye.' He stopped for a photo opportunity, then visited a hospital and chatted warmly with wounded children.

When they reached Swansea's dock area, the reception was even more enthusiastic. The dock workers crowded so thickly around Churchill that the rest of the onlookers were unable to see anything.

'Stand back, my man!' growled Churchill to one of the dock-workers standing beside him. 'Let the others see!'[9] He then put his hat on the end of his cane 'and whirled it around for the crowd to see'. There was a roar of approval.

On such trips, Churchill was always anxious to show off his new American friend. 'When he made a speech on trips like this one,' wrote Averell, 'he would introduce me as President Roosevelt's personal envoy. That was his way of letting the crowd know that America stood with him.'[10]

Mary Churchill was at Averell's side for much of that day and was deeply moved by the reception her father was given. 'They swarmed around Papa, clasping his hand, patting him on the back, shouting his name.' She was proud but concerned. 'It's rather frightening how terribly they depend on him.'

Averell felt a similar sentiment as the day's visit came to an end. He was alone with the prime minister when the train pulled out of Swansea Station. Both of them peered out of the window until the last of the crowds disappeared from view, then Churchill slumped back into his seat, visibly exhausted. Averell noticed him screening his tear-filled eyes with a newspaper. 'They have such faith,' he said at length. 'It is a grave responsibility.'[11]

Back in London, Bob Meiklejohn found himself having to adapt to life in a time of war. The blackout was one inconvenience, casting a sinister calm over the city streets. 'Most impressive thing is the silence,' he wrote. 'Almost everybody walks about like a ghost.' Equally impressive was the London Underground, which had been transformed into a gigantic air raid shelter. 'Astonished to see hundreds of people sleeping in the stations, with passengers going by them and paying no attention.'

Meiklejohn had been anticipating nightly Luftwaffe attacks on London, but it was not until 16 April, four weeks after his arrival, that he experienced a major bombing raid. Excited by the sound of the alarms, he clamped a tin helmet onto his head and headed to the top floor of the embassy. 'A fine view in all directions.'

It was around eight o'clock when the first wave of Luftwaffe planes crossed the night sky. As they passed overhead, Meiklejohn heard the whistle of falling bombs. 'Did a couple of tumbling acts, in which I had plenty of company, to dodge bombs that fell blocks away.' It was difficult to judge how close they were falling, although it was clear they were causing damage. 'Pretty soon there were six to ten big fires about the city, and I saw some amazingly big bomb explosions in the distance. It looked as if whole houses were sailing up in the air.'

Meiklejohn found the experience strangely gripping. 'About midnight, flares started coming down. Lit up the city like a full moon and made one feel pretty uncomfortable.' A few small bombs fell nearby, but at half past twelve the raid became altogether more dangerous. 'An enormous bomb hit what I was told was Battersea Power Station. One of the gas containers blew up in a column of fire that seemed to go up miles.' Just a few minutes later, a stick of bombs fell very close to the embassy itself, sending a cloud of acrid dust over the roof.

The raid lasted for a further three hours, as 450 German bombers launched one of their heaviest attacks on the capital. 'The most amazing sight I have ever seen in my life,' wrote Meiklejohn when it finally came to an end. 'A whole section of the city, north of the financial district, was a solid mass of flames, leaping hundreds of feet in the air.'

A five-minute walk from Grosvenor Square, at the Dorchester Hotel, Averell had been spending that night attending a dinner hosted by Lord Charles Cavendish. The dinner was in honour of Cavendish's wife, Adele, the sister of Fred Astaire, and many society figures had been invited. Among them was twenty-one-year-old Pamela Churchill, the prime minister's daughter-in-law.

Pamela had first met Averell a fortnight earlier at Chequers but they had exchanged only a few words. Now, at the Dorchester, they were to find themselves in a rather more personal conversation.

Eighteen months earlier, Pamela had married the prime minister's unruly son, Randolph, a marriage that rapidly produced a son, also called Winston. Thereafter, the couple's relationship had lurched from disaster to disaster. Randolph was a gambler, drunkard, and serial womaniser who was never shy of exploiting the family name. 'Wherever he went,' wrote the American journalist Virginia Cowles, 'an explosion seemed to follow.'[12] Few tears were shed when he was despatched to the Middle East as an officer with the 4th Hussars.

His absence lifted Pamela's spirits. She had a magnetic allure all her own, with dimples, freckles, and a mane of light red hair, paired with an infectious giggle and a flirtatious air. Evelyn Waugh described her as having 'kitten eyes full of innocent fun'.[13] The fun was not always so innocent.

Her portrait had made the cover of *Life* magazine that January, introducing her to an international audience. The daughter of Lord and Lady Digby, a solidly dull dynasty of gentleman farmers, Pamela modelled herself on her promiscuous great-aunt, Jane Digby, the scandalous nineteenth-century courtesan. Pamela inherited Jane's free-wheeling sexuality, as well as her canny ability to lure rich and influential men into her bed.

Lord Cavendish's dinner at the Dorchester that night was rocked by exploding bombs and anti-aircraft fire. The guests had assembled for dinner on the eighth floor of the hotel and had a fine panorama across Westminster – better, even, than Bob Meiklejohn's view from the roof of the nearby American embassy. Averell said that the magnesium flares lit up the city 'like Broadway and 42nd Street'.[14]

Pamela spent the evening rather more focused on Averell himself. 'The most beautiful man I had ever met. He was marvellous, absolutely marvellous, with his raven black hair . . . very athletic, very tan, very healthy.' Dressed in gold lamé and thinking only of herself, she was untroubled by the fact that he was twenty-eight years older than her. She was determined to spend the night in his bed.

The atmosphere became strained as the bombing raid grew increasingly intense; the final straw came when a bomb exploded in a nearby street. Everyone scurried back to their bedrooms, signalling the end of the party. In Averell's case, he found himself with Pamela in tow.

What happened next took place behind closed doors. Pamela later said that she was glad to spend the night in his arms, having helped him (as she put it) 'peel off her dinner dress'. One of her friends in the know would later add that 'a big bombing raid is a very good way to get into bed with somebody. It is a known fact, and that is how it started.'[15]

Averell himself wrote to his wife, Marie, about the events of that night, although he omitted the salient details. 'Needless to say, my sleep was intermittent. Guns were going all the time and airplanes overhead.'[16]

The union of the two lovers did not go entirely unobserved. When Winston Churchill's private secretary, Jock Colville, walked across

Horse Guards Parade the following morning, he spotted Averell and Pamela strolling together through Whitehall.

He was surprised, but kept the sighting to himself.

As Averell reflected on his first month in London, he was more than satisfied with his achievements. The mission was working round the clock, with a full-time staff that now numbered twelve experts from America and a dozen or more secretaries. The first supplies of food and essentials had been transported across the Atlantic and Averell had forged a close personal relationship with the prime minister. He had also started a deliciously dangerous affair with Pamela Churchill.

But the war itself was looking increasingly fraught. Greece had been invaded by the Wehrmacht and was in imminent danger of falling to the Nazis, and the beleaguered British troops in Tobruk were now virtually encircled. More alarming, from Averell's point of view, was the recent German wolfpack assault on Atlantic convoy SC26, transporting vital supplies to Great Britain. Four U-boats led a devastating attack, which resulted in ten of the twenty-vessel convoy being sent to the bottom of the ocean. Tens of thousands of tons of essential foodstuffs were lost.

It was a stark reminder of the difficulties of keeping Britain supplied from America. Averell's lifeline to the country was as essential as it was precarious.

7
Kathy and Churchill

KATHY HARRIMAN SPENT the first two weeks of April in a state of uncertainty. She had only recently graduated from Bennington College, a prestigious liberal arts college that, at the time, admitted only women. Now Kathy found herself stranded in her father's Sun Valley ski resort, dispirited and desperate to find a purpose in life.

It was Averell who suggested she join him in England, an idea he first expressed in a note to Steve Hannagan, his public relations man at Sun Valley. 'It is hard to understand the significance in New York of what is going on here,' he wrote. 'I am going to encourage Kathy to come.'

Averell also wrote to his wife, Marie. 'It will make a real person out of her.' And then he sent a telegram to Kathy herself: 'THINGS OK HERE,' he said. 'CABLE WHETHER YOU SERIOUSLY WANT TO COME.'

Kathy didn't need any encouragement: she was desperate to join her father. Popsie had been by her side since she was very young, pushing her to excel. Now, six weeks after he had left for London, she needed him more than ever.

But he also needed her. He adored his beloved Puff and knew that her effortless elegance would add lustre to his image. A lively brunette with a forthright manner, Kathy had an intelligent smile and her father's strong jaw. She also had poise, guts, and an insatiable curiosity. And she looked a million dollars in her Worth skirts and silk stockings.

As co-owner of *Newsweek*, Averell knew he could secure her a job as a neophyte reporter. But first she needed the necessary papers, and this was easier said than done, as Steve Hannagan was quick to point out. 'Urgent passport difficulties,' he telegraphed back. 'No woman reporters granted up to now.'

Averell never took no for an answer: he fired off a cable to Dean Acheson, assistant secretary of state. If anyone could grant Kathy a passport, it was Acheson. But Acheson declined his request, leading Averell to appeal directly to the secretary of state, Cordell Hull. 'I am most anxious to have my daughter join me,' he wrote. 'This battle of Britain, being fought every night and day, is a fight participated in equally by the women. If Kathleen can have a part in describing this to America, I believe it would be of value and well justify the food she would eat. I have consulted Mr Churchill . . . her coming would be well received and appreciated.'

Hull was unmoved. 'I strongly advise against.'

Undeterred, Averell now approached President Roosevelt's top aide, Harry Hopkins, so close to the president that he lived in the White House. Averell told Kathy to contact Hopkins as well.

This time their joint appeal worked. Hopkins recommended the idea to Roosevelt, who gave it the presidential green light.

Kathy was delighted. 'PASSPORT OKAY,' she wrote in a two-word cable to her father.

'THRILLED,' was his one-word reply.

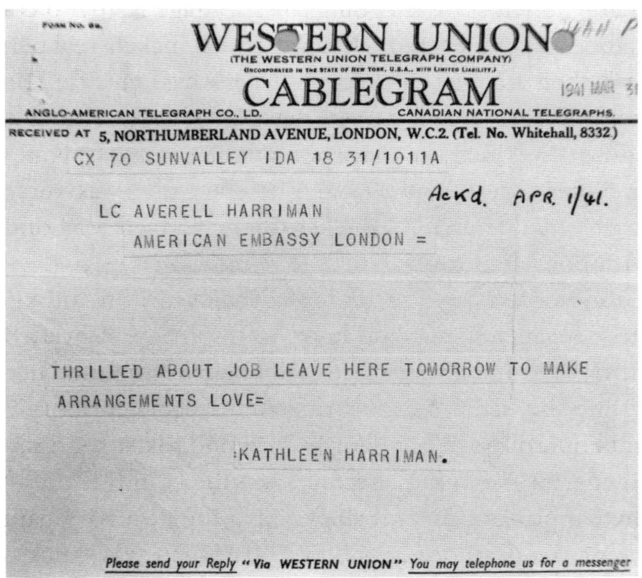

WESTERN UNION
(THE WESTERN UNION TELEGRAPH COMPANY)
CABLEGRAM
1941 MAR 31
ANGLO-AMERICAN TELEGRAPH CO., LD. CANADIAN NATIONAL TELEGRAPHS.
RECEIVED AT 5, NORTHUMBERLAND AVENUE, LONDON, W.C.2. (Tel. No. Whitehall, 8332)

CX 70 SUNVALLEY IDA 18 31/1011A

Ackd. APR. 1/41.

LC AVERELL HARRIMAN
AMERICAN EMBASSY LONDON =

THRILLED ABOUT JOB LEAVE HERE TOMORROW TO MAKE ARRANGEMENTS LOVE=

KATHLEEN HARRIMAN.

Please send your Reply "Via WESTERN UNION" You may telephone us for a messenger

Kathy was desperate to join her father in England and delighted when President Roosevelt sanctioned her trip. 'Thrilled about job,' she wrote in one of several telegrams to Averell.

In the first week of May, Kathy packed her bags and said farewell to Sun Valley as she prepared to embark on the adventure of a lifetime. To the young bachelors working at the resort, it was as if a light had gone out. 'I'm sort of heartbroken,' confessed one. 'She is one young lady who is aces up.'[1]

Kathy's voyage to the British Isles took even longer than it had taken her father. Delayed six days in Lisbon, Kathy lapped up the spring sunshine, swam off the coast of Portugal, and partied late into the night. 'A continual spirit of vacation,' she wrote.[2] Lisbon's nightclubs were packed with revellers and roués, Allies and Nazis. 'I'm getting in all the rhumbas possible before I board the Clipper.'[3]

Yet there was a desperation to the gaiety and the war loomed large over everything. 'It gave one a rather odd feeling, eating dinner with an American expert waiting to go to London,' she later wrote, 'while at the next table were leading members of the German Gestapo.'

Finally, on 16 May, there was an onward flight to London. Kathy boarded the Clipper with all the necessary essentials for a chic young lady: cocktail dresses, nylon stockings, and Guerlain lipsticks, as well as a dozen packs of Stim-U-Dent toothpicks requested by her father.

She arrived in a city still recovering from the mid-April Luftwaffe raid that had helped facilitate Pamela Churchill's seduction of her father. As she was driven by cab to the Dorchester, her first impressions were of the terrific bomb damage. 'Hardly a block has gone unscathed,' she wrote in her first letter home. 'I've read about blocks on end of flattened houses, but it's something quite different to actually see it.'[4]

On the day after her arrival, Saturday, 17 May, Averell hosted a lavish soirée at the Dorchester for his beloved Puff. 'Last night was my coming-out party,' she wrote to her sister. Everyone who was anyone was invited. 'The newspaper world, our foreign correspondents, English reporters, as well as a general or two thrown in to give the party a uniformed and medalled touch.'[5] More than fifty guests showed up, including Pamela Churchill. 'The nicest, sanest girl I've met so far,' wrote Kathy of that first meeting, unaware that Pamela was sleeping with her father. 'She's doing a great job here.'[6]

But so was her father, who was praised by everyone. 'I'm beginning to feel what Ave is,' she wrote. 'He seems to stand for something secure that people can hang onto. They all have great faith in him.' She was amazed by his popularity. 'Just in this short time he literally knows everyone of note. They all love him.'[7]

Averell and Kathy had an unusually close relationship. She admired her Popsie as much as he adored his Puff. Their lives were to be transformed by their wartime service in London and Moscow.

At the end of that glamorous evening, Kathy and guests scrambled through the blackout to the 400 Club in the West End, where they danced through the night. Life felt not so very different from Lisbon. 'London is a gay place, nervously gay,' she wrote in a letter home. 'There is not much time to sleep.'[8]

Averell was delighted that his daughter had been such an instant hit. 'Kathleen has had a royal reception,' he wrote proudly. 'She is the center of attention.'

He secured her work as a reporter for Hearst's International News Service. Her first assignment was to write a series of articles on British women in wartime. The brief from her editor was succinct. 'Just give us everything you can observe and think of, sobbing all over the front page.' She was told not to be precious about her work. 'Don't worry too much about fine writing or licking the yarn into first-class shape. We want the color and the facts.'

Her first article was frothy and upbeat, exactly what was required. She got the idea for it while travelling on a train. An English woman in the same carriage turned to her and asked: 'I've been admiring your silk stockings. Are you American?'

The chat that followed was set down verbatim by Kathy; it told of hardship and fortitude, and was pitch-perfect for readers back home who relished tales of plucky Brits holding out against the Nazis. Better still, her article ended with a feisty payoff line. 'These English women may not have my silk stockings,' she wrote, 'but they have something else, something I'd like to catch hold of, because it's pretty important.'[9] She would expand on this theme in later articles. British women, she said, had guts of brass.

PRESS PASS
TO
AMERICAN EMBASSY
1, GROSVENOR SQUARE, W.1.

Name
(in block letters)
Representing
Signature
Countersigned
Date of Issue

Kathy worked as a journalist during her time in England. Her upbeat articles proved incredibly popular in her native America.

★

As the daughter of the most important American in Britain, Kathy was the talk of the town that spring and was invited to meet everyone of importance.

'Last weekend we went to Chequers,' she wrote to her sister, in a long letter describing her first encounter with Winston Churchill. 'It's rather a shock meeting someone you've seen caricatured so many times.' Churchill was so enchanted by Kathy's presence that he invited her to sit next to him at dinner. 'The Prime Minister is much smaller than I expected and a lot less fat. He wears a blue Jaeger one-piece (the only way to keep warm in that house) and looks rather like a kindly blue teddy bear.' Churchill was utterly charming when chatting with her and gushed with kindly sentiments. 'He expresses himself wonderfully and continually comes out with delightful statements. I'd expected an overpowering, rather terrifying man. He is quite the opposite, very gracious, has a wonderful smile and is not at all hard to talk to.' She added that 'he has the kind of eyes that look right through you'.[10]

Shortly before that weekend at Chequers, Averell had been forwarded some journalistic advice from Herbert Swope, veteran reporter on the *New York Herald* – intended for his daughter. In the words of Swope, 'she has to keep in mind the fact that she is never off duty. That stories occur everywhere, all the time, to everybody.'[11]

Kathy took this advice to heart, observing everything and everyone that weekend at Chequers and thereby providing a unique insider's view of the Churchill household. 'Mrs C is a very sweet lady. She's given up her whole life to her husband and takes a back seat very graciously.' Kathy couldn't help feeling sorry for Clementine. 'Everyone in the family looks upon him as god and she's rather left out, so that when anyone pays her any attention, she's overjoyed.' Averell offered to play croquet with her that weekend, a sport at which they both excelled. 'She was so grateful . . . it seems as though she seldom gets any fun.'

Yet Kathy detected a steely core to Clementine Churchill, viewing her as a point of stability in a household where nerves were often on edge. 'She has a mind of her own,' she told her sister. 'Only she's big enough not to use it unless he [Churchill] wants her to.'

And then there was Mary Churchill, five years younger than Kathy. 'Full of enthusiasm – childish in some ways and terribly grown up in others. She cornered me the moment I got to Chequers and asked about public opinion in the US and questioned me about all sorts of things.' Kathy liked her and found her intelligent, 'but so naive that it hurts'.

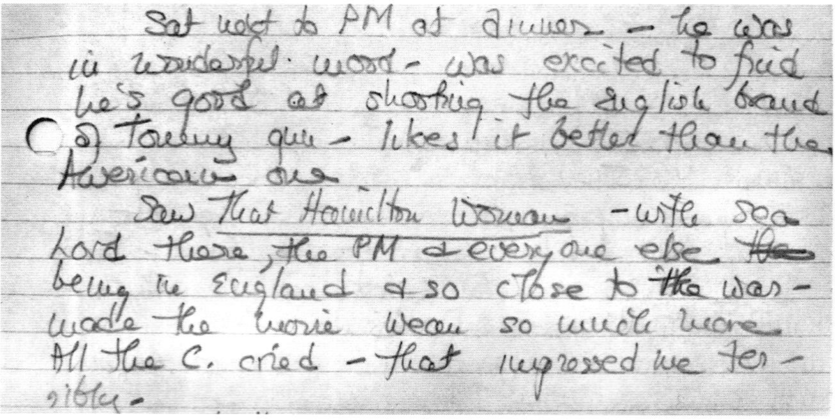

Sat next to PM at dinner – he was
in wonderful mood – was excited to find
he's good at shooting the English brand
of Tommy gun – likes it better than the
American one.
Saw *That Hamilton Woman* – with Sea
Lord there, the PM & everyone else
being in England & so close to the war –
made the movie mean so much more.
All the C. cried – that impressed me terribly.

Kathy's letters to her family are full of fascinating detail. Here she records one of her many visits to Winston Churchill and family. 'Sat next to PM at dinner – he was in wonderful mood.'

During that first night's dinner, Kathy had an enthusiastic discussion about Tommy guns with the PM – 'he was in wonderful mood' – and chatted confidently with Sir Dudley Pound, the First Sea Lord. Senior RAF officials were also there, strategic planners who were continually updating the prime minister on that night's bombing raids. 'Getting their reactions is like entering another world. The war, the bombing, is so completely objective to them.' At one point that evening, they informed Churchill of the terrible news that Crete had just capitulated to the Nazis. 'I don't think I'll ever forget the look on the PM's face when he came in and told us. Words can't describe it.'

That weekend at Chequers was Kathy's induction into the world of power and privilege that she was to inhabit for the next four years. Her own background, education, and wealth provided a buttress to any nerves she might have felt, yet her performance was nevertheless remarkable. Breezily confident, she sailed through that first evening with the prime minister.

After dinner, everyone adjourned to the drawing room to watch *That Hamilton Woman*, the latest film by Alexander Korda. Kathy was moved by it, but not as much as her hosts. 'All the Churchills cried,' she wrote. 'That impressed me terribly.'[12]

Churchill was infamous for his mood swings, as Kathy was to witness the following day. The prime minister, so gay the previous evening, seemed deflated. At that night's dinner, she plucked up the courage to ask him why. His answer reflected his mood.

'Turkey is giving in,' he told her. 'All Europe is swaying towards a Hitler victory. They are giving in. We need a victory.' There was a long pause, as if the cares of the world had left him drained. And then he turned to her and said: 'I'd like to be a cat – without worries.'[13]

Kathy soon found herself in demand. Her first work had been with the International News Service, but she had such a good eye – and such good access to those in power – that she began working as a guest reporter for the *Daily Express*. This was Lord Beaverbrook's flagship newspaper. He placed her under the wing of his finest female journalist, Hilde Marchant, whom Kathy found 'tiny, terribly efficient and terribly cold blooded'. Marchant took her to the less glamorous areas of London: the docks, the wreckage of factories, and the badly damaged East End, 'where the poorer working classes live'. One of her more traumatic visits was to a plastic surgery hospital in East Grinstead, where she met a group of badly burned pilots. 'I expected to be horror-struck and depressed,' she wrote. 'God knows I was.'

This was a story too grim to make the newspapers, for the censors would never allow it to be published. So she set down her experiences for her family back at home. 'Imagine walking up to a guy and shaking hands with a fingerless stub. Badly burned fingers curl under and then grow together. After a while they can be operated on and separated.' She met one young lad who was halfway through surgery. 'His hands are ok, his face isn't. He still has to have a new set of false eyelids grafted on.'

Kathy found the experience difficult to stomach. 'It's not easy talking to an earless, eyelidless boy of about twenty-one, who also has very little nose-structure left. You can't let him realize what you feel. While I was at the hospital I was all right, but I still haven't completely recovered.'[14]

Other visits were more pleasurable. She struck up a friendship with Quentin Reynolds, the best-selling *Collier's* correspondent, borrowed her father's Bentley, and whisked him off to the Derby. And she was also introduced to scores of eligible young officers, 'very dashing, good-looking in their regimental evening uniforms, but not very intelligent'.

She met a pantheon of stars during her first weeks in London: Lord Beaverbrook, minister of air production (and newspaper magnate); Lord Woolton, minister of food; the distinguished politician Duff Cooper. She stayed with Lord and Lady Derby at their stately mansion, Knowsley Hall, and was amazed to find life little changed since the eighteenth century: 'At dinner, a lackey in livery stands behind your chair.'

She gave each acquaintance her own private assessment, expressing a grudging appreciation for Churchill's parliamentary private secretary, Brendan Bracken. 'He likes to think himself the glamor boy of the West End,' she wrote, 'though so far no one's consented to marry him. He's very pompous, wonderful dry sense of humor – has a head of hair like Harpo Marx – only Brendan's is real.' Kathy was particularly fond of General Hastings Ismay, whom she met the same evening. 'Absolute heaven – nicknamed Pug – that's what he looks like.'

Kathy also got to meet the queen, who left a lasting impression. 'She's perfectly beautiful – too bad she hasn't the photogenique type of looks. She's got more poise than anyone I've met yet.' Kathy met her with a small group of foreign journalists. 'All of us American reporters stood around like a bunch of apes and she was wonderful, kept up her end of the conversation, asked questions and seemed interested in the answers. You might have thought she was doing the interviewing.'[15]

Averell Harriman had been living at the Dorchester for nine weeks by the time of Kathy's arrival in London. Pamela was also living at the hotel. Kathy's presence prompted her father to rent a more spacious suite, and she suggested that Pamela also move in. This seemed only natural, for she and Kathy had become firm friends. 'We get on beautifully, thank God, because I see her a hell of a lot,' wrote Kathy. 'She knows everything about everything, political and otherwise.'[16] But she also realised that Pamela was always looking out for herself. 'Pam is a bitch,' she added in another letter.

As for Pamela herself, she adored Kathy. 'Wonderful. The sort of typical American college girl. Long-legged and attractive-looking, totally captivating.'

Kathy soon discovered her father was sleeping with her closest friend in London, just as she had known of his other extra-marital affairs. But she never mentioned it in her letters home, nor did she raise it with Pamela. She inhabited a world of quiet discretion, and it was simply not a matter to be discussed. Pamela herself would later say that it was a case of 'she knows, and I know that she knows, and I know that she knows that I know'.[17]

Only once did Kathy allude to the affair, and even then she did so elliptically. 'She and I were driving down to the country on a Friday,' recalled Pamela years later, 'and something happened, and she said to me, "Well, you know, I am not a total fool." I knew immediately, and I was very surprised, and I said, "Uh, what?" And she said, "I had a big decision to make. I had to decide whether to go home and not be part of it – but I thought I should protect my father, and the best way to do that was by staying."'[18]

Kathy Harriman (second from right) was befriended by Pamela Churchill (left), the PM's daughter-in-law. It was some time before she realised Pamela was sleeping with her father, Averell (right).

Kathy certainly displayed no reticence when her father offered to rent the two girls a country house. Petersfield Farm was in the Surrey hills some twenty miles south-west of London. It was an idyllic place, a Tudor cottage with five bedrooms, a summer house, and a kitchen garden. 'I can rave until Domesday about the old, crooked beams and bricks,' wrote Kathy.

On their first weekend in the house, she and Pamela drove to nearby Dorking to buy supplies – 'rationed food, such as a joint for Sunday lunch, butter and a sliver of cheese'. They managed to get other supplies as well. 'Being Mrs Churchill, Pam gets more than we otherwise would – six extra eggs and things like that. Without any pull, it would have been impossible to have gotten what we need, with guests coming tomorrow.'

Petersfield was glorious, especially in the first warmth of spring. The two of them sat in the garden, surrounded by friends, and ate fresh peaches from Fortnum's and drank chilled champagne. 'If it hadn't been that three of the boys were in uniform,' wrote Kathy, 'it might have been Long Island.'[19]

Life was good and her work was going well. The future had never looked brighter, even though it was wartime. 'The telephone never stops ringing in our suite,' she wrote. 'Combine war and journalism and you'll never have a moment of boredom.'[20] This was certainly the case on the morning of Sunday, 22 June, when Kathy was woken with the sensational news that Nazi Germany had invaded the Soviet Union.

PART III

Seeking Stalin

Moscow
Summer 1941

8

Unwelcome Guests

WINSTON CHURCHILL'S BBC broadcast on Sunday, 22 June, had been a bold throw of the dice. In announcing his support for the Soviet Union, he had turned the country into an ally – albeit an uncertain one. Now his priority was to forge links with the enigmatic Soviet leader. But this was no easy matter, for Stalin was a reclusive figure hardly ever seen in public. Churchill had once described Russia as 'a riddle wrapped in a mystery, inside an enigma'. Its dictator was cast in the same image.

Ambassador Cripps was unable to provide Churchill with much information about the Soviet leader, despite having spent two years in the country. He never got to see Stalin and was never invited into the Kremlin. He had only recently completed a biographical profile of the Soviet leader for the Foreign Office's Northern Department, which oversaw relations with the Soviet Union. Just eighty-six lines in length, it placed most of its emphasis on what was *not* known about Stalin. 'He deliberately makes himself a figure of mystery, rarely emerging from the Kremlin.'[1]

The few things that Cripps knew about Stalin were hardly reassuring. He described the Soviet leader as blinkered and introverted, a lawless gangster who had spent much of his youth engaged in criminal activities. He was known to have been a leading figure in the infamous 1907 Tiflis bank heist in which dozens of people had been killed or maimed. Imprisoned and exiled to Siberia, Stalin had eventually been freed during the 1917 revolution.

Cripps's profile also revealed that the Soviet leader was terrifyingly ruthless when dealing with any potential challenger. 'The *alias* Stalin means Man of Steel . . . he has been remarkably successful in removing any possible rivals from his path, his greatest triumph being the downfall of Trotsky. By surrounding himself with mediocrities and by the employment of an iron discipline, he has reached a position of absolute despotism.'

In the wake of Churchill's BBC broadcast, the PM's imperative was to establish a relationship with Stalin, and that meant sending someone to Moscow who could win the Soviet leader's confidence. The most qualified candidate for the job was Averell. He had spent the previous three months establishing the transatlantic lifeline between America and Britain and knew exactly what munitions were available. He also had the ear of both Roosevelt and Churchill.

But Averell was in Cairo at the time of the invasion, sent there by Churchill to analyse the disastrous performance of the Eighth Army. The Wehrmacht's spring offensive had turned into an Allied rout, with British troops beating a sorry retreat to the Egyptian border. The situation in North Africa was now precarious, with morale sinking to an all-time low.

Averell was not due back for another three weeks and was therefore unable to head to Moscow. Since time was pressing, with the Wehrmacht driving ever deeper into Soviet territory, Churchill was obliged to look elsewhere. It was unfortunate that he settled upon the worst possible candidate. Ambassador Cripps was to be sent back to the Soviet capital.

The choice was regrettable, but it served a purpose. Cripps was one of Churchill's staunchest political enemies (he had remained an MP while serving as ambassador) and had a powerful voice in the House of Commons. In posting him back to Moscow, Churchill was keeping him in political exile.

Cripps left England on Wednesday, 25 June, just three days after the Nazi invasion, accompanied to the Soviet capital by a small military mission. They were given a hero's welcome when they landed at Moscow airport. 'A great assemblage of distinguished people met us,' wrote Cripps, who couldn't stop marvelling at the fact that he had left that same airport in disgrace just three weeks earlier.[2] It was pouring with rain, drenching everyone, but this did little to dampen Cripps's enthusiasm.

He was even more delighted to be taken straight to the Kremlin for a wartime briefing by Foreign Commissar Molotov. The news he received from the battle-front was grim indeed, with Molotov confessing that the Wehrmacht was crushing everything in its path. Hitler's panzer divisions were racing eastwards under a cloudless Soviet sky, virtually uncontested. Army Group North had slashed its way through Lithuania and was now pushing towards Leningrad. Army Group Centre had been equally successful: just three days after crossing the frontier it was heading for Minsk. In the south, the situation was yet more critical. Hitler's panzers were lunging towards Kiev. Cripps was left in no doubt that the entire front line was in danger of collapse.

Later that evening, Cripps dined with his colleagues in the splendour of the British Embassy. He had previously hated his time in Moscow, writing gloom-filled letters about life in the Soviet Union. 'Hopeless . . . very trying . . . quite the worst day I have had.'[3] He had also disliked the palatial British Embassy, a stucco-fronted mansion on Sofiskaya Embankment. But now, on that first night back in Moscow, he felt reinvigorated. He had a task to fulfil – befriending the Soviet regime – and he intended to succeed.

'We all sat on the balcony till eleven o'clock,' he wrote in his diary. 'It was the most perfect night with just a gentle breeze and the most marvellous colouring in the sky behind the Kremlin. As the evening wore on a misty haze came up from the river and shrouded the Kremlin in the most wonderful purple light, softly translucent.'[4]

Despite the warm welcome from Molotov, there was one ingredient missing. Ambassador Cripps had expected to be received by Stalin. But Stalin was nowhere to be seen.

Stalin's invisibility had not gone unnoticed in Moscow. He had been seen by no one since retiring to his Kuntsevo dacha in the aftermath of the Nazi invasion. Foreign diplomats began wondering if the Soviet leader had left the capital and gone into hiding.

'They inferred that he had fled to Turkey or Iran or Afghanistan or China,' wrote Associated Press correspondent, Henry Cassidy. 'Others agreed Stalin was not there [in Moscow] but believed he simply had been spending a holiday in his villa at Gagri, on the Black Sea coast.'[5]

The truth was far worse. According to Molotov, Stalin had shut himself away and was in such a state of prostration 'that he was not interested in anything, didn't show any initiative and was in a bad way'.[6] He couldn't sleep, hadn't changed his clothes, and spent most of his time wandering aimlessly around his dacha, as if in a trance. For a leader used to micro-managing every aspect of life in the Soviet Union, his absence was a disaster.

On Monday, 30 June, an inner circle of Politburo members drew up an emergency plan to form a State Defence Committee responsible for the entire Soviet war effort. It was the first important initiative they had ever taken without Stalin's approval. All agreed that the Soviet leader alone had the authority to lead this committee, and they now drove out to the dacha to plead with him to return to Moscow.

It was gloomy inside the dacha on that afternoon, with the surrounding pine trees casting the dark green interior into deep shadow. The visitors found their leader seated alone in the little dining room. All were struck by how thin, haggard, and depressed he looked.

On any normal occasion they were terrified of him, for he was always blunt-spoken and often unpredictable. But this time, it was Stalin who seemed terrified.

'Why have you come?' he asked nervously. He clearly feared they were going to arrest him.

They informed him that the war situation was so grave that they had formed a State Defence Committee.

'With whom at its head?' he asked.

'You, Comrade Stalin.'

'Can I lead the country to final victory?' He seemed unsure.

'There is none more worthy,' ventured one of his comrades.[7]

After some persuasion, Stalin agreed to take up the onerous task of leading the Soviet Union through the unfolding catastrophe. Henceforth, he was to be the supreme war leader in command of every aspect of the ongoing conflict. Once taken, the decision seemed to breathe new life into him, for his spirits suddenly lifted. He returned to the Kremlin the following day 'a new man', noted one, who added that he was now fully engaged in organising resistance to the Nazi invasion. Two days later, on Thursday, 3 July, Stalin made his defining radio address to the nation. First broadcast at dawn, it was heard by one of the very few Western visitors to Moscow at the time, the celebrated American photographer Margaret Bourke-White. She was taking a stroll when she heard the public loudspeakers crackle into life.

Comrades, citizens, brothers and sisters! Men of our army and navy! I am addressing you, my friends!

It was a voice that Bourke-White didn't recognise. She summoned the porter of the Metropole Hotel and asked him who was speaking. The porter was speechless, transfixed by what he heard.

The enemy is cruel and implacable. He is out to seize our lands, watered with our sweat, to seize our grain and soil secured by our labour.

Bourke-White asked him once again who was speaking.

'He has a Georgian accent,' said the porter. 'Yes, I am sure of it! That is Stalin's voice.'

Bourke-White realised the significance of what was taking place. Stalin had not spoken to the Soviet nation since 1938. He had been all but invisible, the arch-manipulator who always operated in the shadows. She rushed into the hotel and woke her husband, then returned to the square.

In case of forced retreat of Red Army units, not a single engine must be left to the enemy, not a single railway car, not a single pound of grain or gallon of fuel.

This was the scorched-earth tactic intended to deprive the Wehrmacht of food and supplies.

Stalin added a few details about the ongoing struggle, informing his audience that German troops were advancing with terrifying rapidity.

The enemy must be crushed . . . We must win.

When he had finished, Bourke-White overheard an elderly woman muttering to herself: 'He works so hard! When does he sleep? I worry about his health!'[8]

Ambassador Cripps scored his first diplomatic success on Saturday, 12 July, when he was invited into the Kremlin by Stalin himself. 'The great moment has arrived!' he wrote in his diary.[9] He was in buoyant mood.

The occasion was the signing of an historic Anglo-Soviet agreement, negotiated behind the scenes, in which the two countries were to form a loose alliance. It had two key provisions; first, to render each other assistance in the war against Hitler; second, that neither country would sign a separate peace with Nazi Germany.

Shortly before five, a fleet of Soviet limousines swept up outside the British Embassy to transport Ambassador Cripps to the Kremlin. Embassy staff were also invited, along with attachés and secretaries. Everyone had dressed in their finery, for this was history in the making. They would finally get to meet the elusive Soviet leader.

'Sir Stafford Cripps [was] natty in a costume of white trousers and blue coat,' wrote reporter Henry Cassidy. 'The rest of the staff of the British Embassy were all attired in their best suits. Their heads shone from combing, their cheeks from shaving. They were obviously excited.'[10]

But they were soon to find themselves disappointed, for the Soviet leader remained in the background for the entire evening. He declined to have any role in the proceedings, leaving the signing of the Anglo-Soviet agreement to Ambassador Cripps and Foreign Commissar Molotov.

The treaty itself was a cause for celebration, and Cripps was so exultant that he abandoned his lifelong teetotalism, telling those around him that the occasion was so important that he would break his own self-imposed rule. 'Champagne was brought in, and I took one large gulp of it as a toast to "Down with Hitler!" ' He viewed the Anglo-Soviet agreement as a major turning point in relations between the two countries. 'So closes a chapter in the history of the world,' he proclaimed to his diary, 'and I believe that a far more hopeful chapter has opened.'[11]

Once the official photographs had been taken, Cripps led his team across the room to finally meet Stalin. For everyone present, this was the high point of the evening. Cripps's principal military adviser felt that such an important milestone called for a polite remark. Speaking through the embassy interpreter, he told Stalin he was delighted to be working alongside the mighty Red Army.

Stalin looked at him in disdain and replied: 'How splendid if I thought that you meant what you said.'[12]

9
Moscow Aflame

Dreadful news was received by the Kremlin within a fortnight of the Anglo-Soviet agreement being signed. Hitler's Army Group Centre had swept aside everything in its path and was now just 200 miles from Smolensk, linked to Moscow by a direct highway. The capital itself was in grave danger.

The disaster had begun a fortnight earlier, when the first major city fell to the Nazis. 'Up to a thousand tanks are enveloping Minsk,' warned the Red Army's front-line commander, Dmitry Pavlov. 'There is no way to oppose them.' His forces tried to resist the onslaught, but the city was captured by the Wehrmacht on Sunday, 29 June. Almost simultaneously, German panzers closed their pincers around a massive group of Red Army troops, trapping them in a deadly embrace. Although some managed to escape, many more were taken prisoner.

The losses in Soviet manpower were staggering, as was the loss of territory. In the first eighteen days of combat, Army Group Centre had advanced 360 miles and killed or captured a third of a million Soviet soldiers. Those who tried to escape were gunned down by German Stukas flying at low altitude.

Stalin's reaction to the Minsk disaster was characteristically unforgiving. He recalled General Pavlov to Moscow, along with his chief of staff and seven senior commanders. All were charged with betraying the motherland and sentenced to death. They were executed shortly afterwards. Stalin posthumously stripped Pavlov of his rank so that his family could not inherit his army pension, and also confiscated his property. It was an act of vindictiveness that would be repeated many times in the months to come.

Russia was now in such danger that a monumental effort was under way to dismantle industrial plants and move the heavy machinery eastwards, to the Urals and beyond. Stalin himself had declared the German invasion to be total war, requiring endangered territory to be reduced to a wasteland. 'The enemy must not be left a single engine, or a single railway truck, and not a pound of bread nor a pint of fuel . . . all valuable property, whether grain, fuel or non-ferrous metals, which cannot be evacuated, must be destroyed.'[1]

Martial law was introduced; conscription made compulsory. Stalin would soon issue Order Number 270, which declared that all who surrendered or were captured were 'traitors to the motherland'. In issuing such a decree, he was signalling that the country was engaged in a fight to the death.

In the Soviet capital itself, there was an atmosphere of surreal calm. News of the battlefield losses was being suppressed and the Luftwaffe had yet to appear in the skies above Moscow. When the *Collier's* correspondent Alice-Leone Moats toured the streets in those early days of the invasion she found no trace of alarm. The only sign that Moscow was a city at war was the appearance of anti-German propaganda posters. She noticed that the now-closed Italian Embassy had been plastered with graphic depictions of Soviet soldiers stabbing Hitler.

For staff at the British Embassy in Moscow, the evening of Monday, 21 July, began on an optimistic note. Ambassador Cripps had promised his team an outing to Tchaikovsky Hall, where the Moiseyev Ensemble was performing folk dances from across the Soviet Union. Everyone was invited, even the embassy caretaker, Harold Elvin. He watched as the grandees gathered in the embassy atrium, 'looking very resplendent with gold braid, kilts and all that'.[2]

Halfway through the performance, the leader of the ensemble, Igor Moiseyev, climbed onto the stage, called for silence, and announced that Ambassador Cripps was in the auditorium. There was instant jubilation. 'Up shot the audience and hit the roof shouting,' wrote Elvin. 'They cheered and cheered and nothing stopped them. They began shouting slogans: "For the brave British people" – cheer. "For the gallant English army" – cheer. "For the continued friendship and alliance for all time" – cheer.'[3]

Cripps rose to his feet as the cheering grew ever louder. It was his second moment of triumph. 'I bowed to the audience,' he wrote in his diary, 'and then, according to the usual habit here, we all joined in the clapping.'[4]

Later that night, the younger members of his team headed to Aragvi restaurant, one of the few places in Moscow that served half-decent food. They were still in the restaurant when the city's air raid sirens sounded for the first time. It was 10.10 p.m.

They knew they needed to leave straightaway or risk being trapped by the curfew. The most senior embassy staffer, Counsellor Lacy Baggallay, suggested all ten of them squeeze into his Humber and make a dash back to the embassy. It was to be a race against time.

Fifteen minutes to the south of the restaurant, in the Arbat district, Associated Press journalist Henry Cassidy was admiring the sunset from his apartment building when he also heard the public loud-speaker system click into life: 'Citizens, citizenesses, attention! Air raid alarm!'

A Luftwaffe attack was imminent.

'There was a tense, expectant hush as four million persons awaited the unknown,' wrote Cassidy. 'Then, rolling into the city like a mighty wave from the west, came the roar of the anti-aircraft barrage and, after it, the shrill shriek of bombs, the dull grunt of explosions.'[5] Counsellor Baggallay and the other embassy staff were still crossing Moscow when the first bombs began to fall. Through the car windscreen they could see the sticks of explosives caught in the shafts of searchlights. And then came the inferno. 'Fires everywhere like burning mountains, belching like volcanos; all around, ruby red tracer bullets, shells bursting, literally hundreds of search-lights, the ack-ack guns seemed bursting as if aimed at us.'[6] Shrapnel began to rain down on the car. The driver screeched along the Sofiskaya Embankment, then slammed on the brakes as they reached the embassy gates. Everyone dived into the building and sought shelter.

Henry Cassidy was still in his five-storey wood-and-plaster tenement when the powerful anti-aircraft guns let rip. He felt the building tremble, then buckle. 'It literally danced . . . the floor heaved, the walls swayed.' He watched bombs exploding around Kiev railway station, a mile away, before rushing down to the basement. 'My steps were quickened by the shriek of bombs falling nearby and the sight of black columns of smoke, tinged with red, rising like signals of doom.'[7] Out in the street, young lads with asbestos gloves did their best to extinguish the burning incendiaries.

There were chaotic scenes at the British Embassy, which was hit by four incendiaries. Three were rapidly extinguished, but the fourth had wedged itself into an inaccessible part of the roof. Within seconds, the building was ablaze.

A fire engine eventually appeared and quenched the flames. The embassy was saved, although parts of the building were badly damaged. When Cripps re-entered the main atrium, he found it awash with water: 'A regular cataract down the front stairs.' Suffering from acute physical exhaustion, he splashed upstream and slumped into bed. 'The worst of the fire was over my bedroom,' he wrote. 'But luckily it was all at the end, away from the bed, so that I was able to sleep there to the accompaniment of water dripping into two buckets and the firemen hammering away.'[8]

The first Luftwaffe bombing of Moscow, 21 July 1941. American photographer Margaret Bourke-White was visiting the Soviet capital and took this picture of the Kremlin being bombarded.

The Luftwaffe raid was the clearest sign yet that Moscow itself was in peril. On Wednesday, 9 July, the city of Vitebsk had fallen to the Wehrmacht; it lay just 300 miles from Moscow. Smolensk had been captured shortly afterwards, with Soviet forces suffering catastrophic losses. A further 300,000 men were killed or captured. When the war correspondent Vasily Grossman visited a makeshift hospital, he was horrified by the sight that greeted him. 'Bloodstained rags, scraps of flesh, moans, subdued howling, hundreds of dismal, suffering eyes . . . wounded men kept arriving. They were all wet with blood and rain.'[9]

In Moscow, the inhabitants waited in nervous anticipation, aware that the German panzers were racing towards the capital. Before long, they would be pounding on the city gates.

10

The Big Two

THOSE FEW DAYS in the third week of July, so destructive to Moscow, had been rather more enjoyable for the guests staying at Chequers. Averell Harriman was in attendance, suntanned from his recent trip to North Africa, as were Kathy and Pamela. The prime minister's assistant private secretary, Jock Colville, was also there. He sat next to Kathy at dinner on the Friday night.

'Pretty,' he noted in his diary, 'but convinced of the superiority of the United States in all things.'[1] He argued with her about the merits of *Citizen Kane*. She thought it 'wonderful', whereas he had found it 'deplorable'.

Late on Saturday afternoon, 19 July, the Soviet ambassador, Ivan Maisky, arrived in a blaze of summer sunshine. Short, podgy, and with an unusually moon-shaped face, Maisky was flustered on account of his chauffeur having lost his way in the country lanes of Buckinghamshire. He was half an hour late. But he soon found himself relaxing, for the prime minister's country retreat was an oasis of calm. 'Dark halls, old paintings, strange staircases,' wrote Maisky. 'How it should be in a respectful, solid English house several centuries old.'

The ambassador had come on important business: to hand deliver a letter from Stalin to the prime minister. It was the Soviet leader's first correspondence with Churchill, an answer to the PM's two previous messages. As such, its tone and content were of the greatest possible interest.

Maisky was ushered into one of Chequers' many salons. 'The secretary flung a door open and I found myself in a large lit room . . . noisy and full of life.' Clementine Churchill was busily pouring tea for everyone, and the room was full of young people, 'talking, laughing, exchanging remarks'. Churchill himself was on the far side of the room playing a board game with one of them.

Maisky was taken aback by the PM's idiosyncratic attire. He was dressed 'in strange, grey-blue overalls and a belt (a cross between a bricklayer's work clothes and an outfit suitable for a bomb shelter)'. This was the prime minister's siren suit, destined to be worn on many occasions throughout the war.

'Have a cup of tea while I finish the game,' said the PM to Maisky.

The ambassador drank two cups, served by Clementine, while Pamela Churchill went off to look for some biscuits.

The PM eventually led Maisky into a nearby drawing room so they could both study Stalin's letter, translated and typed up by Maisky himself. Churchill read it attentively, checking the names of recent battles against a large map laid out nearby. Maisky noted that he was 'evidently pleased' at having received a personal message from the Soviet leader. He had been awaiting it for weeks.

The Soviet ambassador to Britain, Ivan Maisky, was an important intermediary between Churchill and Stalin. Here he hosts a lunch at the Soviet Embassy in London.

In that letter, Stalin spoke of the Soviet Union and Great Britain as fighting allies, 'strong enough to crush our common enemy'. The Soviet leader also informed Churchill of the desperate situation on the battle-front, which now stretched from the Baltic to Ukraine. To save the Red Army from destruction, he called for an immediate Second Front in France.

'This cannot be done,' the PM told Maisky. 'It's risky. It will end in disaster for England, bringing no benefits at all.'[2]

That afternoon, Maisky was introduced to an American official who had arrived in England just two days previously. Harry Hopkins was not only a long-standing friend of Averell – a friendship that guaranteed him a warm welcome – but also the closest confidant of President Roosevelt. As such, he was being treated like royalty by Churchill.

Hopkins was the strangest presidential emissary ever to travel to Great Britain. A 'half-man', as Roosevelt called him, he had lived in the shadow of death since undergoing drastic surgery for stomach cancer four years earlier.[3] Churchill had first met him the previous January and was stunned that someone so debilitated could radiate such intellectual brilliance. 'He was a crumbling lighthouse from which there shone beams that led great fleets to harbour.'[4]

That lighthouse had been placed in charge of the Lend-Lease programme, working as Averell's counterpart in the United States. His role was to administer the American end of the operation, acting with near-presidential powers. For the duration of the war, he and Averell were to work as an incomparable double-act.

President Roosevelt had sent Hopkins to London in order to plan the forthcoming Atlantic Conference in Newfoundland, at which president and prime minister were to meet for the first time since the outbreak of war. But there was a problem that urgently needed rectifying, as Hopkins was quick to point out. The conference would be held in a semi-vacuum unless Roosevelt and Churchill could obtain up-to-date news of the situation on the Soviet front line. Stalin had provided no detailed intelligence about the German advance, and no one knew whether the Red Army would be able to hold out against the Wehrmacht. Since this information was crucial to everything, including the flow of weaponry to Great Britain, Hopkins proposed paying a flying visit to the Soviet leader.

But he also had another agenda. 'Stalin was little more than a name to Roosevelt,' he told Ambassador Maisky. 'Roosevelt has no notion of Stalin as a personality, a human being. What are his tastes, views, habits and sentiments? Can he be trusted or can't he?'[5]

Three days after Hopkins's departure for Moscow, Averell's aide, Bob Meiklejohn, received an out-of-the-blue phone call. 'Left the office in a tremendous flurry', he later wrote in his diary, 'and drove to Hendon airport in the Bentley.'[6]

Meiklejohn was not alone in that Bentley. Seated behind him was a familiar trio: Averell, Kathy, and Pamela. The two women had come to wave off the men on what was to prove a circuitous voyage to see President Roosevelt.

Their trip to America was completely unforeseen. Meiklejohn didn't even have time to pack. 'Took only my office papers and one bag half full of knick-knacks for the folks.' Kathy was also taken by surprise at her father's last-minute voyage, scarcely having time to scrawl a list of items she wanted him to bring back from America: lipstick, an eyelash curler, bobby pins, and some elasticated Bloomingdale's girdles. She also asked for a Hammacher Schlemmer cigarette lighter engraved with Pamela's initials, PSC.

That Wednesday, Averell and Meiklejohn were to embark on a 6,500-mile whistle-stop tour that would take them to Newfoundland, Washington, and then back to Placentia Bay in Newfoundland. It was here, in just over a week's time, that Winston Churchill and President Roosevelt were to have their first wartime meeting. Averell's presence was required because he was an intimate of both leaders. If disagreements were encountered, he could be relied upon to put things straight.

'I wonder if he will like me?' mused Churchill to Averell.[7] It was a question the prime minister would ask repeatedly, but one that Averell was unable to answer. Much depended on how Churchill conducted himself.

The prime minister was to travel to the rendezvous on one of the Royal Navy's latest battleships, the 35,000-ton *Prince of Wales.* She had been camouflaged with black stripes and her decks were bristling with turreted big guns and anti-aircraft guns. Churchill boarded the vessel at Scapa Flow in the Orkney Isles, excited by the prospect of a voyage through waters infested with German U-boats. The vessel had been well stocked with victuals: Scottish beef, ninety grouse (a gift for President Roosevelt), Pol Roger champagne, Hine brandy, and crates of Romeo y Julieta cigars.

Also aboard the vessel was Harry Hopkins, who had miraculously survived the twenty-four-hour flight from Archangel. 'Ah, my friend,' were Churchill's first words of greeting to Hopkins. 'How are you? And how did you find Stalin?'

'I must tell you about it,' said Hopkins vaguely, although he had very little to say about the Soviet leader.[8] Stalin had proved characteristically impenetrable during their meeting. He had described the battlefield situation in detail and provided Hopkins with a list of the most urgently required weaponry. But he had revealed nothing about himself.

Having failed to garner any information about Stalin, Churchill bombarded Hopkins with questions about President Roosevelt, with whom he was clearly obsessed. 'You'd have thought Winston was being carried up into heaven to meet God!' noted a bemused Hopkins.[9]

At 9 a.m. on Saturday, 9 August, after five choppy days at sea, HMS *Prince of Wales* arrived at its rendezvous in the still waters of Placentia Bay, where the presidential vessel, USS *Augusta*, was already at anchor. That same morning, shortly after eleven, Churchill was ferried over to the *Augusta* looking dapper in his blue naval attire. Roosevelt was wearing a light tan Palm Beach suit and stood unsteadily, supported by his steel leg braces and clutching the arm of his son Elliott. It was a solemn moment, with the ship's band playing the national anthems of Great Britain and the United States. As the last notes of 'The Star-Spangled Banner' faded into the mist, Churchill gave a slight bow before presenting Roosevelt with a letter from King George VI.

'At last we have gotten together,' said the president with a smile, extending his hand.

'We have,' beamed Churchill.[10]

The two leaders dined that evening with Averell and Hopkins, and everything went smoothly, although Averell was dismayed to discover they were served spinach omelette.

Later that night, writing in bed, Averell would type a note to Kathy and Pamela. 'The historic meeting of the great men and their staffs has taken place,' he wrote. 'It is to be seen whether the seeds sown will bloom. The PM has been on his best form. The President is intrigued and likes him enormously.'[11] The two men had already begun calling each other Franklin and Winston, which everyone took to be a good omen.

The most publicised aspect of the four-day meeting at Placentia Bay was the signing of the Atlantic Charter. This pledged a set of lofty post-war principles: freedom from fear; disarmament; and the rights of individuals to be respected 'after the final destruction of the Nazi tyranny'. But another decision had more immediate significance. Churchill and Roosevelt agreed to send a high-level delegation to Stalin to lay the building blocks of a necessary, if disagreeable, relationship. It was to be a joint Anglo-American mission, headed by two figures of sufficient stature to command Stalin's respect.

Hopkins was the obvious choice to represent America, but he was too frail to undertake another gruelling voyage. So Roosevelt offered the role to Averell, believing that he was the only other person with the necessary qualities to deal with the dictator.

Winston Churchill chose Max Aitken, better known as Lord Beaverbrook, to be Great Britain's representative. A Canadian-British press baron, he owned the *Daily Express*, the world's largest-circulation newspaper.

Lord Beaverbrook had been one of the first to meet Averell on his arrival in England, thanks to his role as minister of aircraft production in Churchill's government. He had overseen a massive expansion of productivity, doing so in typically Beaverbrook fashion – bullying, flattering, and energising, with a slash-and-burn approach to red tape. His secretary, Betty Bower, disliked his brusque manner but confessed to admiring him. 'We wouldn't perhaps have won the war without him,' she would later write. 'I was there and I know he did it.'[12] Churchill agreed. 'All his remarkable qualities fitted the need . . . This was his hour. His personal force and genius, combined with so much persuasion and contrivance, swept away many obstacles.'[13]

Beaverbrook had resigned as minister in May, on the grounds that he was incapable of teamwork. 'I am not a committee man,' he told

Churchill. 'I am the cat that walks alone.'[14] Some of those close to the prime minister, including his wife, Clementine, hoped it would stay that way. 'My darling,' she said, 'try ridding yourself of this microbe which some people fear is in your blood – exorcise this bottled imp and see if the air is not clearer and purer.'[15]

Nicknamed 'the Toad' by the foreign secretary, and 'the Beaver' by everyone else, he was also referred to as the 'Minister of Midnight', an arch-manipulator who relished playing with the levers of power. But Churchill was addicted to him and refused to listen to any criticism. 'Some take drugs,' he said. 'I take Max.'[16]

Beaverbrook's country residence was Cherkley Court, a Victorian-era neoclassical mansion that stood just a short distance from Kathy and Pamela's Petersfield cottage. It was huge and ugly, 'of remarkable hideousness both inside and out'.[17] But it could accommodate large numbers of guests and had acres of gardens. Before long, Kathy and Pamela were regular weekend guests.

'Exceedingly terrifying', was Kathy's opinion of Beaverbrook after her first encounter with him. 'Our host looks like a cartoon out of *Punch*. Small, baldish, big stomach and from there he tapers down to two very shiny yellow shoes. His idea of sport is to surround himself with intelligent men, then egg them on to argue and fight among themselves.'

She watched in fascination as he directed the fiery table talk in the fashion of a virtuoso conductor, goading and insulting his guests. 'Even his best friends are half scared of him, because he's got a fearful temper and no one seems to know when it will break.'

His face was a mottled tan and his mouth was cartoon-like, 'a satchel mouth, bisecting the face in an enormous grin'.[18] His voice still had a Canadian resonance, loud and rasping when he was in a bad mood. But when he was in good humour, it would change to a coaxing purr.

He was a widower, for his wife had died in 1927, but he adored women – especially Kathy and Pamela. Always unconventional, he insisted they remain at the dining table for port and cigars. Then, when the last cigar was extinguished, he would escort them down to his private cinema, where they would watch his favourite film, *Destry Rides Again*, which he had seen sixteen times.

Kathy asked Beaverbrook if she could interview him for the International News Service. He readily agreed and proved as outspoken as ever. 'I would like to see the United States in the war,' he said unequivocally, 'and to a higher measure.'[19]

Kathy and Pamela were not alone in enjoying Beaverbrook's company: Averell also relished his visits to Cherkley Court. These two multimillionaires had been engaged in a political dance ever since Churchill had first introduced them back in March. Averell's instinct had always been to push himself towards those in power, while Beaverbrook knew that only Averell – with his links to President Roosevelt – could supply Britain with munitions.

It was inevitable that they would find themselves working closely with each other, especially when Churchill made Beaverbrook his minister of supply. The appointment was to form an interlocking bond between the duo, two business tycoons charged with keeping Britain afloat. 'Averell and Beaverbrook have started a mutual admiration society,' wrote Kathy in one of her letters. 'They spend their time patting each other on the back.' She found it hilarious. 'It reminds me of two children.'[20]

This eminent duo was now entrusted with a crucial four-day mission to the court of Joseph Stalin. Roosevelt hoped that Averell's natural charm would enable him to overcome the hostility of the Soviet leader, while Churchill hoped Beaverbrook's charisma would work magic inside the walls of the Kremlin.

At stake was the future course of the war.

11

Meeting Stalin

AVERELL AND LORD Beaverbrook set off for Moscow on Sunday, 21 September. It was a portentous day on the Soviet battle-front. That very morning, Hitler's panzers had captured the embattled city of Kiev, ensnaring 700,000 Red Army troops in their encirclement. German morale had never been higher, for the path was now open for the Wehrmacht to occupy the rest of Ukraine, as well as the Crimean Peninsula.

Winston Churchill bade a personal farewell to Averell and Beaverbrook, aware that the stakes for their mission could not be higher. It was essential for them to establish a personal relationship with Stalin and thereby get an insight into his character and resolve. 'All good wishes to you both and your colleagues for your memorable journey, on which you carry with you the hope of the world.'

They travelled by train from London to Thurso, in the far north of Scotland, undertaking this first leg of the journey in considerable luxury. Each tycoon had his own private carriage, and the train was also equipped with a club car, a dining car, and a so-called 'parlour car', to be used by the team accompanying the two men to the Soviet Union.

Beaverbrook was dismissive of everyone in his party, taunting them for being superfluous hangers-on. They were 'coming along for the ride', he said mockingly, adding that he and Harriman 'would handle all the important negotiations with Stalin'.[1] He even had the temerity to tell General Ismay he was 'being taken along for the scenery', a comment that Averell found boorish.

On arrival in Thurso, the party boarded HMS *London*, a 14,000-ton cruiser equipped with four big-gun turrets and a forest of anti-aircraft guns. Lord Beaverbrook caused some amusement by informing everyone that his on-board toilet was strictly private. He even hung up a sign that said 'Reserved for Lord Beaverbrook'. Bob Meiklejohn was no stranger to big egos, but he felt Beaverbrook was in a league of his own. 'You'd think that would be enough,' he wrote in his diary. 'But today I noticed they had gilded the lily by rigging up an electric light to shine on the sign so nobody would make a mistake at night.'[2]

After six days at sea, the delegation arrived at the White Sea port of Archangel. From there they headed to Moscow in four Russian-built Douglas DC-3 transports. The flight was not for the faint-hearted. The planes had no radio equipment, requiring them to navigate under the clouds. 'So close to the treetops', wrote Averell, 'that I felt I could touch them if I put my hand out of the window.'[3]

As they approached Moscow, the flight took a yet more precarious turn. 'I heard a thump that sounded as if it came from beneath the plane,' wrote Bob Meiklejohn, who peered outside and saw they were being fired on by a ground battery.

Another of those on board, Captain Harold Balfour, was terrified by the way in which the pilot sought to dodge the shells. 'I felt we were like a much shot-at covey of partridges, very wild and determined to get away from the guns.'

Averell and Beaverbrook finally touched down in Moscow at 3 p.m. and were met by dozens of Soviet officials. 'Much cinema-turning, camera clicking and inspection of the Guard of Honour,' wrote Captain Balfour.[4]

Averell was taken by limousine to Spaso House, the ambassadorial residence, a large neoclassical mansion situated just a stone's throw from the Kremlin. It had been badly damaged in one of the many Luftwaffe raids, and its shattered windows were now boarded up.

Lord Beaverbrook had elected to stay at the National Hotel, because he wanted to avoid having to socialise with Ambassador Cripps. In common with Churchill, he had a long-standing hatred of Cripps. He told everyone he was 'always ill at ease with teetotallers, especially socialist teetotallers who were candidates for sainthood'.[5]

Shortly after arriving at the National, Beaverbrook held a meeting with the senior members of his team. He warned them that their chauffeurs were spies and that the hotel's staff were informers. He added that their rooms would be bugged. Whenever they spoke with each other, they must do so with the radio on full blast.

Averell and Beaverbrook met with Stalin on their very first night in Moscow. 'The most dramatic feeling that I ever had,' wrote Averell of his arrival at the Kremlin. 'We went into Stalin's room, which was a largish office with pictures of Lenin, Engels and Marx.' It was simply furnished, with a writing desk in one corner and a green baize table on the left. Stalin was there with Foreign Commissar Molotov and his interpreter, Maxim Litvinov.

The Soviet leader was shorter and broader than Averell had been expecting and wore a simple tunic without any decorations. It hung loosely from his frame. One of his arms was shorter than the other and almost completely hidden inside the sleeve.

'His face was swarthy, with a black mustache covering much of his mouth. His hair was quite gray. His face was pock-marked, his teeth broken and stained. When he lit a cigarette, I noticed that his left arm was slightly deformed.'[6] Such were the impressions of the American Embassy's interpreter, Charles Bohlen. The most disturbing feature was Stalin's eyes, which were almost yellow. He looked as if he had jaundice.

Averell was surprised to find no hint of the sinister tyrant. Rather, Stalin seemed bashful, quiet-spoken, and devoid of emotion. 'Blunt but amazingly frank,' he wrote. 'When I looked straight at him, he did not avoid my eye.' But nor was there any sign of warmth, perhaps on account of the glaring ideological gulf between him and his two guests. This was a meeting of different worlds, opposing systems, and conflicting values. At the head of the table sat the gangster-turned-dictator, who scorned the capitalist West and had long sought to destroy it. Beside him sat two of the wealthiest representatives of that hated system, a duo of multimillionaires. Both had long been scathing in their criticism of Stalin's Communist dictatorship, with its command economy and enforced collectivisation. The Soviet regime was particularly offensive to Lord Beaverbrook, press baron extraordinaire, who despised the tight noose that Stalin kept on the press. It ran counter to his most cherished beliefs.

Stalin invited his two guests to be seated and then described the grim tactical situation in microscopic detail, speaking candidly of the numerical superiority of the Wehrmacht. German panzers were within striking distance of the Sea of Azov, from which, if captured, they could besiege the Crimea. And they had almost encircled Leningrad, cutting all access to the city and its two and a half million inhabitants. Now the only route into the city was across the expanse of Lake Ladoga. Moscow, too, was in increasing danger of falling to the rapidly approaching Wehrmacht. The Red Army troops charged with keeping Hitler's panzers at bay were a hotchpotch of battle-weary survivors and poorly trained militia units; these *opolchenie* were comprised of retired men and women with no experience of fighting.

The Soviet leader told Averell and Beaverbrook that he would defend the capital to the very last man but warned that 'the loss of Moscow, the nerve centre of all Soviet operations, would gravely handicap any offensive action in the future.'[7] His visitors were left in no doubt that the situation was on a knife-edge, with the very real prospect of the Red Army being annihilated.

Stalin remained calm while describing the situation on the battlefield, but his mood changed abruptly when he had finished. It was as if someone had flicked a switch, for he became jumpy and aggressive. 'Very restless', noted Beaverbrook in his pocketbook. 'Walking about and smoking continuously.'[8] Everything he now said seemed calculated to offend. He openly questioned his two visitors' good faith and outraged them both by suggesting they were secretly hoping that Hitler would destroy the Soviet regime: 'The paucity of your offers clearly shows that you want to see the Soviet Union defeated.'[9] When Beaverbrook presented Stalin with a warmly worded letter from Churchill, the Soviet leader ripped open the envelope, then tossed the letter unread onto a nearby table. He was angry and increasingly unpleasant.

Averell had not been expecting Stalin to be so captious, nor so disagreeable; he felt their relationship with him was over before it had even begun. 'Very rough going,' he wrote later that night.

Stalin's commissars made some effort to welcome their visitors to Moscow, organising sightseeing trips for those with time on their hands. Bob Meiklejohn went on one of these trips and was amazed to discover that the city's most iconic palaces and museums had been camouflaged with vast stage canvases.

'The wall of the Kremlin has been painted to look like actual trees, planted in pots, to change their appearance. Open squares have whole blocks of imitation house roofs made of canvas to make the highway look like a developed area.'[10] A fake wooden cottage had been constructed over Lenin's tomb on Red Square. As for Lenin himself, his embalmed corpse had been spirited off to the countryside.

The Grand Kremlin Palace was camouflaged behind vast canvas screens to confuse Luftwaffe pilots; the Cathedral of the Annunciation (far right) has yet to be concealed.

Meiklejohn and company were also taken around the city by limousine, with their NKVD minders at the wheel. 'They never stop for traffic lights but just blow their horns continuously and the cops stop all other traffic to let us proceed. We have a grand time barging around from place to place in big Packards, Buicks and Russian ZIS cars.' The scars of the Luftwaffe bombing raids were everywhere visible, with bomb craters in the streets and heaps of rubble where apartment blocks once stood.

Meiklejohn took himself off to the Bolshoi for a special performance but was not impressed. 'Personally I'll take the Radio City Rockettes any day,' he said, 'but it was good to say I'd seen the ballet.' The rest of his time was devoted to writing up Averell's memos, which took up much of each night. 'Here it is, five a.m., and I have just finished transcribing my notes . . . it's an interesting life, if you can stand the pace.'[11]

Morale was at a very low ebb when Averell and Beaverbrook returned to the Kremlin for another meeting with Stalin on the evening of Tuesday, 30 September. They feared for the worst but had decided to make one last attempt at finding common ground with the Soviet leader. To their astonishment, they found Stalin completely transformed. He puffed on his pipe, appeared relaxed, and even allowed himself the occasional smile.

Averell seized the opportunity and got down to business. He had brought a list of seventy items the United States could supply to the Soviet Union over the longer term: 1,800 aeroplanes, 2,250 tanks, and hundreds of trucks and scout cars. He also offered barbed wire, half a million miles of telephone cable, and near-limitless quantities of chemicals and explosives.

As Averell went through each item, Beaverbrook kept a close watch on Stalin. He was intrigued by his obsession with drawing doodles of wolves. Each time the conversation paused while his interpreter translated his words, he picked up his red pencil and drew yet more wolves. The sheet of paper was soon covered with them.

Averell's generous offer of military supplies eventually worked its magic. As the evening wore on, the atmosphere grew increasingly relaxed.

'You are pleased?' ventured Beaverbrook at one point.[12]

Stalin broke into a rare smile, at which point his interpreter leaped from his chair and cried out excitedly: 'Now we shall win the war!'[13]

It is never easy to talk through an interpreter, but on this occasion the conversation began to flow quite naturally.

'Why don't you ask Churchill to come and see you?' asked Beaverbrook as he sought to build on Stalin's good humour.

'Will he come?'

'He might well if you ask him.'

The Beaver had long been a master of small talk and he was at his raconteur best that evening, spilling gossip, anecdotes, and unsubstantiated rumours. He delighted Stalin with an account of his visit to the recently incarcerated Rudolf Hess, Hitler's deputy, who had astonished the world by landing in Scotland four months earlier. Beaverbrook said that Hess had been hoping to lead a coup d'état backed by right-wing British aristocrats.

Stalin broached the subject of Ambassador Maisky in London, asking if he bored everyone with lectures on Soviet doctrine.

'I don't give him a chance,' chortled Beaverbrook, who responded with a question of his own. 'What about our fellow?' he asked – a reference to Ambassador Cripps.

Stalin gave a negative shrug. 'Oh, he's all right.'

'He's a bore,' said Beaverbrook.

'Like Maisky?' asked Stalin.

'No,' said Beaverbrook. 'Like Madame Maisky.'[14]

Stalin guffawed with laughter, because he also thought that Agniya Maisky was a tiresome gossip.

The meeting with Stalin was a triumph. Not only had the two businessmen offered something concrete, but they had chipped away at the wall of suspicion. A partnership with the Soviet leader at last seemed possible.

Bob Meiklejohn noticed a complete change in Averell's spirits on his return to Spaso House. '[He] came in about eleven o'clock from his meeting at the Kremlin looking like the cat that swallowed the mouse,' he wrote. 'His nibs was obviously very pleased with himself – said that he had accomplished the most important thing he had ever done, a matter of immense importance, and that if he had been a bit nasty in the last few days, he didn't really mean it.'[15]

Stalin was so delighted by the outcome of the meeting that he proposed a banquet on the following evening, Wednesday, 1 October. It was to be held in the imperial throne room of the Grand Kremlin Palace, a vaulted banqueting hall built of malachite and marble. Not since the days of Tsar Nicholas II had Moscow been the setting for such an opulent feast.

The 130 guests were transported to the Kremlin in a fleet of chauffeur-driven Packards and ZISs. Bob Meiklejohn had hitherto seen only drabness in Moscow; now his eyes fell upon a world of gilded extravagance. The double doors to the state banqueting hall stood fully sixteen feet high and were adorned with gold-leafed carvings, with Catherine the Great's imperial crest sculpted into the centrepiece.

Meiklejohn blinked in disbelief. 'A mass of gargantuan chandeliers that really puts one's eyes out,' he wrote. The malachite pillars were glinting in the candlelight and the highly polished banqueting tables stretched to the farthest end of the room. Gigantic silver salvers were spilling with ripe peaches and grapes, and ornamental vases sprouted arum lilies and other freshly cut blooms. The tables were also charged with bottles: pepper vodka, red and white Caucasian wine, champagne, brandy, and rare vintage liqueurs.

Stalin arrived without fuss or ceremony, escorted into the room on the arm of the florid-cheeked General Kliment Voroshilov. The room fell silent. The effect of his entrance astonished everyone. Some observers would later say that it was like a ghastly parody of a bride on the arm of her father. But Captain Balfour disagreed, thinking it a masterful entrance on the part of Stalin. 'Mussolini or Hitler would have had flags; perhaps heralds; quite likely a band; and they would have made their entry in gorgeous uniform, surrounded by pomp and splendour. Stalin got his effect by simplicity. He walked slowly, with his hands held behind his back, clasped.'[16] He had no need for the vanities and outward trappings of power.

'When he saw Harriman and the Beaver, his face broke into animated welcome. He shook hands with the two mission heads, and those of us who were seeing him for the first time were stricken dumb.'[17] So wrote *Collier's* reporter Quentin Reynolds. One of the delegates was heard to whisper that Stalin looked like a kindly old gardener you'd have in once a week to pull up the weeds.

The Soviet leader seemed a little confused as to who was who and wandered over to a small group of Americans gathered around Bob Meiklejohn. 'We edged away, knowing it wasn't us he was after, but he kept on coming, looking quite meek and mild.' Meiklejohn and friends took a few more steps backwards, 'but it began to look silly, us backing away from him, so we all stopped and shook hands.'[18] Meiklejohn noted that Stalin's handshake was rather feeble. He was disappointed, having expected an iron grip.

The dinner started punctually at seven o'clock and was a sumptuous affair, with twenty-three courses. Platters of caviar and sturgeon were followed by roast turkey, chicken, grouse, and quails. Averell had not seen such an abundance of food since leaving the United States. It was particularly striking after his lean months in London. 'Churchill was always careful to conform to the British rations,' he wrote, 'whereas the tables of the Russian officials were groaning with all kinds of delectable foods.'

Stalin was seated between Averell and Beaverbrook, his two guests of honour. While Averell tackled yet another hors d'oeuvre, Beaverbrook played the journalist and made a mental note of everything Stalin said and did. 'His curiosity about Churchill was insatiable . . . his hatred of Hitler appears to be real . . . his confidence in the Americans and Great Britain is limited . . . his power, I should have thought, is absolute, and the bottleneck is the most effective in history.'[19] He noticed that the Soviet leader's food was served from special bowls, which he took as a sign of paranoia.

At one point, Stalin suddenly rose to his feet and tapped his glass with a knife. He spoke for about fifteen seconds before his words were translated into English. His toast was for President Roosevelt, 'who has the very difficult task of leading a country which is non-belligerent and yet wants to do all it can to help the two great democracies of Europe in their fight against Fascism'. This was followed by a moment's silence as the guests digested the idea of Stalin leading a democracy.

There were thirty-two toasts that night, with each toast requiring everyone to knock back a full shot of vodka. They drank to brave Soviet soldiers; to Allied fighters; to victory over Hitler. No sooner had they done so than the air raid sirens warned of an imminent attack, a sign that the war was inching ever closer to Moscow.

Averell and Beaverbrook were used to thinking big, and their deal with Stalin was no exception. The list of weaponry to be shipped to the Soviet Union filled nine closely typed pages. It covered not only the monthly supply of vehicles and munitions, but fuel, chemicals, and medical equipment.

Every four weeks there was to be a delivery of 500 tanks, 400 planes, 152 anti-aircraft guns, 500 anti-tank guns, and 5,000 scout cars (over nine months), along with huge quantities of aluminium, tin, lead, nickel, and zinc. There was also provision for army boots and cloth, wheat, sugar, and cocoa beans. And there was a list of eighty chemicals, including 750,000 kg of strophanthin, 100,000 kg of chloramine, and 100,000 kg of lanolin.

Lord Beaverbrook (fourth from left) and Averell Harriman (seated) travelled to Moscow in September 1941. They are signing an agreement to supply Stalin with vast quantities of equipment.

Journalist Quentin Reynolds felt the two tycoons had performed their roles to perfection, overcoming years of mistrust on the part of Stalin and his commissars. 'In one week, Beaverbrook and Harriman swept away much of this feeling,' he said. 'They loved the Beaver's showmanship, his loud laughter, his jokes and his absolute disregard of protocol and red tape. They admired Harriman's sincerity, his obvious knowledge of the problems involved and his eagerness to work all night every night, if need be, to help solve those problems.' He said that Averell had already become 'a very popular figure among members of the official Soviet family'.[20]

There was to be one minor scandal that threatened to overshadow the success of the mission. Beaverbrook had asked one of the British Embassy staff, John Russell, to buy twenty-five pounds of caviar. He intended to give some of it to Winston Churchill. This came to the attention of one of the Moscow correspondents, Philip Jordan, who duly published a largely inaccurate article about Churchill's greed for caviar.

The prime minister was furious when the story broke and sent a blistering telegram to Beaverbrook, blaming him for such negative publicity. The idea that caviar was being brought back for his personal consumption was deeply embarrassing.

The Averell-Beaverbrook mission left Moscow on Saturday, 4 October. Ambassador Cripps was glad to see the back of the two men. 'I have held myself at Beaverbrook's disposal every day and all day,' he wrote wearily, 'but he has not vouchsafed anything to me at all.'

Cripps criticised them to anyone who would listen, but more often than not his diary was the only receptive ear. 'The whole thing comes down to a sort of Father Christmas party,' he wrote, 'with America and England declaring what they are prepared to do.' He was disgusted by the two of them playing at being Santa Claus. 'Poor Russia,' he wrote. 'This is the wrong atmosphere altogether.'

He was particularly infuriated not to have received any recognition from Beaverbrook for the embassy's generous welcome: 'He didn't even thank me or my staff for what we had done for him.' Cripps remained philosophical. 'That is the Beaver,' he wrote. 'He is what he is.'[21]

After a five-day sea voyage to Scotland and an overnight train ride to London, Averell and Beaverbrook finally arrived back at Euston Station. The stationmaster had been forewarned of their arrival and appeared on the platform in a morning suit and top hat, with a fresh flower in his buttonhole. Also awaiting them was 'a young woman in a gay red costume'. It was Kathy, come to meet her Popsie.

Winston Churchill invited them all to dinner at Chequers that very evening. Beaverbrook was in a foul mood and accused the prime minister of mishandling the caviar incident. But the food and drink soon improved everyone's humour. By the end of the evening, everyone (including the Beaver) was in good spirits.

As they left the Chequers dining room, Churchill turned to Beaverbrook with a mischievous grin.

'Now,' he said, 'after all this talk, where is that caviar?'[22]

COMING DOWN TO EARTH

DINNER IN HONOUR OF

LORD BEAVERBROOK AND MR. AVERELL HARRIMAN

BY THE

AMERICAN AND BRITISH DELEGATES TO THE MOSCOW CONFERENCE

DORCHESTER HOTEL 13TH OCTOBER, 1941

Averell and Beaverbrook's mission to Moscow was viewed as a triumph. A drawing by the celebrated cartoonist David Low illustrates the menu card for their homecoming dinner.

12

Taking Flight

'COME TO THE embassy at once!'

The American ambassador, Laurence Steinhardt, was bawling down the telephone to the *Collier's* reporter Quentin Reynolds. It was just after luncheon on Wednesday, 15 October.

'This is urgent,' he said. 'The balloon has gone up. Cripps and I were summoned by Molotov this morning. He told us that a train would be waiting at Kazan Station at seven o'clock tonight for the diplomatic corps.'[1] All foreign nationals were to be evacuated from Moscow and Ambassador Steinhardt was engaged in a frantic effort to contact every American in the city.

Journalist Charlotte Haldane had received a similar summons from Ambassador Cripps, who was trying to reach everyone in his own little community. 'Come here immediately!' he told her. 'With all your baggage.'[2]

Ever alert to breaking news, embassy caretaker, Harold Elvin, had been one of the first to learn of the evacuation order. 'We're off!' he scribbled in his diary that afternoon. 'The Germans have made a clean breakthrough sixty miles away and are driving hell for leather.' When he stepped outside the embassy, he saw huge quantities of Soviet supplies being rushed to the nearby front line. 'Lorryload after lorryload after lorryload of stuff. Stacks of ammunition covered with tree camouflage, guns after guns . . . I have the feeling, as never before, that everything's being chucked in, old horses, broken wagons, primitive dressing ambulances.'[3] He was warned that Moscow would be in Nazi hands within days, if not hours. It was imperative for everyone to leave the city while it was still possible.

The crisis was real and imminent. A twelve-mile column of German armour was rapidly advancing on the capital, and everyone, everywhere, was fleeing in the face of the impending catastrophe. 'Exodus! Biblical exodus!' wrote war correspondent Vasily Grossman as he fled the advancing Germans. 'Vehicles are moving eight abreast, there's the violent roaring of dozens of trucks trying simultaneously to tear their wheels out of the mud. Huge herds of sheep and cows are driven through the fields . . . crowds of pedestrians with sacks, bundles, suitcases.'[4] It felt like the end of the world.

Even Stalin panicked, putting in an urgent telephone call to the Moscow district command. 'Mobilise everything you have,' he barked. He then summoned an emergency meeting of the State Defence Committee and ordered a ferocious last stand on the western fringes of Moscow. The Mozhaisk Line, though thinly manned and poorly armed, was to square off against the advancing enemy.

In the German capital, Adolf Hitler was so confident of crushing the last vestiges of the Red Army that he addressed a vast audience at the Berlin Sportpalast, informing them that victory over the Soviet Union was now assured. The Wehrmacht, he said, had fought 'the greatest battle in the history of the world' and had emerged triumphant. The Soviet war machine was broken 'and would never rise again'. The triumph was best told through statistics: two million Soviet prisoners of war, 18,000 tanks destroyed, 14,500 aircraft shot down. Newspapers in Berlin ran banner headlines announcing the victory: 'Campaign in East Decided!', 'The Great Hour Has Struck!'[5] The war in the Soviet Union had ended in victory, as Hitler had always promised.

When Molotov summoned Ambassadors Cripps and Steinhardt to the Kremlin on the morning of Wednesday, 15 October, he told them that the regime 'intended to defend Moscow at all costs and to continue the fighting to the end'. But he also warned that it would be a fight to the death, which required the immediate evacuation of both diplomats and civilians. Advance units of German troops had been sighted just a few miles from the city's perimeter.

Cripps was shocked to see how the strain was showing on Molotov. 'I have never seen him look so tired and ill,' he wrote in his diary that afternoon. The foreign commissar was normally so starched and dapper. Not any more. 'He was deadly pale and his collar all awry . . . he looked completely exhausted.'[6]

The foreign community was to be evacuated by train that evening, leaving them just a few hours to pack their belongings. At the British Embassy, staff spent the rest of the afternoon burning secret papers in a brazier installed on the tennis court. Someone asked Ambassador Cripps what to do with the embassy wireless. 'Smash it,' he said.[7] It was duly despatched with a few blows of a sledgehammer.

The evacuees had no idea as to their destination, although it was clear they would be heading east. Reporter Alice-Leone Moats was one of the many who learned of the evacuation from Ambassador Steinhardt. 'Be here at five-thirty,' he ordered, 'and bring only the baggage you can carry.'

On arriving at Spaso House, she found the entrance hall piled high with suitcases. 'People were leaping over them like goats, tying on tags which had been provided by the embassy.'[8]

She found her fellow American refugees sprawled on the gilded divans that furnished the drawing room. The ambassador's flustered wife, Dulcie, was preparing a last supper of spaghetti, cold meats, and baked beans. Mortars and cannon boomed ominously in the near distance, heralding the arrival of the Nazis.

Snow was teeming from the night sky when the Americans and British left their respective embassies and were transported to Moscow's Kazan Station in a hastily assembled fleet of cars. When Charlotte Haldane peered through the windscreen, she saw tens of thousands of Muscovites following in their wake: 'Workers of key factories and industrial undertakings, researchers, mothers and children, every civilian who was not required in Moscow.' The entire city was on a one-way ticket east.

'Complete chaos,' wrote Ambassador Cripps on arriving at the station. A mass of humanity was jostling its way across the concourse: wizened babushkas, factory workers, cleaners, nurses, and scores of frantic mothers clutching at screaming babies and children. It was pitch black, for lights were forbidden, and the air was suffused with panic.

Earlier that evening, Cripps had put his most senior staffer, Counsellor Lacy Baggallay, in charge of the embassy's fleet of cars. Baggallay and a few others were to travel by road to their as yet unknown destination, transporting all the embassy essentials. The rest of the team were to travel with nothing but hand luggage.

Amid chaotic scenes, they were led to the station waiting room, reserved for the diplomatic corps. Cripps found it crowded with foreign nationals: Turks, Yugoslavs, Czechs, Persians, Chinese, Afghans, Mongolians, and Japanese. 'The oddest assortment of persons I have ever set eyes on,' thought Charlotte Haldane. Most of the British staff were in khaki fatigues, although the naval attaché had pitched up in full dress uniform. The British Embassy's second secretary, Richard Ferrier, was wearing a white sheepskin hat 'at least two feet tall' and a magnificent white fur Afghan coat. He might have been heading to a fancy-dress party. When journalist Philip Jordan looked out over the dense crowd forcing its way across the station concourse, he felt as if the whole of Moscow was passing through the gates of hell. 'A cavern of damned souls for whom this retreat meant, perhaps, the end of all things.'

At around midnight, the British and American embassy staff were escorted to a waiting train, aided by Soviet police who forced a passage through the crowd. 'Comrades, comrades! Make way there. Stand back, order please. Please!'[9]

The concourse was awash with muddy slush that spilled into everyone's shoes. It took an age for the Brits and Americans to push their way through to the twenty-eight-carriage train, equipped with a mix of hard- and soft-class compartments. Soft class was stiflingly hot, for the winter heating had been set to maximum, while hard class was so cold that the windows were frosted on the inside. There was no water in the lavatories, no drinking water, no food. Everyone was worried they would be attacked by the Luftwaffe, whose low-flying pilots had already strafed scores of trains heading east.

When they eventually pulled out of Moscow at around 2 a.m., it began to snow in earnest. 'The first real snows of winter,' wrote Philip Jordan. If the train got stuck, they would be a sitting target.

The five days that followed were to test the nerves of everyone. Food was their most immediate concern. 'How we were to feed ourselves during the next week, no one knew,' wrote Philip Jordan, 'for the excellent reason that the authorities would not tell us how long the journey was to last, nor where we were going.' The extreme cold was also a challenge. Quentin Reynolds had been allotted a place in hard class, along with Henry Cassidy and a few other reporters. He was accustomed to hardship, for it came with the job, but this was off the scale. 'The cold filtered through the windows and caught us in its terrible grasp. It got under our skin and into our bones, and we breathed it into our bloodstream and somehow it got into our brains.'

Ambassador Cripps was rather more comfortable. He had been allocated a wagon-lit compartment that he was to share with his pet terrier, Joe. When Alice-Leone Moats poked her head through Cripps's door, she found him munching raw carrots. He told her of his concern for Joe, also a vegetarian, who had nothing to eat for the long journey ahead.

The train crawled, stopped, then crawled again. The first long halt came just twenty miles east of Moscow, where the track had been wrecked by a Luftwaffe bombing raid. It was the first of scores of such stops on the long voyage east, many caused by priority westbound trains heading to the battle-front.

Hundreds of trains were also heading east, laden with industrial equipment, heavy plant machinery, and turbines. These had been hastily dismantled from factories close to the battle-front and were to be rebuilt in the east of the country, beyond the reach of the Luftwaffe. Also travelling east were hundreds of thousands of factory workers, mostly women, who were to fill the shoes of their conscripted husbands.

Ambassador Cripps and company eventually learned that their destination was Kuibyshev, a provincial city at the confluence of the Volga and Samara rivers. It lay some 800 miles to the south-east of Moscow, safely out of range of both the Luftwaffe and the advancing Wehrmacht. Cripps was told that the entire Soviet government was moving there so the fight against the Nazis could continue from afar.

By the end of the second day, everyone on the train was hungry. 'Although hundreds of boxes of iron rations had been prepared against such an emergency,' wrote Charlotte Haldane, 'in the flurry of the exodus practically the whole lot had been left behind.' When Cripps finished his carrots, he kept hunger at bay by eating a pot of Tiptree Little Scarlet jam.

The Americans were faring better because Charles Thayer had packed a small stash of beans and tinned salmon. For breakfast, he made everyone gin and pineapple juice cocktails, using a shaker crafted out of a bully-beef tin.

They were not able to acquire food until they reached Ryazan, 150 miles south-east of Moscow. Everyone's mood was suddenly lifted. 'We fed hugely on fried eggs, soup and a dish of veal, washed down with fresh vodka,' wrote Philip Jordan. He also managed to buy tomatoes and a chicken for the next leg of the journey.

The train was filthy by the third day of travel, with the floor strewn with cigarette butts and eggshells. Everyone was unwashed and the waterless lavatories were overflowing.

After five torturous days of stop-and-start travel, the train finally crossed the River Volga at Syzran. They were now just fifty miles from Kuibyshev, whose tenements swung into view at dawn the following morning.

'This was Kuibyshev,' wrote Quentin Reynolds when they finally arrived, 'so far from the war zone that it was not even blacked out.' When he alighted onto the platform, he saw a sign that said 'Moscow: 630 miles'. 'We had taken exactly one hundred and five hours to make the trip,' he wrote. 'In short, our average speed had been six miles an hour.'[10]

'Well, well, well!' wrote Ambassador Cripps in his diary on the day of their arrival. 'Here we are at last!' He was relieved to have made it in one piece, but his cautious optimism turned to dismay when he was escorted to the accommodation reserved for his British contingent.

Kuibyshev Boys Gymnasium School was a crumbling two-storey brick building that had been hastily converted into a series of dormitories equipped with narrow iron beds and filthy mattresses. The dormitories were infested with bedbugs and there were only two semi-working lavatories.

Cripps fretted and fumed. 'Here we are expected to live and do all our work,' he wrote angrily. 'There is absolutely nothing in the way of eating or cooking utensils . . . there is not a pantry at all, and of course, no blinds or curtains.'[11]

The Americans were marginally more fortunate. They had been assigned an apartment block with six kitchens and scores of individual rooms. The block had been freshly painted in advance of their arrival, and Ambassador Steinhardt even had his own bedroom, complete with a brass bed and a sofa. The downside was that the plumbing didn't work and the toilets were therefore unusable.

The small group of journalists had fared best of all. They were lodged in the Grand Hotel, an imposing *hôtel particulier* on the main street. There was no heating – a major drawback – and no working baths. 'Not so blooming grand,' wrote one of Cripps's team after visiting the place.[12] But it was bug-free and had individual bedrooms. It was better than the train.

As they settled in for their first night in Kuibyshev, everyone had an uneasy feeling that Stalin had transported them to this far-flung city in order to get rid of them. 'The end of the world,' wrote Henry Cassidy.[13] And there was more bad news to come. When Ambassador Cripps contacted Vice Commissar Andrey Vyshinsky the following morning, he received news that left him fuming.

Stalin, he was told, had decided to stay in Moscow.

13

At Chequers

KATHY HARRIMAN'S BIRTHDAY was on Sunday, 7 December: she was turning twenty-four. When Winston Churchill learned this, he proposed a festive weekend at Chequers for herself and Averell. Pamela Churchill was also invited, along with Ambassador Winant and John Martin, the prime minister's private secretary. It was to be a celebratory long weekend.

An inadvertent mix-up with dates meant that the birthday dinner was held on the Saturday evening, rather than the Sunday, but this did little to dampen the festive atmosphere. Churchill was in fine fettle, offering a birthday toast to Kathy and presenting her with an autographed copy of his book *The River War*. It was not her usual choice of reading material (it was an account of Lord Kitchener's 1899 conquest of the Sudan) and even in its abridged form ran to more than four hundred pages. But it was a gift from the heart. Churchill also presented Kathy with a specially baked cake, a rare luxury in wartime. The evening ended in high spirits.

The mood was rather gloomier the following morning, perhaps on account of the number of bottles that had been emptied. Clementine was unwell and remained upstairs, not even appearing to greet her husband's luncheon guests. Winston was also below par. 'Tired and depressed,' noted Averell, who added that the PM's mood grew darker as the day progressed. 'He didn't have much to say throughout dinner and was immersed in his thoughts, with his head in his hands part of the time.'[1]

The grim news from the battle-front was one reason for his depression, with the situation on the Eastern Front growing increasingly precarious. Moscow looked certain to fall to the Wehrmacht, bringing the possibility of the complete collapse of the Red Army. Tensions were also rising in the Far East, and Averell and Churchill spent much of that evening discussing the consequences of a Japanese attack on Siam. Churchill expressed his willingness to take on the Japanese, who had signed the Tripartite Pact with Germany and Italy in the summer of 1940, but only if Roosevelt would provide 'some assurance of support'.[2]

It was almost nine o'clock when Churchill's butler-valet, Sawyers, entered the Chequers dining room with the little flip-top radio that Harry Hopkins had given the prime minister. It was small and practical, perfect for Churchill to listen to the nightly BBC news. As Sawyers handed it to the PM, he turned to address the room at large. 'There was something in the news about a Japanese attack on the American fleet.'[3]

Churchill fumbled when opening the radio and therefore missed the lead item. The second piece of news concerned a tank battle in a remote area of Libya, somewhere south of Tobruk. Averell was depressed to learn that the British had once again been bested.

The BBC announcer, Alvar Liddell, eventually returned to the day's top story, providing a more detailed account of what had taken place. 'Japanese aircraft have raided Pearl Harbor, the naval base in Hawaii,' he said. 'The announcement of the attack was made in a brief statement by President Roosevelt.'

In a flash, the mood in the room was transformed. 'We looked at one another incredulously,' said Ambassador Winant. Kathy detected a frisson of panic. '*What was that?* Pearl Harbor. *Where is that?*'

The announcer continued. 'Naval and military targets on the principal Hawaiian island of Oahu have also been attacked. No further details are yet available.'

Another moment of suspended silence. 'I was thoroughly startled,' recalled Averell, 'and I repeated the words, "The Japanese have raided Pearl Harbor."' Churchill's aide-de-camp, Tommy Thompson, disagreed. 'No, no . . . he said Pearl River.'

But everyone else had heard the words Pearl Harbor, including Churchill, who suddenly leaped to his feet. Averell had never seen the prime minister's mood change so abruptly. 'Recovering from his lethargy, [he] slammed the top of the radio down and got up from his chair.' Addressing the room at large, he boomed: 'We shall declare war on Japan!'[4]

'Good God!' responded Ambassador Winant. 'You can't declare war on a radio announcement.'[5]

Churchill's private secretary, John Martin, had slipped out of the room a few seconds earlier; he now reappeared with news that the Admiralty was on the phone. The prime minister was urgently required.

Averell and Winant followed Churchill in order to eavesdrop on the telephone conversation. The Admiralty confirmed the BBC's sensational news: Japan had indeed attacked America at Pearl Harbor.

Kathy and Pamela had remained by the fireplace during this kerfuffle. They were awaiting confirmation of the news from Ambassador Winant, who was trying to place a call to President Roosevelt. He eventually succeeded, but the line was not secure and required Roosevelt to be guarded in what he said. He provided no details of the scale of the assault, nor did he reveal how many ships had been sunk. In the absence of specific information, Winant assumed the attack had been a minor one. 'That's fine, Mr President, just fine,' he could be heard saying in his customarily soothing tone, before informing Roosevelt that he was with a friend who wished to speak with him.[6] 'You will know who it is as soon as you hear his voice.'[7]

Churchill didn't bother with the usual pleasantries.

'Mr President, what's this about Japan?'

'It's quite true,' said Roosevelt. 'They have attacked us at Pearl Harbor. We are all in the same boat now.'[8] He told Churchill he would go to Congress the following morning and ask for a declaration of war. Churchill promised to do the same.

The prime minister would later try to reconstruct the exact details of that momentous evening: 'We then went back into the hall and tried to adjust our thoughts to the supreme world event which had occurred, which was of so startling a nature as to make even those who were near the centre gasp.' Churchill admired the cool reaction of Averell and Winant. 'My two American friends took the shock with admirable fortitude.'[9]

Averell's overwhelming feeling that night was one of relief – relief that America was at long last in the war. This was the moment both he and Churchill had been awaiting ever since his arrival in London nine months earlier. 'The inevitable had finally arrived,' he wrote. 'We all knew the grim future that it held, but at least there was a future now. We both had realized that the British could not win the war alone. On the Russian front there was still a question whether the Red Army would hold out.' Now a more positive thought was running through Averell's mind: 'At last, we could see a prospect of winning.'[10]

TELEGRAMS BUTLERS·CROSS
STATIONS
LITTLE·KIMBLE·1·MILE
WENDOVER·2½·MILES
PRINCES·RISBOROUGH·3½·MILES
TELEPHONE WENDOVER·70·77

CHEQUERS
BUTLER'S CROSS·AYLESBURY
BUCKS

Dear Mary –
Was it a hope? I always hoped – wondered – to be in London
the night we got into the war. Somehow it's been more
exciting – Since here –
We heard the news of the bombing of Pearl Harbor – just like
everyone else – over the 9 o'clock news – It took a while to sink
in – the words had a too new association to – Then there was
a clamour – "What was that? Pearl Harbor – Where's that?" Then
Martin left to get a confirmation – Ave & Winant wondered – a rumor
no doubt – It couldn't be true – but it was –
I don't remember much else of dinner – the P.M. had cheered up –
he kept leaving to phone – Winant kept leaving – then finally we &
the coffee pot were left alone in the dining room – I left, & the
men came back to finish & talk –
I sitting by the fire place when Winant came in – "It's come
at last – It's exciting –" Winant spoke of his son – "He'll be in it." Why in
hell did he have to get personal at the moment?
Plans were made – Parliament called for tomorrow – Washington called –
Winant was nervous he smoked down an all-night cigar in
a short hour – "I'm glad we're together –"
"The light that flickered – the light that gleamed, the light that
shone" – perhaps he'll use that in tomorrow's speech –
"We must see our cinema." For a hour perhaps we did – Came
down for the midnight news –
"Japan declared war on U.S. & Brit. Emp." Then 16 min. of news.
P.M. pacing in dragon wrapper – Ave standing by fire place – Winant in
overcoat buttoned up – standing at different places – puffing a new cigar –
God save the King – Argument ensues – about yesterday or tomorrow in
Singapore –
"The 1st day of war is always exciting."

Kathy found herself at the centre of momentous events. In this letter, written at Chequers, she describes being with Churchill on the night of Japan's attack on Pearl Harbor.

Kathy was busily making notes as Chequers moved seamlessly into crisis mode. 'Plans were made . . . Parliament called for tomorrow.' Churchill was already composing phrases for his following day's speech, testing them out on those in the room. 'The light that *flickered* . . . the light that *gleamed* . . . the light that *shone*.' Ambassador Winant looked visibly nervous, perhaps because his son was likely to be conscripted. 'He smoked down an all-night cigar in a short hour,' noted Kathy.

At midnight, the assembled company once again turned on the BBC news. Churchill was by now in his Chinese dressing gown – 'pacing in a dragon wrapper', as Kathy put it[11] – while Averell was lounging nonchalantly by the crackling hearth. Winant had slipped on his overcoat, protection against the December draughts, and was shuffling around the room as he consumed another of Churchill's cigars.

None of those gathered at Chequers had any idea of the scale of American losses. It would be several days before they learned that the raid on Pearl Harbor had been catastrophic. No fewer than 350 Japanese planes had participated in the attack, and they had sunk or seriously damaged seven of the eight battleships stationed in the port, as well as destroying 180 aircraft and killing almost 2,500 American servicemen. 'What a holocaust!' said Churchill when eventually told of the American setback.[12]

It was late by the time the midnight news had been digested and everyone began shuffling off to bed. Kathy had clean forgotten it was her birthday, which had been superseded by international events. Before going to sleep, she scrawled a hasty letter to her sister, recalling everything that had just happened. 'The first day of war is always exciting,' she wrote.[13]

America declared war on Japan within twenty-four hours of the attack on Pearl Harbor. Britain followed suit that same day. Three days later, on Thursday, 11 December, Hitler declared war on America and Roosevelt responded in kind. In the space of four short days, an already convulsed world had been pitched into global turmoil.

Churchill's immediate reaction to these events was to call for another meeting with President Roosevelt. 'Now that we are, as you say, "in the same boat", would it not be wise for us to have another conference?' He wanted to discuss the crisis face to face. Roosevelt agreed and invited Churchill to Washington.

Accompanied by his inseparable duo of advisers, Averell and Beaverbrook, the prime minister boarded the *Duke of York* at Greenock in Scotland in the second week of December, along with a team of lesser officials. The Atlantic crossing was so rough that almost everyone was seasick, with the exception of the PM himself, who took unseemly relish in regaling his companions with nauseating tales of seasickness. Averell said Churchill particularly enjoyed telling the story of a ship's passenger who held in his vomit as he raced for the deck. The steward protested, 'But you can't be sick here.' To which the unfortunate passenger spewed up his stomach contents with the words, 'Oh, can't I?'[14]

On their arrival at Hampton Roads, Virginia, the three men flew directly to Washington, arriving on Monday, 22 December. The ensuing conference, code-named Arcadia, succeeded in establishing a Grand Coalition of all the nations at war with Germany and Japan. This would eventually bring together twenty-six countries, including the Soviet Union. 'The declaration could not by itself win battles,' admitted Churchill, 'but it set forth who we were and what we were fighting for.'[15]

Averell and Beaverbrook were meanwhile involved in the nuts and bolts of winning battles. They installed themselves in the Mayflower Hotel, the grandest in the capital, and thrashed out a blueprint for victory. Four months earlier, they had launched their radical plan to transform America's civilian industries into munitions factories. Now they set their sights on an altogether more ambitious programme. It would see the entire industrial might of America focused on one overarching goal: the mass production of weaponry.

It was so radical that the country's car production would fall to zero as the great Detroit automobile companies turned over their assembly lines to the production of tanks, trucks, and bomber aircraft. Some factory bosses complained bitterly at such unreasonable demands, but Averell and Beaverbrook didn't care. Production targets were doubled, trebled, quadrupled. The two millionaires were accustomed to thinking big and no figure was too large for them. They demanded 45,000 new aircraft over the next twelve months, and a staggering 100,000 by the end of 1943. That meant a daily output of almost 300 planes. The annual tank target was set at 75,000, more than 200 a day.

Both men were acutely conscious of the need to get supplies to the Soviet Union. Just twelve weeks earlier, they had promised Stalin a massive injection of weaponry, but the Arctic convoys had so far been scantily laden. The first convoy, PQ1, had delivered just twenty tanks. Nor had there been as many convoys as projected. By the time of the Arcadia meeting, just six had reached the northern ports of Archangel and Murmansk, where a small team of Allied personnel had been stationed to offload them.

While Averell sent messages to Stalin promising an imminent increase in weaponry, Beaverbrook reprimanded his juniors for not working hard enough. 'This won't do!' he admonished Captain Harold Balfour, undersecretary of state for air. 'We want the planes to get to Russia. If the Russians can fight in the snow, surely we can move airplanes in the snow.' Beaverbrook was once again displaying that uncompromising spirit that made him so reviled by his staff. He would brook no dissent, allow for no compromise. 'England will send the promised planes to Russia,' he told Balfour.[16]

It was an order, not an aspiration.

The Wehrmacht was still making huge advances as winter approached, but the battle for Moscow was proving tougher than expected. Adolf Hitler's declaration of victory at Berlin's Sportpalast had proven premature, as had the victorious headlines in Berlin's newspapers.

The Wehrmacht had launched its final drive towards the Soviet capital on Sunday, 16 November, and swept through everything in its path during the first fortnight. But German commanders had not reckoned on a blistering Soviet counteroffensive, spearheaded by eighteen divisions newly transferred from Siberia. They were supported by 2,000 tanks that continued to operate even as the temperature fell to minus forty.

Stalin's Red Army soldiers fought with consummate bravery in those dying days of November, despite facing a catastrophic shortage of weaponry. One officer complained to Molotov that he had only one rifle for every five soldiers. The foreign commissar replied bluntly,

'If they have no rifles, let them fight with bottles.'[17] This was later said to have been the origin of the Molotov cocktail, a bottle filled with flammable liquid.

The Soviet troops defending Moscow eventually managed to recapture a string of towns and villages to the west of the capital, forcing the German army into its first retreat. By the end of December, it was clear that the Wehrmacht's great winter offensive had failed in its principal objective. Although the Luftwaffe's bombardment of the capital would endure and intensify, the immediate danger to Moscow was over.

Stalin had a brief moment of respite.

Ambassador Cripps had grown increasingly depressed since his enforced move to Kuibyshev. Not only was he shunned by the Kremlin, but he was also treated as an irrelevance by Whitehall. 'Intolerable,' he wrote.[18] 'I feel that I am so useless here.'[19] He suspected that Churchill was keeping him in the Soviet Union for the sole reason that it was a long way from Westminster. He had tendered his resignation on several occasions, but each time it had been refused. Now, in December, he once again announced his desire to quit. This time his resignation was accepted. Cripps was returning home.

His final weeks in Russia were more miserable than ever. He was suffering from acute catarrh, a sickness compounded by the icy-damp climate of Kuibyshev, and his vegetarian diet was increasingly difficult to sustain in the depths of a Russian winter. Finally, on Thursday, 8 January, he boarded a flight from Kuibyshev to Moscow, the first stage in a long voyage.

Most departing ambassadors were given an official farewell from senior commissars, along with an all-trumpets-blazing guard of honour. Not Cripps. 'All a bit odd,' he wrote on the night of his departure, 'as there was no one to see me off at the aerodrome. It looks as if for some reason they want to show their displeasure.'[20]

He flew to Moscow to say farewell to Stalin, but the Soviet leader refused to see him. 'I cannot think there is any political reason,' he wrote, 'and if that is so, it must be a personal one.'

Insulted and dejected, he finally flew out of Moscow on Friday, 9 January. 'No one from the government,' he noted on his arrival at the airport. 'It seems clear that they have decided to do the minimum of seeing me off.'[21]

This was indeed the case. Cripps was leaving Moscow as he had arrived, unwanted and unloved. His relationship with Stalin throughout his ambassadorship had mirrored the relationship between the Soviet Union and Great Britain – frosty and dysfunctional, with a few brief interludes of semi-warmth.

Cripps felt that whoever replaced him would need to be of radically different temperament; someone who could connect with the Soviet leader. Unless a personal relationship with Stalin could be established, Britain would be unable to sustain a long-term relationship with the country.

Cripps had a clear idea as to who that replacement should be. 'I rather feel the best man might be Archie Clark Kerr,' he wrote.[22] Archie was currently serving as Britain's ambassador to China, and Cripps had visited him the previous year. He had been charmed by Sir Archibald, describing him as 'an absolutely first-class man . . . one of the most enlightened men I have met'.[23]

But Archie had more to offer than enlightened views. He had also displayed a remarkable ability at befriending China's feuding warlords and bandits, carousing with them and striking up relationships with them.

To Sir Stafford Cripps, it was as if Ambassador Clark Kerr had a set of skills uniquely suited to the needs of the moment.

PART IV

A Fresh Start

Moscow
Spring and Summer 1942

14

Call Me Archie

AT APPROXIMATELY THE same time each day in the Chinese city of Chungking, a curious little scene was played out on the banks of the River Yangtze. A middle-aged Westerner, burned to bronze after many years abroad, would strip off his garments and plunge into the dangerously swirling waters.

No one else in the city swam in the Yangtze, for its current was treacherous and unpredictable. And no one else was prepared to face the oft-present risk of Japanese warplanes spitting bullets onto the shoreline. But then no one else was quite like Sir Archibald Clark Kerr, His Britannic Majesty's ambassador to war-torn China. Oblivious to danger – or rather revelling in it – he took pride in displaying his suntanned torso and powerful physique. 'Tough?' he scoffed after meeting Ernest Hemingway. 'I'm tougher than he is.'[1]

By November 1941, Archie Clark Kerr had been in China for more than three years. It had proved one of the most demanding assignments in the world. The Chinese were at war with the Japanese, who had captured Peking and Shanghai, but China was also at war with itself, with frequent clashes between Nationalist forces (led by Chiang Kai-shek) and Communist forces (led by Mao Tse-tung). The two warlords had struck an uneasy truce in the wake of the Japanese onslaught, but they remained irrevocably divided.

Sir Archibald Clark Kerr brought three decades of diplomatic experience to the post, having previously served in half a dozen trouble spots. To those who watched his rise, it was as if he had been specially designed for the world's war zones – a charismatic adventurer with an uncommon ability to charm bandits, warlords, and dictators. '[He had] many traits of character associated with a Renaissance *condottiere*,' wrote one journalist. 'Outstanding courage, immense and obstinate self-assurance, opportunism, and a resolve to succeed.'[2]

He certainly had none of the usual attributes of the Whitehall diplomat, that faintly ludicrous caricature equipped with pinstripe, bowler, and despatch case. Nor did he have the requisite schooling. Far from being educated at Eton and Oxford (de rigueur for entry into the pre-war diplomatic corps), Clark Kerr had gone to a little-known day school in Bath. And in an age in which many ambassadors still hailed from hereditary dynasties, he possessed neither pedigree nor fortune. Born into a family of Scottish émigrés living in New South Wales – and transported to Britain at an early age – he would remain proudly Scottish for his entire life.

In the corridors of power and within their splendorous embassies, ambassadors of the period were always addressed as Your Excellency. Not so Archibald Clark Kerr. Everyone called him Archie – he insisted upon it. It was his way of cutting a ray of warmth through the diplomatic ice.

Not everyone was impressed by his happy-go-lucky manner. 'One of the most bizarre human beings ever to rise to the rank of ambassador,' wrote Rebecca West, at the time a highly opinionated journalist. She said that his posting to China 'left many an astonished traveller marvelling at the Foreign Office system of promotion'.[3] Others felt there was a flaw in Archie's character, 'a tendency to hero worship some of the great men to whom he has been accredited'.[4] So wrote journalist and MP Tom Driberg, who added that Archie was so over-awed by those in power – especially dictators – that he lost all sense of objectivity. If true, it was a potentially serious failing.

Winston Churchill had known Archie for almost two decades by 1942 and had supported him on a number of occasions during that time. Back in 1925, when Churchill was chancellor of the exchequer, he had defended Archie against the old guard in the Foreign Office. He would continue to champion Archie throughout his career, perhaps because he viewed him as a kindred free spirit. Yet the political views of the two men were radically opposed. Archie was anti-imperial, egalitarian, and liberal; politically, he was closer to the Labour Party than the Conservatives. But his charisma was such that he found himself with high-ranking backers in both political parties. And however much he disagreed with Churchill's imperial policy, there developed a genuine friendship between the two men.

Archie Clark Kerr was radically different from the average British diplomat. A flamboyant bisexual maverick, he forged a close personal relationship with Stalin. 'Two old rogues' is how he described the pair of them.

Archie's ambassadorial predecessor in China, Sir Hughe Knatchbull-Hugessen, had been severely wounded when his car was strafed with Japanese machine-gun fire. By the time Archie arrived to replace him, Shanghai was under Japanese control and the British Embassy had been evacuated to provincial Chungking. Even here, it came under constant attack from Japanese fighters. When Archie rolled into town, he found the embassy destroyed and the adjoining building severely damaged.

The Foreign Office ordered him to abandon the place, considering it too dangerous. Archie defied this order and insisted that the Union

Jack be kept flying over the charred wreckage. It was his way of giving a diplomatic two fingers to the passing Japanese bombers. At a decidedly dangerous cocktail party on the embassy lawn, he gave his Chinese guests a rousing speech. 'The Foreign Office has ordered me to move the embassy,' he thundered, 'but they cannot order me to move my body!'[5] His defiant stance endeared him to the local population. Before long, they viewed him as their greatest champion.

Archie had long taken a mischievous delight in scandalising his peers. In 1929, while serving as Britain's minister in Chile, he fell in love with a stunningly attractive Chilean woman, María Teresa Díaz Salas, the daughter of a millionaire businessman. Blonde, refined, and with an impeccable Chilean pedigree, this 'Pocket Venus' (as she was known) was twenty-nine years Archie's junior. Within a month they were married, and 'Tita' became an entertaining addition to the diplomatic cocktail circuit.

She didn't mince her words. On arriving at her husband's posting in Sweden, she declared that 'the three things I hate in life are darkness, smoked fish and bridge'. In one sentence, she managed to offend both the Swedes and the bridge-playing embassy staff. Archie was equally blunt. 'Swedes are only interesting when they are stark naked,' he declared. 'Dressed, they are the worst of bores.'[6] He himself was rarely fully dressed, at least not in the summer months, when he conducted his ambassadorial meetings from a deckchair.

Women adored Archie and Archie adored women, especially those of high birth. In his formative years he had dated Princess Sophie of Prussia (a granddaughter of Queen Victoria) and formed a close attachment to Lady Elizabeth Bowes-Lyons. 'Wonderful, beautiful', he mused after an evening in her company, 'the stuff of dreams'.[7] The feeling was mutual, but there was no lasting romance and she later sent him word that she had become engaged to 'Bertie', the future King George VI.

The young Archie had also formed close friendships with young men. These 'naturally gave rise to gossip', according to journalist Walter Bell, although such friendships were far from unusual at the time.[8] Among the young men in Archie's circle was Harold Nicolson, who wrote him soppy and intimate letters when they were both still bachelors. 'Dear Arch, I want you so. You are very remote tonight. How long it is. How careless we were to let it all slip away!'[9]

In those heady days that followed the Great War, sexuality was fluid and promiscuity a virtue. When one of Archie's male friends ran off with a princess, they mocked him for being 'frightfully Lesbian'.[10] Life was a game for the youthful Archie, often reckless and always full of promise. It was to remain a game for the rest of his life.

The Japanese raids on Chungking grew so menacing during the course of 1941 that the city's 250,000 inhabitants took to hiding out in caves hacked into the steep riverside cliffs. As Japanese bombs exploded around the embassy, Archie would withdraw to his study, 'taking snuff like an eighteenth-century cavalier', and compile his weekly despatches for the Foreign Office.[11]

Once a raid was over, he would change into his Argyll tweeds and stroll over the clifftops, smoking his pipe and exercising Hodge, his huge German shepherd. It was a dangerous stroll, for he was a wanted man: his constant support for the Nationalist Army had earned him the enmity of the Japanese occupying forces. Before long, they were darkly muttering that their real enemy in China was neither Chiang Kai-shek nor Mao Tse-tung, but Sir Archibald Clark Kerr.

Archie took their threats seriously. In his back study, in the third drawer of a locked steel cabinet, he had an index file of all the known terrorists, traitors, and gangsters who wanted him dead. Some were Japanese. Others, like the Yellow Way, were Chinese Communists. All were seeking to kill him.

His reports so alarmed the Foreign Office that he was instructed to buy a bullet-proof car. The most affordable offer came from Bills Motors in Shanghai, authorised Ford dealers in China, who offered him a customised Lincoln Zephyr sedan. Its roof, sides, and dashboard were to be lined with pistol-proof armour plate while its mild steel floor served as a shield against grenade fragments. Most impressive was the windscreen of four-ply bullet-proof glass. It was like driving in an armoured fish tank.

But Archie was not destined to spend much time in that fish tank. On the evening of Friday, 16 January, the Foreign Office in London made an important announcement. 'The King has been graciously pleased to approve the appointment of Sir Archibald Clark Kerr, GCMG, as His Majesty's Ambassador in the Soviet Union.' The communiqué added that Clark Kerr was considered the best man for the job, 'with the added asset of four years in war-time China'.[12]

The news was greeted with sadness in China, with the local press labelling him 'the most popular diplomatist Great Britain has ever sent to China'. Archie was no less effusive in his praise for the Chinese. In a farewell message, he said he was proud to have watched them fight so heroically against Japanese aggression, 'a matter for amazement and the highest admiration'.[13]

But now he had a new field to furrow, a new dictator to befriend. Within days, Archie was to leave his old friends in Chungking and head for distant Kuibyshev. His life was about to take a wholly new turn.

15

In Stalin's Bunker

ARCHIBALD CLARK KERR's official title was Ambassador Extraordinary and Plenipotentiary to the Soviet Union, for which he was to be paid £2,500 a year, with a further £4,150 in allowances. It was a princely salary for service in a country in which there was almost nothing to buy.

Before leaving Chungking, he was given a farewell banquet by Chiang Kai-shek, who hailed his achievements as a miracle of diplomacy. 'The Chinese people shall never forget him.'[1] Now, in Soviet Russia, Archie would need to pull off a far greater miracle if he was to succeed where Ambassador Cripps had so glaringly failed.

Archie had suffered a succession of personal blows in the weeks before leaving Chungking. Most crippling of all was the loss of his beloved Tita, who had walked out of the marital home and headed for a more glamorous existence in New York. What prompted her departure remains unclear, but the stresses of life in bomb-torn Chungking cannot have helped their marriage, nor the prospect of several more years in provincial Kuibyshev. Archie was heading to his new posting without his greatest pillar of support.

A further blow was the death of his faithful dog, Hodge, who had accompanied Archie on some of his more dangerous hikes into the Chungking countryside. And then came more bad news: that spring, Archie's London apartment in Grosvenor Square was flattened by a Luftwaffe bomb, destroying all his belongings. At around the same time, the ship carrying his personal effects from China to Russia was sunk by a Japanese torpedo. The only items he would eventually recover were those he had left behind in Chungking: a set of Scottish tartan napkins and a crate containing Yardley soap, Mennen shaving cream, and De Reszke cigarettes, along with boxes of Bromo toilet paper and a silver bell for summoning servants.[2]

If he was depressed by these setbacks, he kept it hidden behind a veil of bonhomie. After leaving Chungking on Wednesday, 4 February, he flew via Karachi, Baghdad, and Teheran before finally touching down in Kuibyshev. Embassy staff and journalists who greeted him at the airport were delighted to see that he alighted from the plane with a warm smile and a twinkle in his eye. The shadow of Ambassador Cripps had been replaced by a ray of brilliant sunshine.

Archie's first task was to get to know the staff serving under him, a heady mix of depressives, mavericks, and comedians. His deputy was Lacy Baggallay, an old-school gentleman with refined manners and a heart of gold. Even the Soviets admired him. 'We would like more Mr Baggallays in this world,' said one commissar. 'Then there would be no more wars.'[3]

Next in the hierarchy came Daniel Lascelles, a less endearing character. Lascelles was a humourless workaholic who informed his colleagues that he was 'perfectly prepared to go to parties for the purpose of representation, [but] he absolutely refused to go any place to be amused'.[4] Similarly morose was the embassy's elderly interpreter, Charles Dunlop.

Archie steered clear of the doomsters and befriended instead the handful of young blades diverted by the absurdities of life in Soviet Russia. These included Tom Brimelow, newly recruited and full of good cheer; Harold Elvin, the bright-eyed Cockney who worked as embassy caretaker; and First Secretary John Trant, who had been a stand-up comic before entering the Foreign Office. Trant even looked like a pantomime clown – short and stout, with an impressively voluminous belly.

Archie also got to know the locally based staff, whose most flamboyant representative was the ambassador's diminutive Greek butler, Timoleon. He doubled as the embassy's major-domo, riding out of town in search of much-needed food. He would return from these expeditions like a triumphant corsair, bearing a piratical smile and a crate of ill-gotten gains: sheep, chicken, or (on one notable occasion) half a dozen turkeys.

All these staff had their allotted duties in the embassy, but a few were to play a more significant role in the events to come. Among these was Archie's personal interpreter, Arthur Birse, who had spent his youth in tsarist St Petersburg but fled the country at the time of Britain's disastrous military intervention in 1919. Inquisitive and modest, the balding Birse was to remain at Archie's side through everything that was to follow. 'An extraordinary man who pretends to be ordinary,' wrote one of his colleagues.[5] Before long, Birse would find himself accompanying Archie into the Kremlin.

Archie was horrified by the provincial backwardness of Kuibyshev. 'A frozen little place,' he wrote in a letter to Stafford Cripps. 'What is a fellow to do?'[6] It was a good question. Kuibyshev was cold, dull, and entirely lacking in charm. There was nothing to do except watch the relentless snowstorms rage in from the eastern steppes.

This city of half a million souls was overflowing with evacuees from Moscow and elsewhere. Swarms of famished refugees shambled along Kuibyshev's streets with colourless faces and exhaustion in their eyes. There was little food, less alcohol, and no fresh fruit or vegetables. Several members of the American Embassy had contracted scurvy and a few had gone down with typhus.[7] The *Collier's* reporter Alice-Leone Moats caught influenza, then conjunctivitis, then dysentery.

'Our work was temporarily at a standstill,' wrote Arthur Birse of the long weeks that followed Archie's arrival. 'We visited each other in our dormitories, listened to the radio and speculated on the limits of Hitler's advance.'[8] The Wehrmacht was driving ever deeper into Soviet territory, with the cities of Kerch and Kharkov in imminent danger of capture by the Germans. Army Group North had also tightened its grip on Leningrad, where starvation and extreme hypothermia were claiming the lives of thousands. The city was being systematically strangled by the German siege, with the only lifeline being the ice road over Lake Ladoga. It was not enough. The most desperate inhabitants staved off death by resorting to cannibalism.

In Kuibyshev, which lay beyond the reach of both the Wehrmacht and the Luftwaffe, the mighty Volga might have afforded some distraction, but it was still locked in ice at the time of Archie's arrival. The famous boatmen would not return to work until the great thaw. Kuibyshev's only other attraction was the Bolshoi ballet, whose dancers had been transferred to the city from Moscow. But even *Swan Lake* lost its magic after the umpteenth performance.

Archie soon found himself oppressed by the constrictions of life in the Soviet Union. The regime had established special agencies to cater to foreigners, thereby restricting any contact with Soviet citizens. Intourist handled travel arrangements; Burobin oversaw the rental of apartments; Sovinformburo censored articles and letters home. The word he heard most often was *nyet*.

It was impossible to meet any locals, for it was a criminal offence for a Soviet citizen to fraternise with the foreign community. 'I want to plunge into the mind of the Russians,' wrote Archie, 'and that seems to be impossible . . . I came here prepared to offer a hell of a lot – all I have – but there is no one to take it!'

In a letter to Anthony Eden, he contrasted the bustle of Chungking with the moribundity of Kuibyshev. 'My little four-room house was always full of Chinese bursting with useful and stimulating talk,' he wrote. 'Here, so far, in my little three-roomed house, there has been nothing but the smell of cooking, Stafford's Airedale and silence.'

It dawned on him that his greatest asset, his gregarious charm, might not work the same magic here as it had done in China. 'People have been at pains to make clear to me that being oneself – they call it personality – counts for nothing in Russia.' It was all rather troubling. 'A fellow like myself needs – I won't say an audience – but a sympathetic readership.'[9]

Within a week of arriving in Kuibyshev, Archie got permission to undertake a two-week trip to Moscow, travelling there with a few of his staff. The official purpose of his visit was to present his ambassadorial credentials to the Soviet head of state, Mikhail Kalinin, but he was already eyeing the possibility of an early meeting with Stalin. He was equipped with a letter from Churchill, in the hope it might gain him access to the Kremlin.

He travelled to Moscow by plane, arriving at 4.30 p.m. on Friday, 20 March. The trip began well. His little team was given a far more convivial welcome than had ever been accorded to Ambassador

Cripps, despite a biting Arctic wind. They were then escorted to the still-functioning Metropole Hotel, where rooms had been reserved for them.

A week after arriving in the capital, Archie received an unexpected summons to the Kremlin. The invitation came directly from Stalin, who expressed an interest in meeting the new ambassador. The visit was arranged for the evening of Saturday, 28 March.

After being led through a maze of corridors, Archie was ushered into a large but sparsely furnished room. At the farthest end, diminutive in stature, stood Joseph Stalin.

'My first surprise was the shape and size of him,' he wrote. 'I had expected something big and burly. But I saw, at the end of the long room, a little, slim, bent, grey man with a large head and immense white hands.' The all-powerful Soviet leader cut a less-than-imposing figure and seemed strangely furtive. 'As he took my hand, I noticed that he averted his eyes, setting them not upon mine, but upon my middle button. He gave me a chair at the end of the long green baize table, almost as long as the room.'

Archie was also struck by Stalin's physiognomy. 'His face seemed to droop, loose and slightly dew-lapped . . . When he talks, this drooping remains almost unrelieved until something pleases him, and then the whole thing tightens up and crinkles into the most engaging and disarming smile.'

Archie had heard others describe Stalin as being like a well-fed cat, but he chose a different analogy. 'To me, he suggests a possum rather than a cat, and the kind of possum you would like to have about you as a pet.' But possums could be dangerous and unpredictable. Stalin was 'a possum you would get very fond of, against your better judgement, but would have to keep a sharp eye on, lest he nip you in the buttocks out of sheer mischief'.

Standing next to Stalin was Foreign Commissar Molotov, whose defining features were his expressionless eyes and monochrome pallor. Archie took an instant dislike to him and would refer to him as 'Old Bootface' (or 'Football Face') from that day forth.

'As I was reaching for Mr Churchill's message, which was the pretext for my presence, a young officer burst into the room and shouted that German bombers were over Moscow.' Stalin asked

Archie if he would like to take shelter in his private bunker below the Kremlin.

'I replied that I was fresh from Chungking, which for three years or so had been bombed night and day, and that I was attuned to the crashing of air raids.' He was happy to remain in Stalin's study.

It was the wrong answer. 'Stalin suggested it would be quieter in the shelter and led the way, very swift-footed, to a lift and pushed into it Molotov and me, banging the door upon us and remaining behind himself.'

Archie felt he had blown a unique opportunity to get acquainted with Stalin. 'I was much inclined to bite my thumbs . . . and cursed the German bombers for spoiling my talk with him.'

The lift descended rapidly before shuddering to a halt. The doors opened onto another brightly lit corridor. 'It was kind of a dog-leg journey. One lift and a quick scuttle along a corridor, Molotov making the pace, then another lift, and we found ourselves in the bowels of the Kremlin.'

Archie was astonished by the scale of this underground labyrinth, which seemed to spread under half of Moscow. No foreigner had ever been down there before. Molotov led Archie along another narrow corridor, which eventually led to Stalin's private shelter. 'Great steel doors admitted us to a long, vaulted, almost floodlit room. Before I had wholly got over the dazzle, there was Stalin standing mysteriously in our midst.'

He couldn't work out how the Soviet leader had beaten them to it. 'I can only imagine that he came down by some special, extra-speedy one-man chute. I was glad to see him, for I had assumed that, as he had remained behind, he had escaped me altogether.' Stalin looked relaxed and was already smoking an immense curved pipe whose bowl was so heavy he was unable to clamp it between his teeth.

Archie realised he had been presented with a unique opportunity to break the ice, for both he and Stalin were avid pipe smokers. As they sat down at a green baize table, with the interpreter squeezed between them, both men produced their pipes and tobacco pouches. 'Claiming some expertise in the matter of pipes, I fairly smashed it with Stalin's pipe and three of my own, which happened to be about my person.'

There now began a delicate ritual that came naturally to both men. 'His tobacco and mine were brought out and sniffed by two practised noses, rolled in the palm of the hand and teased with the fingertips.' It was smokers' chat, and Archie excelled at it. They discussed the art of pipe smoking, which then led to an earnest discussion about different types of tobacco. 'Inevitably, my tobacco went into Stalin's pipe and his into mine,' wrote Archie. 'Common and really solid ground had been reached. It was by no means unimportant. And so, through a cloud of friendly reek, the long talk began.'

The two-and-a-half-hour conversation that followed was a mixture of banter, boisterous bonhomie, and serious political debate. Archie knew he had been handed the opportunity of a lifetime and was determined not to squander it. This was the sort of convivial meeting that Ambassador Cripps had dreamed of during his long stint in the country.

'It was not my function as His Majesty's Ambassador to go too deeply into Stalin's past,' wrote Archie. 'We were Allies of the Soviet Union in a major war and my first duty, as I saw it, was rather to establish myself in the confidence of the man who was the unquestioned master of that vast country. Into this task I entered with zest.'

He was at his gregarious best during this first meeting, deftly steering the conversation from pipes to sex, thereby covering two of his favourite topics. What the two men had to say on this latter subject was sadly not recorded in Archie's memorandum to the Foreign Office. They next moved on to marital relations, a painful topic for the recently separated Archie. But it was also painful for Stalin, whose second wife, Nadezhda Alliluyeva, had committed suicide. Stalin said he was always strict when dealing with women 'and was inclined to the early use of the stick'. Archie said he always preferred the carrot.

'These digressions were pleasant enough, for they crackled with jokes.' The more they chatted, the more Archie was enjoying himself. 'I found him to be in many ways what in homespun English we call "just my cup of tea", and I conceived a liking for him personally and got stimulus from his company.'

Stalin next asked him about China and the private life of Chiang Kai-shek, 'about which he had some queer ideas, that I had to dispel'. And then came the serious stuff, 'prolonged and diverting digressions into such matters as democracy and its weaknesses'. Once or twice, Molotov attempted to join the conversation, but Stalin swiftly silenced him. 'He did not hesitate to sweep Molotov aside when Football Face ventured to intervene.'

They talked for so long that Archie feared he might be outstaying his welcome. But Stalin persuaded him otherwise. 'He resisted all attempts I made to bring the talk to an end, feeling, as I did, that I must be squandering the time of one of the busiest men in the world.'

In fact, Stalin was enjoying himself as much as Archie, and urged him to stay 'until the German bombers had done their work'.

There were moments when the Soviet leader seemed to speak from the heart. He told Archie of his genuine gratitude 'at the promptitude and regularity with which supplies were arriving from Great Britain, which he confessed had taken him and his people by surprise'. This was Averell's doing, and Stalin knew it. He next spoke of the profound misunderstandings that existed between Russia and the West, which he hoped would one day be overcome. When Archie decried the fact that Ambassador Cripps's military advisers had been poorly treated ever since their arrival in the country, Stalin offered his apologies. But he also had a criticism of his own, blaming the BBC for broadcasting negative comments about the Soviet Union. He said that free speech was the great weakness of democracy.

'As time went on he seemed to get restless, for he began to walk up and down at the far end of the room. I made, therefore, appropriate efforts to go.' But still Stalin was having none of it. 'He waved me back to my chair and asked if I was bored.'

Only now did Archie realise the reason for Stalin's restlessness. 'His belly, which is biggish and rather *schlap*, was rumbling – not as yours or mine might, but stupendously. I mean, really on the dictator level. He was a bit shy about it and he was trying to drown its booming voice with his own . . . But sometimes he had to pause and my translator was not man of the world enough to raise his voice too. So as the rumbling went on echoing down the long room, Stalin was driven to banging his pipe loudly on a tinny ashtray.'

As time went on he seemed to get restless for he began to walk up and down at the far end of the long room. I made therefore appropriate efforts to go in the belief that I had allowed the interest I felt to blind me to the passage of time. But with a sweep of that [illegible] short pipe of his he waved me back to my chair and asked if I was bored that I wanted to go. I soon discovered the reason for his restlessness. His belly, which is biggish and rather [illegible], was rumbling – not as yours or mine might, but stupendously. I mean really on the dictator level.

Archie wrote with a goose-feather quill, which made his memos extremely hard to read. Here he describes his remarkable first meeting with Stalin, who greatly enjoyed Archie's company.

Archie didn't leave until the Luftwaffe raid was finally over and the all-clear had sounded. It had been a remarkable encounter with the Soviet leader, unique in its informality and banter. 'At all times I was impressed by the calm and quiet of his approach to events. Nothing seemed to disturb his serenity.'

He felt he had made significant progress in that first meeting, forging the beginnings of a close personal relationship. 'The huddle I went into with Stalin proved to be cosier and pleasanter than I ever dared to hope,' he wrote. 'Probably it was no more than a juxtaposition of two old rogues, each one seeing the roguery in the other and finding comfort and harmony in it, and chuckling over it – chuckling all the more because of the governessy presence of that boot-faced Molotov.'[10] They may have been two old rogues, but one was assuredly more roguish than the other.

16

Spring Thaw

FOR THREE LONG months, the great winter chill sent the Wehrmacht into enforced hibernation. The world froze, and so did Hitler's army. But as the sun rose with enough warmth to melt the snows, German soldiers were suddenly rejuvenated. Panzer divisions were re-equipped, crippled tanks repaired, and new artillery was delivered from the Fatherland. Operation Barbarossa may have faltered during the deep freeze, but it was now relaunched with renewed vigour.

That spring, General Erich von Manstein launched an all-out offensive against Soviet forces in the eastern Crimea. In ten days, he annihilated the opposing Red Army. Some 175,000 men were killed or captured along with 347 tanks. But this was but the prelude to an even greater disaster. When Stalin ordered his commanders in the south to retake the city of Kharkov, his troops advanced in a giant pincer movement. Their intention was to trap and kill the bulk of Army Group South. But those Soviet soldiers walked into a trap that rapidly turned into a rout. A further 240,000 Red Army troops were captured, along with hundreds of tanks and field guns.

Stalin recalled to Moscow Nikita Khrushchev, one of his senior commanders in Ukraine, and blamed him for the defeat. He then publicly humiliated him by tapping the ash from his pipe onto Khrushchev's bald head. 'That's in accordance with *Roman* tradition,' he said to his astonished audience, explaining that defeated Roman commanders were ordered to take the ashes from a bonfire and rub them into their scalp.*[1]

* Khrushchev would never forget this humiliation and would later speak about the Kharkov disaster – and Stalin's role in it – in his famous denunciation of the Soviet leader in 1956.

In the city of Kuibyshev, 1,300 miles to the north-east of these cataclysmic battles, spring arrived all in a trice. When the CBS correspondent Larry LeSueur sauntered down to the River Volga after lunch on Tuesday, 21 April, he was witness to the breaking of the winter ice. 'There was no roar of crashing floes,' he wrote, 'just a slow languid movement of mile-long ice pans down the river.'[2] Finally the sun had mustered enough heat to weaken and crack the vast Volga sheet ice. Five hundred miles downstream, in distant Astrakhan, it had already melted, and scores of diesel-powered oil and grain barges were on the move. Within weeks, the entire river would be navigable.

The end of winter was one cause for optimism. Another was the thaw in relations with the Soviet regime. Archie returned from Moscow to Kuibyshev with a spring in his step, still basking in the afterglow of his meeting with the Soviet leader. Stalin had sent a telegram to Winston Churchill expressing his approval of such a genial ambassador. 'A good start,' wrote the foreign secretary, Anthony Eden.[3]

Stalin also wrote to Archie himself, sending boxes of pipe tobacco to Kuibyshev. Archie was genuinely touched and wrote an enthusiastic thank-you letter. 'I confess that I still have enough of the schoolboy left in me to make me eye an unopened parcel with some impatience,' he said. 'The young messenger indulged my weakness and was therefore witness to the delight I felt on seeing the generous heap of golden boxes that emerged from the paper, and on sniffing the sweetness they held . . . You have warmed my heart. I am indeed amazed and touched that, in the midst of your countless preoccupations, you should have found the time to think so kindly of the stranger and newcomer to your country.'[4]

As the spring weather grew warmer, Archie moved his office outside and conducted his affairs from the embassy garden. When the recently recruited Tom Brimelow was summoned to a formal meeting, he found the ambassador dressed in nothing more than a pair of skimpy black bathing shorts. 'He sunbathed as much as he could,' wrote Brimelow. 'Brown as a berry. Over six feet tall. With his barrel chest and broken nose, he looked like a retired bruiser.'[5]

Archie had the physique of a Hemingway hero. Sun-burnished and handsome, he was also uncommonly vain. His passport photo was not a photograph at all, but the copy of a painting of him when young. 'Overtones of Dorian Gray,' sighed one of his staff.[6]

He declined to provide his age to the editors of *Who's Who* – a most unusual departure from convention – and was an enthusiast for physical fitness, exercising outdoors for an hour each day. He thought nothing of plunging into the icy Volga – it was more bracing than the Yangtze – and acquired an old motorboat for himself and his staff. At weekends, he would take Brimelow, Arthur Birse, and a few others out to the islands where they would strip off and swim. The boat's engine would invariably stall on the return journey, threatening to float off downstream. But they were always tailed by four NKVD officers in a motor launch who would obligingly tow the stranded diplomats to safety.

One of Archie's staff described his conversation as 'a combination of Mark Twain, Churchill and Jesus Christ', and listened in wonder as he spilled extravagant stories of his ancestral Scottish home.[7] He led everyone to believe that it was a rambling baronial pile on the shores of Loch Eck in Argyll. In fact, it was nothing more than a modest bungalow furnished with glass-fronted cabinets. These were filled with rare editions of erotica.

Archie's interpreter, Arthur Birse, got to know him intimately and found him free from all pretence. 'His quizzical manner and witticisms hid his capacity for deep feeling, intense sympathy and understanding of human nature; and also, I think, his loneliness.'[8] Archie wrote to Tita constantly, obsessively, but she never replied. The marriage, it seemed, was over.

Archie's sexuality was a subject of much backstairs gossip in the embassy, but none of it – as yet – was substantiated. 'He certainly liked the company and presence of good-looking young men,' wrote one of the young attachés. 'But how far he went in these relationships is anyone's guess.' Besides, it wasn't just men he invited into his home. 'He equally relished the company of good-looking young women.'[9]

A few were less equivocal. 'There was no doubt in my mind that he was bisexual,' said Robert Cecil, who had worked alongside him in Iraq. Archie had an insatiable appetite for sex, which Cecil summed up in six words: 'If it moves, go for it.'[10]

★

Archie Clark Kerr took great delight in writing witty telegrams to his friends back in Whitehall, most of them composed from the comfort of his deckchair. They were never typed. Rather, he wrote with a goose quill, pausing at the end of each sentence to stab its nib into the precariously balanced inkpot.

'He kept a few geese,' noted an increasingly wide-eyed Tom Brimelow. 'When his current quill pen had worn out, he would grab a quill from a protesting gander, cut a nib and resume his work.'[11]

Brimelow and company found it almost impossible to decipher Archie's memos, because he wrote in a cursive eighteenth-century hand, with elongated twirls and calligraphic flourishes. He used the antiquated *ſ* instead of the pedestrian *s* and contrived lengthy and languid sentences. Words were chosen with care. He never spoke of 'diplomats' (preferring the less-used 'diplomatists') and would scatter his reports with esoteric terms such as 'atrabiliousness', which had even erudite Whitehall mandarins reaching for their dictionaries.* Nor did he shy from letting rip with the vernacular. 'Christ, god, damn, fuck and bugger', was his opinion of one truculent politician.

His private missives were particularly alive with wit, with the most celebrated being this letter to his old friend Lord Reginald Pembroke:

> My Dear Reggie,
>
> In these dark days man tends to look for little shafts of light that spill from Heaven. My days are probably darker than yours, and I need, my God I do, all the light I can get. But I am a decent fellow, and I do not want to be mean and selfish about what little brightness is shed upon me from time to time.
>
> So I propose to share with you a tiny flash that has illuminated my sombre life and tell you that God has given me a new Turkish colleague whose card tells me that he is called Mustapha Kunt.

* Atrabiliousness: melancholic, hypochondriac, splenetic, acrimonious.

> We all feel like that, Reggie, now and then, especially when Spring is upon us, but few of us would care to put it on our cards. It takes a Turk to do that.*

Many of Archie's official telegrams were addressed to Christopher Warner, head of the Foreign Office's Northern Department, which oversaw relations with the Soviet Union. Warner relished his salacious memos and begged for more. 'We know that you are all against sending us what may be pure gossip,' he wrote, 'but nonetheless, we would like to receive a certain amount.'[12] Over the months that followed, Warner and his colleagues would not be disappointed.

While Archie kept London informed of events in the Soviet Union, Kathy Harriman was getting to know some of the most influential voices in Britain. Her greatest coup that spring was to secure an exclusive interview with General Władysław Anders, commander-in-chief of all Polish forces stationed in Russia, while he was on a visit to London. Kathy had first met him at a cocktail party hosted by Poland's prime minister in exile, Władysław Sikorski: 'a cosy little affair for about five hundred of us'. Anders made quite an impression: 'Terrific to look at, if you don't mind a shaven head and bad teeth.' After befriending the prime minister's aide-de-camp, she secured her interview, conducting it in fluent French.

General Anders had a remarkable story to tell. Captured while defending his country during the 1939 Soviet invasion, he was repeatedly tortured by Stalin's thuggish security squad. 'A year ago he was in the dark and damp of Moscow's most gruesome prison, Lubyanka, wounded, half starving.'

He told Kathy he'd thought it unlikely he would survive. But everything changed with Hitler's invasion of the Soviet Union. Poland was suddenly an ally of Russia, albeit an uneasy one, and the large contingent of Polish soldiers deported to the USSR from

* Some have argued that the letter is not genuine. But it is entirely in character, and it is clear from other letters that Archie was amused by Mustapha Kunt's idiosyncratic name. According to Clark Kerr's biographer Donald Gillies, 'the contents are genuine but it has been typed up from the original by a third party, as Archie would never resort to "modern technology".'

Soviet-occupied Poland were now placed under the command of General Anders. 'His cell door was opened, Russian officials saluted him, told him he was commander-in-chief, their ally and friend; and, please, to have his baggage ready in an hour.'

He reminded his prison guards that he had no baggage. 'But in Russia, all great and important guests must have baggage,' he told Kathy, 'so he was brought shiny luggage and it – empty – was carried with him in state through the streets of Moscow to a grand apartment.'

Kathy was smitten by this rugged war hero who had been gravely wounded fully nine times. 'A nice general chat about his home, his family and the war. He spoke of the dazed feeling – the sudden transition from prison, twenty months of it – to complete luxury and importance.'

Almost twelve months had passed, but the transformation in his fortunes still hadn't sunk in. The Soviets had pillaged his country and liquidated thousands of his compatriots. And now they were hailing him as a war hero. 'Ex-enemies made friends by a great foe,' he said.[13] He might have been speaking for Great Britain and America, as well as for Poland.

Kathy's interview with General Anders was followed by a long lunch with Winston Churchill. 'The PM was in great form,' she wrote to Mary. 'Madagascar battle starting [and] a tussle with a man who is running for parliament.' This would-be Member of Parliament was trying to sue Churchill for libel, a source of great amusement to the prime minister. He was in ebullient mood and optimistic about the future. The meal that day was followed (for Kathy, not Churchill) by a languorous afternoon in the rear garden of No. 10 Downing Street. It was a glorious day and the war suddenly seemed very far away. 'I almost got a suntan,' she wrote.[14]

Kathy soon clocked up another success when she secured an interview with Sir Stafford Cripps, a man she privately found insufferable.[15] Cripps might have left Moscow under a dark cloud, but he had returned to London in triumph. He was hailed as the man who had brought the Soviet Union into the war on the side of the Allies, a perception he did everything possible to encourage.

Cripps had remained a Member of Parliament during his time as ambassador, which enabled him to re-enter front-line British politics on his return. He also gave a number of popular broadcasts about the Soviet war effort, in one of which he declared, 'If it hadn't been for the determination of the ordinary Russian peasant and his wife, and indeed of his child too, to take every conceivable step to prevent the advance of the Germans, I don't think the Russian Army alone would have succeeded.'[16]

This particular broadcast, exclusive to Paramount, was viewed by millions and caused such a surge in Cripps's popularity that Winston Churchill reluctantly brought him into the government as Lord Privy Seal and leader of the House of Commons.

In his interview with Kathy, Cripps told her how entire industrial plants had been dismantled from the Nazi-occupied areas of the Soviet Union and transported east, where they were being rebuilt. He felt that the scale of this reconstruction programme was not appreciated in the West. 'Many of these factories moved east of the Urals are only now beginning to come into production,' he said. When fully functioning, they would be able to produce enormous quantities of weaponry. But this would not happen for many months, leading to a drastic shortage of munitions for Stalin's front-line troops.

Cripps assured Kathy that Stalin would ultimately prevail over Hitler's Wehrmacht, although he added an important caveat: 'I am convinced that success for our cause in Russia this spring is dependent upon supplies from Great Britain and America.' It was imperative to get ever-increasing deliveries to the Soviet Union, and the responsibility for that, as Kathy well knew, fell entirely on her father's shoulders. It was to prove a very tall order.

17

Old Bootface

FOREIGN COMMISSAR MOLOTOV rarely left Stalin's side that spring, especially as news from the battle-front grew increasingly desperate. But in the third week of May, the Soviet leader despatched Old Bootface to London. It was a tangible sign of improving relations.

Molotov had two goals. The first was to sign a comprehensive alliance in which the two powers would reaffirm their commitment to destroying the Third Reich. His second goal was more controversial: to demand the immediate opening of a Second Front, with Britain and America launching a joint invasion of Nazi-occupied Europe.

Molotov landed at a military airfield near Dundee on Sunday, 17 May, having made the journey to Britain aboard a state-of-the-art TB-7 Soviet bomber, one of only six in existence. It flew at a record-breaking 30,000 feet, beyond the reach of any Luftwaffe bomber, and completed the journey in just over seven hours. This was also a record. Molotov almost froze to death during the flight and emerged from the plane dressed in a flamboyant set of fur-lined flying leathers. For the first and only time in his life, Old Bootface looked like a First World War fighter ace.

His trip was overshadowed by suspicion. The RAF offered Molotov an onward flight from Dundee to London, but he insisted on travelling by train. He privately feared that anti-Soviet elements in the British establishment might shoot down the plane. And he was so wary of MI6 spying on him during his visit that he had all his briefing documents sewn into the waistcoat of his interpreter, Vladimir Pavlov.

Winston Churchill proved a generous host, inviting Molotov and his team to Chequers. The prime minister was taken aback by their obsession with security. They demanded long-mislaid keys to their bedrooms (these were eventually found) and kept their doors locked at all times. Molotov's bodyguards went as far as to search every item of furniture in his bedroom, paying special attention to the bed and mattress. 'When the staff at Chequers succeeded in getting in to make the beds,' wrote Churchill, 'they were disturbed to find pistols under the pillows.'

Molotov and company also brought their own maids, who ensured that someone remained in each room at all times. Churchill was astonished to learn that 'the sheets and blankets were rearranged by the Russians so as to leave an opening in the middle of the bed out of which the occupant could spring at a moment's notice, instead of being tucked in . . . At night, a revolver was laid out beside his [Molotov's] dressing gown and his despatch case.'[1] It was as if the foreign commissar was expecting a nocturnal assault.

Molotov (left) was Stalin's unsmilingly monochrome foreign commissar, whom Averell (centre) met frequently. Archie hated Molotov and nicknamed him Old Bootface.

The proposed Anglo-Soviet Treaty of Alliance was swiftly agreed: it reaffirmed mutual military assistance and forbade either party from concluding a separate peace with Hitler. It was signed on the evening of Tuesday, 26 May, and Molotov's reward was an audience with King George VI at Buckingham Palace. This brought pleasure to neither party. His Majesty was underwhelmed by Stalin's most senior diplomat – 'a small quiet man with a feeble voice' – while Molotov was equally dismissive of the king. 'Nothing remarkable', he told Stalin.[2]

The discussion about a Second Front proved more problematic. At Stalin's insistence, Molotov demanded an invasion of Nazi-occupied Europe before the end of the year, arguing his case with the dry logic of a lawyer. One observer described Molotov as having 'all the grace and conciliation of a totem pole'.[3]

Churchill did his best to deflect Molotov's demands. After one Chequers dinner, he led the foreign commissar over to a giant globe and waxed lyrical about the feisty resilience of Great Britain, 'these small islands representing an almost microscopic fragment of land amid vast continents and boundless oceans'.[4] Old Bootface was unmoved by Churchill's animated oration, because it lacked any mention of a Second Front.

The prime minister eventually confessed to Molotov that an invasion of Nazi-occupied Europe was inconceivable in the near future. The country was not ready, the troops were not trained, and there were not enough weapons. The Western allies would get only one chance of liberating occupied Europe, and now was not the moment.

Molotov was disappointed. On Wednesday, 27 May, after ten fruitless days in London, he flew to Washington to try his luck with President Roosevelt.

Molotov was welcomed in the American capital as an honoured guest, with lodgings in the White House and a formal banquet on his first night. When a White House valet unpacked the foreign commissar's bags, he was bemused by what he found. Wrapped inside Molotov's clothes were an old sausage (somewhat rancid), a loaf of rye bread (somewhat stale), and a loaded pistol.

President Roosevelt was informed about both the weapon and the food. 'The Secret Servicemen did not like visitors with pistols,' he remarked, 'but on this occasion nothing was said.' The president was nonetheless tickled by the foreign commissar's eccentric luggage. 'Mr Molotov evidently thought he might have to defend himself and also he might be hungry.'[5]

Their first White House business meeting took place on the afternoon of Friday, 29 May. Molotov was uncharacteristically upbeat and even managed some small talk. He chatted about the speed of his flight to America and apologised for not bringing his military adviser, who had broken his kneecap in a London car crash. Roosevelt was pleasantly surprised by Molotov's amiable manner but reasoned that the Soviets must be wanting something.[6]

The president and commissar met again at 11.30 the following morning, and this time the discussions were more combative.[7] Molotov made the same blunt demand that he had issued to Churchill: an Anglo-American invasion before the end of 1942. Such an invasion would draw forty Wehrmacht divisions away from the Soviet battle-front, enabling the Red Army to strike Hitler a decisive blow.

Roosevelt summoned his two senior advisers, General George Marshall and Admiral Ernest King. In Molotov's presence, he asked Marshall a direct question: were plans sufficiently advanced to inform Stalin that America and Britain were indeed preparing for a Second Front?

'Yes,' said General Marshall.

Roosevelt, speaking through his interpreter, repeated this to Molotov, adding that the foreign commissar could 'inform Mr Stalin that we expect the formation of a Second Front *this year*'.[8]

It is never easy to translate a conversation, but Roosevelt was fortunate to have an expert interpreter in Samuel Cross. Dr Cross was a professor of Slavonic languages at Harvard and editor of the *American Slavonic Review*. It was not his fault that the president's choice of words introduced a fatal element of ambiguity into the translated conversation.

The British and Americans were indeed preparing for a Second Front, but these preparations involved two quite separate operations. One was a massive cross-channel assault on Nazi-occupied Europe, with the code name Operation Roundup, later changed to Overlord. It was scheduled to take place in 1943. The other was a smaller emergency raid on the French coast, with the aim of drawing German divisions away from the Soviet front line. This was Operation Sledgehammer.

Was the president committing to Roundup or to Sledgehammer? His meaning was lost in translation, with Molotov thinking one thing and President Roosevelt meaning another. When Winston Churchill learned of the discussions, he hoped the president had committed to neither, for he had serious doubts about any assault on occupied France in the near future. 'Impossible, disastrous,' he had told Averell just a few days earlier. British troops were 'not up to strength and seriously under-equipped'.[9]

Molotov left Washington delighted with the president's commitment to a Second Front. He now returned to London in order to fine-tune the details with the prime minister. Churchill reluctantly signed the president's communiqué committing the Americans and British to a Second Front within six months. But he attached an all-important caveat: 'We can therefore give no promise in the matter,' he wrote, 'but provided that it appears sound and sensible, we shall not hesitate to put our plans into effect.'[10] It was dangerously imprecise language when dealing with a dictator as fastidious as Stalin.

After a final champagne reception in Downing Street on the evening of Wednesday, 10 June, the Soviet delegation flew back to Moscow. Churchill and his advisers were relieved at the departure of Old Bootface and his entourage, whose ungracious demeanour had tested their endurance. One of the least impressed was the PM's permanent undersecretary, Alexander Cadogan. 'What savages!' he wrote in his diary.[11]

18

Troubled Waters

Averell's trusted aide, Bob Meiklejohn, had never worked as hard as he did that summer. Not only was he helping to organise the transport of millions of tons of weaponry to Stalin, but he was also in charge of the day-to-day running of the Harriman Mission. It was a stressful sixteen-hour-a-day job that left him exhausted. There were times when he could hardly keep awake at his desk.

The nerve centre of Averell's empire was No. 3 Grosvenor Square, an imposing five-storey Victorian mansion block with direct access to the adjacent American Embassy. Here on the first floor, seated behind a dictatorial-sized desk, Averell played the role of a Roman proconsul.

'His nibs has acquired an authoritative, imperious way of announcing his views on even the most inconsequential matters, such as the weather, that is extremely irritating,' wrote Meiklejohn, 'most of all when he is correct.'[1]

Meiklejohn had to manage a constant stream of experts flying in from New York, Washington, and California. 'At the rate our personnel come and go,' he wrote on one particularly bothersome afternoon, 'we'll have to install a traffic director.'[2]

The mission headquarters had acquired seventeen full-time members of staff and seven part-time, fifteen stenographers, two clerks, two chauffeurs, two messengers, and five cleaning ladies. The offices were spread over twenty-seven rooms, and senior staff had three cars at their disposal, including Averell's Bentley. There was also an ever-changing roster of staff on secondment from Washington. All were focused on one goal: getting supplies to Stalin.

Averell had promised to ship industrial-size quantities of munitions to the Soviet Union: tens of thousands of tanks, planes, and guns, along with fuel, chemicals, and medical equipment. Transporting this from America required numerous hurdles to be overcome, including the establishment of a hazardous transatlantic supply chain.

Ships sailed to Hvalfjördur on the west coast of Iceland, where their cargos were transferred onto British merchantmen. They were then transported under naval escort to Archangel or Murmansk, the two principal ports in northern Russia. This was the most perilous part of the voyage. Not only was the Arctic Ocean often ice-bound, but its waters were patrolled by German warships and U-boats. Hitler's forces included the battleships *Tirpitz* and *Scheer*, a fleet of modern destroyers, twenty U-boats, and numerous fighters and bombers.

Averell's difficulties increased as the Arctic spring brought twenty-four-hour daylight. His fourteenth convoy, PQ14, was harried by German U-boats, which sank the lead vessel, *Empire Howard*, and sent fourteen others scurrying back to Iceland. Only eight ships made it to Murmansk.

And the news only got worse. The seventeenth convoy, PQ17, was the largest yet despatched to the Soviet Union: thirty-five merchant ships accompanied by an escort of forty-three warships. This protective ring of steel included two American cruisers, the battleship *Washington*, and the aircraft carrier *Victorious*. With thirteen submarines operating ahead of the convoy, PQ17 was the most formidable fleet ever to sail to Archangel.

Far from discouraging the Kriegsmarine, this armoured shield presented them with an enticing target. The first sign of trouble came on Wednesday, 1 July, the convoy's third day at sea, when the lead ships passed Bear Island, deep inside the Arctic Circle. Here, solid pack ice prevented the fleet from heading further north, leaving them exposed to German aerial surveillance. By the early hours of Saturday, 4 July, the convoy was being shadowed by the Luftwaffe.

The first attack came that very morning, when the *Christopher Newport* was struck by a torpedo. The weapon punched a huge hole in the hull, which flooded the engine room and forced the crew to abandon ship. She sank shortly after 8 a.m. A further three vessels were attacked by torpedo bombers, with the *William Hooper* the next to sink, along with her cargo of tanks, trucks, and ammunition.

Back in London, Averell and Churchill were kept informed in real time of the unfolding disaster. Events spiralled out of control just before nightfall. 'That evening', wrote Averell, 'Sir Dudley Pound, the First Sea Lord, sent signals to the convoy escort from London, ordering the cruisers to withdraw at high speed and the smaller vessels to scatter.'[3] Sir Dudley hoped the dispersal of the fleet would render it less vulnerable: instead, it was one of the most disastrous commands ever issued by the Royal Navy. Within minutes of receiving his order, the protective shield of PQ17 began to peel away, leaving the merchantmen to fend for themselves.

Deprived of its naval escort, the defenceless ships presented easy pickings for the marauding German U-boats and aircraft, which attacked them one by one. Of the thirty-four vessels that left Iceland, twenty-three were sunk over the days that followed. A mere eleven survivors limped into Archangel. PQ17 had proved an unmitigated disaster. Of the 200,000 tons of tanks, planes, and supplies destined for the Soviet battle-front, two-thirds now lay at the bottom of the Arctic Ocean. This was the equivalent of 4,000 Sherman tanks. Averell's supply line to Stalin had been broken.

Averell's Arctic supply line to Stalin faced constant attack from the Luftwaffe: here convoy PQ18 comes under assault. The previous convoy, PQ17, was all but annihilated: only eleven of the thirty-four vessels survived the voyage.

Winston Churchill had the painful task of informing the Soviet leader that such losses were unsustainable, sending him an unusually convoluted telegram with news that he was suspending the convoys.

Stalin's response was received six days later, on Thursday, 23 July, when Ambassador Ivan Maisky hand delivered it to Downing Street. It was uncompromising in both tone and message. The Soviet leader angrily denounced the prime minister's decision to suspend the convoys – 'wholly unconvincing' – and sneeringly informed him that fighting a war entailed taking risks. He was equally furious at the rumoured postponement of the assault on Nazi-occupied France. 'I must state in the most emphatic manner that the Soviet Government cannot acquiesce in the postponement of a Second Front in Europe until 1943.'[4]

Ambassador Maisky was a keen observer of people and watched Churchill's reaction with interest. The PM was already in an irritable mood that night because of recent setbacks in North Africa. Stalin's letter was to prove the last straw. 'Churchill must have had a drop too much whisky,' wrote Maisky. 'I could tell from his face, eyes and gestures. At times his head shook in a strange way, betraying the fact that in essence he is already an old man and that it won't be long before he starts sliding downhill fast. It is only by terrific exertion of will and mind that Churchill remains fit for the fight.'

Perhaps it was whisky, perhaps it was melancholy. Whatever it was, Churchill's mood turned maudlin. 'The thought even seemed to flash through his mind that the USSR might withdraw from the war,' wrote Maisky. It was a perceptive piece of mind reading, for Churchill was indeed having such a thought.

'Well . . .' was the prime minister's halting reaction. He paused for a moment before launching himself into the opening phrases of what looked set to be an emotionally charged speech. 'We have been alone before . . . we still fought . . . it's a miracle that our little island survived . . .'

Ambassador Maisky had had enough histrionics for one evening.

'Drop this nonsense!' he snapped in his thick Russian accent.[5]

To his surprise, Churchill did.

As with every successful entrepreneur, Averell knew that crisis brings opportunity. For him, the destruction of PQ17 was undeniably a crisis. Now he sought the opportunity.

In the second week of July, he found himself staring at a map of Persia, invaded and occupied by British and Soviet forces the previous summer. As he studied the map more intently, his eyes focused on a thin black line that stretched from sun-baked Bandar Shahpur on the Persian Gulf to Bandar Shah on the Caspian Sea. This line represented one of the principal arteries of the Iranian State Railway and Averell immediately realised it threw a potential lifeline to Joseph Stalin. There *was* an alternative to the Arctic convoys. If supplies could be shipped from America to the Persian Gulf, they could then be freighted northwards by train to the Soviet Union.

That Monday, 13 July, he cabled President Roosevelt and informed him that the railway offered a unique opportunity for sending supplies to Stalin. The only problem was the British, who were operating the entire system as if it were a suburban branch line. Averell wanted it placed in American hands, with him at the helm. He, after all, ran the world's most successful railway company. Railways were his heritage.

Roosevelt agreed. Three days after receiving Averell's cable, he sent his own telegram to Churchill suggesting that the Americans take over the Iranian State Railway.

'Have you an opinion about this?' he asked. 'Americans are first class at this sort of thing.'[6]

Averell had another reason for cabling President Roosevelt, and it was no less important. He felt it vital for the president to meet face to face with Joseph Stalin. The two men needed to develop a personal relationship, just as Roosevelt had done with Churchill.

The president was receptive, for he was extremely keen to meet Stalin in advance of Churchill. He even admitted as much in a forthright letter to the prime minister. 'I know you will not mind my being brutally frank when I tell you that I think I can personally handle Stalin better than either your Foreign Office or my State Department. Stalin hates the guts of all your top people. He thinks he likes me better and I hope he will continue to do so.'[7]

Behind the scenes, Averell began planning a meeting between Roosevelt and the Soviet leader. He discussed the practicalities with Ambassador Maisky and the two of them considered where it might take place, with Archangel, Astrakhan, or the Bering Strait at the top of their list. But Roosevelt would not travel to Astrakhan, because it was too far, and Archangel was deemed too dangerous. As for the Bering Strait, it was vetoed by Stalin.

In the event, Churchill stole Roosevelt's thunder by heading to Moscow himself. He wanted to explain to Stalin in person why the convoys had been suspended and why there could be no immediate Second Front. But most of all he wanted to establish a close personal relationship with the Soviet leader. If he could do this in advance of Roosevelt, then so much the better.

He knew that his mission was likely to be disagreeable. 'Like carrying a large lump of ice to the North Pole', was how he described it.[8] His wife, Clementine, called it 'a visit to the Ogre in his Den'.[9] Both she and Churchill knew he would be reliant on his ambassador, Archie Clark Kerr, to ensure the visit was a success.

Averell suggested accompanying the prime minister to Moscow, on the grounds that it was crucial for Stalin to see that the two Western allies were united. To his surprise, Churchill welcomed the offer and wrote to Roosevelt: 'Would you be able to let Averell come with me? I feel that things would be easier if we all seemed to be together. I have a somewhat raw job.'[10] The president was more than willing to give his consent, ordering Averell to accompany the PM to Moscow.

'He got off in great spirits,' wrote Kathy in a letter to her sister. 'He's certainly been lucky getting in on all the big shows!'[11]

For the second time in eleven months, Averell was heading into the Kremlin.

19

Mission from Hell

WINSTON CHURCHILL'S FORTHCOMING visit to Stalin was kept strictly secret. Very few people knew about it. Principal among them was Archie Clark Kerr, responsible for organising the trip. Security was paramount. The prime minister was to fly to Moscow via Cairo, with his route taking him over the Caspian Sea towards the Soviet capital. Only Archie, Molotov, and Moscow air traffic control knew the secret call sign of Churchill's plane: BE2EH239. The rest of Churchill's entourage would fly in a second B-24 Liberator. The intention was for them to land just a few minutes after Averell and the prime minister.

Churchill and Averell met in Cairo and set off for Moscow on Monday, 10 August, breaking their journey in Teheran before continuing on to the Soviet capital. They were accompanied by a few others, including Churchill's bodyguard, Commander Walter Thompson, and his doctor, Sir Charles Wilson. Conversation was impossible over the roar of the engines, so the prime minister and Averell passed handwritten notes to each other. At midday, Churchill demanded lunch. Commander Thompson duly produced a ham sandwich prepared by the British Legation staff in Teheran, only to find himself castigated by the PM. 'Ten de-merits,' roared Churchill over the din of the engines. 'You should know that no gentleman eats ham sandwiches without mustard.'[1]

As they entered Soviet air space, Churchill became pensive. 'I pondered on my mission to this sullen, sinister Bolshevik state I had once tried to strangle at birth . . . I had regarded [it] as the mortal foe of civilised freedom.'[2] Now he was trying to save it from the Wehrmacht.

The plane carrying Churchill's advisers had suffered engine trouble and been forced to return to Teheran. It was just Churchill and Averell who stepped onto the tarmac at Moscow airport, accompanied by the PM's valet, bodyguard, and doctor.

'Quite a formidable crowd was there to greet them,' wrote Archie Clark Kerr, who had also headed to the airport that afternoon. 'Molotov and his gang, Marshal Shaposhnikov, hardly able to stand on his feet, the American ambassador and all his guys.'

Archie knew that his old pal at the Foreign Office, Christopher Warner, would be expecting a colourful account of the visit, so he didn't hold back. 'The first glimpse I had of the PM was a pair of stout legs dangling from the belly of the plane and feeling for terra-firma. They found it, and then came the plump trunk and finally the round football head, and quite a normal hat. All this stooped under the machine, but it scrambled successfully out and drew itself up.'

Churchill made two wartime visits to Joseph Stalin. Archie (left) offered constant support to both Churchill and Eden (right).

Archie was impressed with Churchill's increased girth and wild expression. 'It was like a bull at the corrida when it first comes out of its dark pen and stands dazzled and bewildered and glares at the crowd. Like the bull's, the PM's eyes were bloodshot and defiant and like the bull he stood and swayed as if uncertain where to make the first charge. But the charge came from the crowd, headed by Molotov, and the bull was lost to sight in a wild scrum.'

Archie could hardly believe his eyes. 'It was like the mobbing of a movie star,' he wrote. Archie himself remained in the background, but Churchill soon caught sight of him. 'Hello, Archie!' he called out with a cheery smile. Clark Kerr was touched. Even the prime minister referred to him as Archie.

Churchill's arrival was met with a great deal of pomp. A Soviet band crashed out 'God Save the King', followed by 'The Star-Spangled Banner'. A guard of honour then marched by in an impressive goose-step.

It was unfortunate that Churchill raised his hand and gave his trademark two-fingered gesture to the crowd. This was misconstrued – not as an insult, nor even as a sign of victory, but as a sign that he had come to Moscow to announce the launching of a Second Front in Europe. It was the worst possible start.

Churchill, Averell, and Archie were then escorted to a waiting Packard and driven at high speed to their accommodation in the countryside, just outside the capital.

'Is this the Nevsky Prospekt?' asked Churchill as they sped past the Kremlin.[3]

Archie politely informed him that the Nevsky Prospekt was in Leningrad.

Among the few Western journalists in Moscow that day was Larry LeSueur, a correspondent for CBS. He had already heard vague rumours of Churchill and Averell's visit. Now, on seeing the American B-24 Liberator flying low over the city, he rushed to Gorki Street, the direct route into town from Moscow airport. 'Within twenty minutes a line of big, black limousines rolled swiftly through the traffic lights,' he wrote, 'and in the first car, a shining black Packard, we saw Churchill himself, in the back seat, getting his first sight of the Russian capital through the bulletproof windows and leaning over in a well-known posture, lighting up a big black cigar.'

LeSueur dashed over to the still-damaged British Embassy, where a skeleton staff had been flown in from Kuibyshev. But when he asked where Churchill was staying, he was met by blank expressions.

'I know nothing about it,' said the doorman disingenuously. 'Who told you he was in Moscow?'[4]

Winston Churchill and his entourage were housed in State Villa No. 7, a large and luxurious dacha just outside Moscow. It had all the mod cons: refrigerators, a fully equipped kitchen, and an electric lift, as well as a colossal air raid shelter. 'Ten or eleven elaborately furnished rooms,' noted Churchill's doctor approvingly after poking his head inside. 'Like a section of the Strand Palace Hotel gone underground.'[5]

Commander Thompson was pleased to note that the dacha was 'stiff with armed sentries', but rather less delighted to discover that several of those NKVD agents had been assigned to shadow him.[6] He felt they were taking security a little too seriously.

Averell's villa was as comfortable as Churchill's and staffed with servants and chefs. He was informed that breakfast would include caviar, Caucasian wine, champagne, brandy, and vodka.[7]

Churchill, Averell, and Archie were due to meet Stalin later that night and decided to eat together before setting off for the Kremlin. At one point, when Churchill was distracted, Archie whispered to Averell that he hoped to be one day appointed as ambassador to Washington.

'What are you talking about?' asked Churchill, 'with a booming voice and a scowl on his face. Don't you realise that I have just appointed you to the most important job in the world?'[8]

By this point in his career, Archie had known the PM for seventeen years. He had worked with him, dined with him, and been promoted by him. Although never overawed, he nevertheless had a profound respect for Churchill's talents.

'In his bestowal of gifts, God has been uncommonly kind to Winston Churchill,' he wrote. 'Perhaps I envy most his mastery of the English language. That is something very rare. But there is something rarer still and of very high price. This is his ability in a twinkling to transform his face from the rosiest, happiest, the most laughing, dimpled, and mischievous baby's bottom into the face of an angry and outraged bullfrog. I wish that I could do that. It is very remarkable. It is tremendous. I cannot get anywhere near it. Whatever be my emotions, my face remains like a ram's.'

Archie was equally impressed by the quantity of food and alcohol that Churchill consumed, and the fact that it never prevented him from focusing on the matter at hand.

'What did the Russians want?' he asked Archie on that first afternoon in Moscow.

'A Second Front in Europe.'

'Well, they're not going to get it.'

Archie advised Churchill to tackle this unpleasant news as soon as he arrived at the Kremlin, and then reveal the plans for the Allied landings in North Africa. He also warned him of Stalin's likely response. 'Flat disappointment and probably irritation, followed by distinct relief.'[9]

The prime minister's advisers had still not arrived from Teheran, so it was a depleted little group that set off in the embassy limousine to meet Stalin at 7 p.m. that evening: Churchill, Averell, and Archie, together with the elderly Charles Dunlop as interpreter. They were escorted into Stalin's private office, a sparsely furnished room whose only decoration was a portrait of Lenin.

The PM's bodyguard, Commander Thompson, was disappointed to be told to wait in an anteroom. The upside to his exclusion was the Kremlin's generous hospitality. 'An array of drinks, cigarettes and cigars were set out. I could, if I had so desired, have drunk myself into a coma.'[10]

'Welcome to Moscow, Mr Prime Minister,' were Stalin's opening words. He spoke hoarsely and his face was downcast. He extended a limp hand, and a smiling Churchill shook it with seeming confidence. But Stalin's interpreter, Valentin Berezhkov, felt that Churchill's smile was concealing an inner nervousness. He had noticed that all foreign visitors to the Kremlin, with the notable exception of Archie, had the same reaction. Many years later, when living in exile, Berezhkov would write about this phenomenon in his memoirs.

'Maybe his absolute power over his subjects created an aura around the Great Leader that made the people who came in contact with him obsequious toward him against their will. Or maybe it was a manifestation of their subconscious fear in front of a monster.'[11]

Stalin invited everyone to be seated at the long table covered with a green cloth. He positioned himself at the head, with Churchill to his right. He offered a few pleasantries and then came to the point, painting a grim but honest assessment of the situation on the battlefront. 'There is no guarantee that the Russians will beat off their new assault,' he said, aware that the Red Army had only recently suffered terrific losses at Stalingrad.

When he had finished, Churchill addressed the issue that had brought him to Moscow. 'I have come here to speak very frankly about real issues,' he said. 'Let's talk to each other as friends. I hope you'll agree to that and will be as frank in telling me what you consider to be the right course of action at this point in time.'[12]

Stalin signalled his assent, but he reacted angrily and bitterly when told of the postponement of the planned Allied landings in occupied France. 'No risks taken, no victories gained,' he said to Churchill in a deliberately caustic tone, before accusing the Western allies of cowardice: 'The British shouldn't be afraid of the Germans. They are by no means superhuman.'

Churchill was deeply offended by his remarks and struck back hard, alluding to the time in 1940 when Britain stood all alone against the Nazis – a clear reference to Stalin's friendly relations with Hitler at the time. As tempers frayed, the PM grew visibly hot and bothered. 'He got up and had a walk,' wrote Archie, 'pulling from his heated buttocks the seat of his trousers which had clearly stuck to them. There was something about this dumpy figure, plucking at his backside, which suggested immense strength but little distinction.'

Stalin was equally restless. 'He kept getting up and walking across the big room to a writing table into which he delved for cigarettes. These he tore a bit and stuffed into his absurd curly pipe.'

Each man seemed wary of the other. 'It was interesting to watch the impact of the two men clash and recoil and clash again, and then a slow but unmistakable coming together as each got the measure of the other.' But this coming together was not to last, and the gulf that separated them seemed unbridgeable. This might have been anticipated, for their lives and backgrounds stood at opposite ends of the social spectrum. Churchill was a distinguished aristocrat whose illustrious forebears included the Duke of Marlborough, victor of the Battle of Blenheim. He was also an imperialist whose political views could scarcely have been more offensive to Stalin. The Soviet leader, by contrast, was a revolutionary peasant from Georgia whose father had been an alcoholic wife-beater.

Stalin's humour went from bad to worse and he was soon hurling accusations at Churchill. 'With his eyes half-closed, which always avoided mine, he uttered at intervals a string of insults.'[13]

The prime minister was incensed.

'Poles apart as human beings,' wrote General Alan Brooke when he heard what had taken place. 'I cannot see a friendship between them, such as exists between Roosevelt and Winston.' Brooke was one of several in Churchill's entourage who felt the Anglo-Soviet alliance was a huge mistake. 'We have bowed and scraped to them, done all we could for them and never asked them for a single fact or figure concerning their production, strength, dispositions, etc. As a result, they despise us and have no use for us except for what they can get out of us.'[14]

After attacking Churchill for being too scared to fight the Germans, Stalin vented his fury on Averell, lambasting him for failing to deliver essential supplies to Russia. He then turned back to Churchill and accused him of snatching whatever he wanted from the American supply chain before allowing a few inferior scraps to be sent to the Soviet Union. Churchill curtly reminded Stalin that Britain had been abandoned for more than a year while Stalin was fawning to Hitler.

Averell was astounded by the venom in their discussions. 'Very bad tempered,' he wrote. 'The PM wouldn't let the interpreter finish his translation but snapped back after each sentence. The whole show almost broke up when Stalin said he had nothing more to add.'[15]

Only at the close of the meeting did the Soviet leader relent somewhat and propose a dinner at the Kremlin for the two leaders and their advisers. The prime minister accepted with extreme reluctance.

Churchill, infuriated by Stalin's insults, drank far too much Caucasian champagne on his return from the Kremlin. He soon fell into a bilious mood and Archie found himself paying the price. 'His ill humour seemed to focus itself upon me,' he wrote. 'Whenever I was anywhere near, he put on his angry bullfrog face and he addressed me laboriously as ambassador. Throughout the meal he flopped about in his chair complaining that his head, which at times he put on the table, ached.'

He was still in a foul temper when his much-delayed entourage of experts and advisers finally arrived at Moscow airport and were driven to the dacha. In his opening breath, Churchill warned them all that Stalin was an ignorant peasant. Air Marshal Arthur Tedder was horrified and signalled that the room was almost certainly bugged. This only enraged Churchill yet further. 'The Russians are not human beings at all,' he fumed. 'They are lower in the scale of nature than the orang-outang. Now let them take that down and translate it into Russian.'[16] It was unfortunate for Churchill that they almost certainly did.

Archie himself was sick of the whole charade. 'Well, well, boys will be boys!' he wrote. 'What a bloody day.'[17]

Churchill's trip to Moscow went from bad to worse. Archie arrived early at the PM's dacha the following day, Friday, 14 August, but soon wished he hadn't. 'This morning I found the dacha murmurous and uneasy. Everyone seemed to be scuttling about like startled hens.' Churchill was still furious about his meeting at the Kremlin. 'He was like a wounded lion. He declaimed against Stalin in ponderous, Gibbonesque periods.'[18]

Churchill had spent the previous few hours stomping around the dacha in his dressing gown. His clothes had been somehow mislaid, only adding to his anger, and Archie was summoned to join the search for them. He refused. 'The Clarks do not valet anyone,' he declared. 'Not even the PM.'[19]

As the clothes hunt continued, Churchill dropped an unexpected bombshell. 'He was damned', he said, 'if he would keep his engagement to dine with Stalin tonight.'

Archie told him that cancelling the dinner would be extremely unwise, provoking another extended rant from Churchill. 'At lunch, the PM was at his bloody worst. He seemed to concentrate his ill-humour upon me. It was difficult to sit through the meal with any semblance of patience and good manners.' Archie was outraged. 'I felt like giving him a good root up the arse,' he wrote. He was also saddened to see Churchill so diminished. 'My respect for him and faith in him have suffered sadly.'

In the end, a reluctant PM was persuaded to attend Stalin's dinner, a nineteen-course Kremlin banquet held in Catherine the Great's state room. Stalin was dressed in a lilac-coloured tunic and had made an effort to look smart, whereas Churchill turned up in his crumpled siren suit. 'A dreadful garment', thought Archie, 'which he claimed to have designed to wear during air-raids in London. It looked like a mechanic's overalls.'[20]

The dinner was stodgy and unappetising; it was all too much for General Brooke, who was sick of the whole charade. 'In front of me, amongst the many fish dishes, was a small suckling pig covered with a blanket of white sauce. He had a black truffle eye and an orange peel mouth. He was never eaten, and as the evening slipped by his black eye remained fixed on me, and the orange peel mouth developed a sardonical smile.'[21]

Stalin offered a toast to Churchill but was deliberately offensive. He spoke of the catastrophic Gallipoli campaign in the Great War, aware of Churchill's central role in planning it, and said it failed because of 'gross stupidities in concept and execution'.[22] One of the guests described Stalin's toast as 'a deep knife-thrust worthy of a Georgian mountaineer into a quondam enemy for whom he still felt only distrust and contempt'.[23]

Churchill had had enough and announced he was leaving. Archie was fearful of what was to come. 'What a day, my God!' he wrote in his diary late that night. 'Now I must go out to the dacha to see what the morning has to bring.'[24]

20

A Battle of Wills

ARCHIE CLARK KERR arrived at Churchill's dacha at eleven o'clock on the morning of Saturday, 15 August. 'A terrific flurry,' he wrote. 'All was up. The PM had decided to pack up and go. He had had enough of Stalin and was damned if he would see him again.'[1]

This was terrible news. Such a departure from Moscow would throw the Allied partnership into turmoil, as well as emboldening the Nazis. But Churchill was in a stupendous rage that morning. 'Like a bull in a ring maddened by the pricks of the picadors,' wrote his doctor, Sir Charles Wilson (later Lord Moran). The PM kept repeating that 'he would return to London without seeing Stalin again'.

Churchill's permanent undersecretary, Alexander Cadogan, tried to reason with him, but to no avail. When Archie arrived at the dacha, Cadogan alerted him to the desperate situation in which they found themselves. Churchill must be persuaded to change his mind – and fast.

Archie wandered into the garden to collect his thoughts. As he strolled among the raspberry bushes he bumped into Wilson, who had yet more alarming news. Not only was the PM intending to leave Moscow right away, but he was also withdrawing all aid to the Soviet Union.

Sir Charles begged Archie to intervene, believing him to be the only person capable of persuading the PM to change his mind. A reluctant Archie agreed to try, bracing himself for the fight ahead. He told Wilson 'it would have to be with the gloves off, and might provoke a first-class row.'[2] It would also require him to put his job on the line. As he would later explain in a lengthy memo to the Foreign Office, Churchill was in no mood for a lecture:

> I found him lowering and sullen.
>
> 'I hear you want to see me,' said Churchill.

'Yes. Let us go for a little walk. I talk better if I walk, and so, I have observed, do you.'

He didn't like my facetiousness.

'I haven't much time.'

'I shall not keep you long.'

He put a preposterous ten-gallon hat on his head and, arming himself with a stick, went out on to the terrace, leaving me to follow him.

'May I be frank?'

He stopped and stared at me.

'Frank? Why not?'

'I may have something that is unpleasing to you.'

He snorted. 'I've been used to that all my life. I'm not afraid.'

And then began one of the most remarkable talks I have ever had. I wish that I could reproduce it intact. I can't. I didn't compel him to the fatigue of high argument, for I did all, or nearly all, the talking. But it must have been just as fatiguing for him to hold himself in as he did.

It was like this: I talked, and he stomped along in front of me among the fir trees. I addressed myself to a pink and swollen neck and a pair of hunched shoulders, because the path I had chosen was too narrow to let me keep abreast of him. Perhaps he didn't want me to watch his face unless it was ready for me. Every now and then it *was* ready, for as I shot each one of my bolts, he stopped short and turned to stare at me.

On the whole I find it easier to talk to a face than to a neck and, for myself, I should not have chosen a dodging-in-and-out-of-the-fir-trees as the best occasion in which to say something that mattered.

I began by saying that it seemed to me he was going about this whole business the wrong way.

He stopped and stared at me.

Well, perhaps that was a bad start, and I began afresh. God had been particularly kind to him when he bestowed his gifts. I needn't mention them. He knew what they were, and when he cared to use them, he could do so with devastating effect. It had been my own memories of these gifts – and my belief in their power – that had led me to suggest his coming [to Moscow], for deep down in me I had felt that from a meeting between him and Stalin, immense good must flow.

His pace slowed down.

I had had great faith in him, and he had disappointed me. This brought him to a halt and he stared again. By this time there was no withdrawing and, my God, I didn't want to! If his mission to Moscow, on which we had all set such high hopes, were a failure, it was his own fault, as he was making no use of these matchless gifts of his. After the first day, when I had watched him use his charm with admirable effect, he had put them all away. His approach to the Russians had become all wrong. What was wrong was that he was an aristocrat and a man of the world, and he expected these people to be like him. They weren't. They were straight from the plough or the lathe. They were rough and inexperienced. They didn't discuss things as we discussed them. They thought aloud, and in thinking aloud, they said many harsh and offensive things. They had angered him and his pride was hurt. That didn't surprise me. They angered me too. But what did surprise me was to see him letting the hurting of his pride blur his judgement.

He stopped and stared.

'That man has insulted me. From now on he will have to fight his battles alone.' (The very words the doctor had quoted.)

I let the second bit pass, saving it up for my next salvo, and I took him up on the insult. I suggested that nothing had been said at the second meeting that had not been said in the early stages of the first. Why had he felt affronted at the second meeting when he hadn't at the first? It had probably been Stalin's disingenuous memorandum that had put him in bad humour. I confessed that it was an unhappy document, but he had been wrong to let it warp his judgement. Things were too important . . . He must sweep away all that had passed and make friends with Stalin. At the Kremlin dinner, Stalin had made it clear that he wanted to make amends, but the PM had cold-shouldered him. He must meet Stalin halfway.

'But the man has insulted me. I represent a great country and

I am not submissive by nature.' (This sulkily, over his hunched shoulders.)

Then I went on. He had said just now that Stalin would have to fight his own battles. Did he mean that seriously? I couldn't believe it.

He stopped and stared and then dodged on amongst the fir trees, in which he seemed to find some protection.

Had he reflected upon what it would mean to the issue of the war? If Russia went down for want of support, *his* support, which only *he* could give? How many young British and American lives would have to be sacrificed to make this good? Had he thought of that when he decided, as I understood he had decided, to break off his talks with Stalin and to go home?

He stopped to stare again.

And I went on. He couldn't leave Russia in the lurch, whatever Stalin had said to hurt his pride. He would have to swallow his pride, if only to save young lives.

'The man thinks he can upset my government and throw me out.' And here followed quite a long speech about his strength at home, his hold on the public mind, and on the House of Commons. He even enumerated the great chunks of votes he could count on in Parliament.

'If he thinks he can throw me out, he is very much mistaken.'

I asked if I might go on . . . Of course, today he had immense strength. I well knew that. But tomorrow, if he abandoned Russia, he would find his strength falling away. He would soon be alone. He would be the man who had thrown Russia to the Nazis. (A stop and a stare.) And all because he was offended. Offended by a peasant who didn't know any better. That seemed to me to be a pity. It seemed to me a pity to come all this way and to make a mess of things.

That pulled him up short.

'A mess of things? You mean that you think it's all my fault?'

'Yes. I'm sorry but I do.'

'*A mess of things?*'

By this time we had got out of those blasted dodgy fir trees and were walking abreast. We had nearly reached the house. He stopped and glanced at the ground in front of him. After a longish pause he said:

'Well, and what do you want me to do?'

I told him quickly that I wanted him at once to send a message to Stalin to say that he wanted another talk. Just the two of them. I felt convinced that Stalin was ready for it. Witness all the trouble Stalin had taken at the Kremlin dinner (and I enlarged upon what Stalin had done). I assured him that it was within his power to nobble Stalin, if he made good use of those gifts of his which I had spoken of. I was prepared to bet that he would be successful if he allowed himself to be himself. It was very important.

He listened carefully and then he said:

'But I am not a submissive man.'

'I don't ask you to be submissive. I only ask you to be yourself.'

'Myself.'

We were now near to the dacha door and into it he suddenly strode, leaving me in the mild sunshine, to reflect upon what I had said. Somehow or other I didn't feel that any part of it had cost me special effort. It had all seemed to be quite easy and natural. Certainly no effort of courage.

I was just about to look for the doctor and to speculate with him about the probable results when Alec [Sir Alexander Cadogan] called me into the PM's room. They were alone. The PM said he wanted to discuss plans. We sat down.

'Ally [Alexander Cadogan] . . .' he said. '*He*' (pointing at me) 'says that it's all my fault.' (This, with half-a-baby's bottom face.)

And suddenly he chuckled, and Alec laughed, and I knew that it was all right. In a twinkling Pavlov was sent for and told that the PM wanted to see Stalin and see him alone and to have a good man-to-man talk.

The dacha luncheon that followed this event was marked by exuberance and relief. 'The PM was transformed. His form was terrific. He ate and drank with tremendous gusto.' He delivered an extemporaneous monologue in defence of the aristocracy and then ate and drank some more. When he finished, Sir Charles Wilson ordered him to bed.

He needed to be on form for his meeting with Stalin, which had been arranged for 7 p.m. On this occasion, the two leaders were to meet alone, with only their interpreters accompanying them.

Archie made another important intervention that afternoon. He felt that the sickly Charles Dunlop was quite inadequate as an interpreter, having failed to turn Churchill's eloquent prose into equally eloquent Russian. He wanted his personal interpreter, Arthur Birse, to accompany Churchill to the Kremlin. He also hoped that Birse could be persuaded to report back everything that took place.

Birse was horrified when informed he would be interpreting for the prime minister. 'I protested that I had had no experience of political talks, that I should certainly be below the standard required.' But Archie insisted and Birse eventually accepted. 'I understood that it was an order,' he wrote. 'I resigned myself to the inevitable.'

Interpreter Arthur Birse was extremely nervous about working with Churchill and Stalin, as can be seen in his expression. He overcame his anxiety by pretending that he was interpreting for two ordinary individuals.

He was overcome with nerves as he was driven to the PM's dacha. It was so unexpected. 'What would Churchill be like?' he asked himself. And Stalin? It was all so terrifying that Birse had to repeatedly pull himself together. 'I determined to try to forget who these two men were, and to act as if I were interpreting for two ordinary individuals.'

Churchill was in his dressing gown when Birse was first introduced. He told Birse that he wanted to make amends with Stalin before leaving Moscow and warned that the translation of his sentiments needed to be totally accurate. 'Then, looking me up and down, he asked where I had learned Russian and how many years I had spent in the country.' Birse provided a brief outline of his formative years, 'which evoked low, throaty sounds between the puffs of his cigar, which I took to mean approval'.[3]

The two of them set off for the Kremlin shortly before seven o'clock, passing through the Borovitsky Gate in their ZIS. They were then escorted down a long green carpeted corridor to Stalin's antechamber. Churchill was irrepressibly upbeat: he had previously told Sir Charles Wilson that 'he would not leave the Kremlin until he had Stalin in his pocket.'[4]

The meeting that followed was intended to be strictly private, but Archie had indeed persuaded Birse to write a confidential account of everything that took place that night, thereby providing him with a unique peep behind the curtain of the meeting he had done so much to secure.

It began with a handshake in Stalin's office: the Soviet leader greeted Churchill with his soft, limp hand, then shook Arthur Birse's hand in similar fashion.

Birse now prepared himself for the assignment of a lifetime. 'I had my scribbling pad with me, with two or three sharpened pencils which I always carried in my pocket, and I set these in front of me, ready to begin.'

The tone of the evening was markedly different from that of the previous meetings. Churchill was warm, emollient, apologetic; he chose his words with care. 'His remarks were prefaced by a kind of suppressed murmur, as if he were trying out the richness of his words while on their way from brain to tongue; as if he were repeating them to himself, testing them, discarding the inappropriate and choosing precisely the right expression.'

Stalin, in return, was generous and understanding. 'Obviously there are differences between us,' he said calmly, 'but differences are in the nature of things.'[5] He listened intently as Birse sought to render Churchill's discourse into fluent Russian. 'Once or twice during my translation he [the PM] looked at me, the first time with no expression at all, but later something like a look of approval seemed to emerge, like the sun breaking through the dark clouds.'[6] Churchill steered the conversation round to congenial topics: the defence of the Caucasus and the proposed landings in North Africa.

'Are you getting me across?' he boomed. Birse said he thought he was doing all right.

'I think you are doing very well.'[7]

Stalin stressed the importance of the North African landings.

'May God help you,' he said.

'God, of course, is on our side,' joked Churchill.

'And the devil is, naturally, on mine,' retorted Stalin with evident relish, 'and through our combined efforts we shall defeat the enemy.'[8]

Stalin's humour was transformed by Churchill's sparkling conversation. At first, he allowed himself an occasional smile, but soon he had a broad grin on his face and began joking and leg-pulling. 'A complete change of mood,' noted Birse.

When Churchill finally announced that he ought to be going, Stalin protested.

'Why don't we stop in at my Kremlin apartment for a drink?' he said.

'I never refuse offers like that,' replied Churchill.

Stalin led him and Birse to an adjacent building that was hastily being prepared by a female housekeeper dressed in crisp white overalls. Birse realised that this was a unique experience: no foreigner, and very few Russians, had ever seen the inside of Stalin's private apartment.

The dining room was simply furnished, with a wooden table, hard chairs, and a large dresser. 'All rather stiff and cold.' Lots of bottles stood in the middle of the table and there were plates and cutlery for four people. 'Then a pretty, ginger-haired young woman appeared, went up to Stalin and kissed him.'[9] This was Svetlana, his daughter, whom he now introduced.

Svetlana had rarely seen her father in such a cordial frame of mind. 'He was in one of those amiable and hospitable moods when he could charm anyone,' she would later recall. 'Patting me on the head, he said: "This is my daughter," and added, "She's a red-head."'

Churchill spoke to her in English, which Svetlana could understand. '[He] remarked that he had been red-headed too, when he was a young man, but now look – and he waved a cigar in the direction of his head.' He spoke of his second daughter, Sarah, who was in the Women's Auxiliary Air Force, before the subject returned to the war in Russia.

'My father kissed me and told me to go on about my own business,' said Svetlana. She couldn't understand why Stalin had summoned her and only realised some time later. 'He wanted to seem at least a little like an ordinary human being. You could see he liked Churchill.'[10]

Birse was making a mental note of everything, aware that Archie would want to know every detail of what happened that night. There were four or five glasses in front of each plate and Stalin now filled them with vodkas, Caucasian wine, and champagne. 'I noticed that while he was talking to us he kept touching an even number of glasses with his fork, which made me wonder whether he was not superstitious and considered uneven numbers unlucky.'

Birse grew seriously alarmed when Stalin produced a bottle of Pertsovka, an extremely alcoholic vodka, and urged Churchill to drink it. This was a very bad idea: the PM was likely to knock back glass after glass until completely inebriated. Birse intervened.

'May I say, sir, that it is vicious stuff and I cannot recommend it.'

Happily, and wisely, Churchill declined Stalin's offer. But both men ate heartily: two chickens, beef, mutton, every kind of fish, and a whole suckling pig. Churchill politely turned down the head, which he was offered by Stalin. 'He himself tackled it with relish. With a knife he cleaned out the head, putting it into his mouth with his knife. He then cut pieces of flesh from the cheeks of the pig and ate them with his fingers.' It was a peculiarly gruesome little display, but Stalin was clearly enjoying the slimy flesh and brains.

The conversation remained good-natured throughout. When Churchill told Stalin that Britain's greatest general had been his ancestor the Duke of Marlborough, the Soviet leader mischievously disagreed. 'I think England had a greater general in Wellington, who defeated Napoleon, the greatest menace of all time.'

He proceeded to display a comprehensive knowledge of Wellington's military campaigns, 'quoting chapter and verse with regard to some of the battles'. It was a tour de force, and Birse kept a note of it all.

At one point, Churchill expressed the desire to wash his hands. Stalin led him to an ensuite bathroom, with Birse in tow. 'I accompanied them, and thus became the first foreigner to see Stalin's bedroom. It was simply furnished, with an absence of any luxury. A bed and a bedside table, a rug or two on the floor, a few chairs, and a large bookcase made up the total.' There were lots of bookshelves. 'I had a look at the books. They were a collection of Marxist literature, with a good many historical works, but I could see no Russian classics. There were a few books in Georgian.'[11]

At midnight the two leaders were joined by Sir Alexander Cadogan and Foreign Commissar Molotov; by this time, the conversation had turned to banter. When the subject of collective farms came up, Churchill was so bold as to ask whatever happened to the Kulaks, the wealthy peasant class brutally eliminated by Stalin.

Stalin replied with a straight face. 'Some of them had been given an acre or two in Siberia but had proved very unpopular with the rest of the people.'

When the party broke up at 2 a.m., Birse was shattered, for he had been interpreting for fully seven hours.

'I am very pleased with you,' said Churchill at the end of the evening. 'In future I will want you always to interpret for me.'[12]

Archie had spent that evening with General Władysław Anders, the Polish commander whom Kathy Harriman had only recently interviewed in London. Archie slipped away at 1.30 a.m. and slept for an hour and a half before being abruptly woken by the PM, who was in triumphant mood. He drank a large whisky with Anders, who was still at the dacha, then flung himself onto a sofa and yelled for his doctor, Sir Charles Wilson. Archie described what happened next:

'The PM began to chuckle and kick a pair of gay legs in the air.' He said the evening had been grand. 'He had cemented a friendship with Stalin. My God, he was glad that he had come.' He bragged about being served dinner by Svetlana (which was not true) and of being shown around Stalin's private apartment.

'The glee of the PM was a pleasure to see,' wrote Archie. 'He was like a dog with two cocks. I forgave him all his bloodymindedness and even his folly.' The Allied partnership with Stalin was back on track.

Archie assumed that Churchill would want some sleep before flying back to Teheran in the morning, but the PM had other ideas. 'He sprang up, shouted for his man and for his bath.'

Archie made his excuses.

'Don't go!' roared an exuberant Churchill. 'I want to talk to you.'

What followed caused even Archie to blink. The PM 'began to tear his clothes off. In a jiffy he was down to his vest.'

Archie was impressed by his lack of inhibitions. 'I like him for his exhibitionism,' he wrote. 'This is what he looked like' – here, he drew a picture in his account for the Foreign Office. 'From under his skimpy vest, penis and a pair of crinkled creamy buttocks protruded.'

As he clambered into his bath, Churchill regaled Archie with stories from his splendid evening.

'My God, he talked . . . Stalin this, and Stalin that.'[13]

At 4.30 a.m., Molotov arrived at the dacha in order to escort Churchill and his entourage to the airport. 'The PM was bubbling with good spirits,' noted John Reed, one of Archie's staff, 'and continued to bubble until pushed into the aeroplane.'

Churchill was gracious enough to thank Archie for having saved the visit from disaster. 'You were a constant help and wise adviser,' he said. 'I hope my visit will make it easier for you to carry on the arduous and difficult duties you are doing so well.' John Reed agreed with Churchill's assessment, feeling that Archie deserved the highest praise for tackling the PM in a moment of great crisis. 'From that moment, everything went splendidly,' he wrote. 'Thanks entirely, I believe, to His Excellency's zealistic intervention.'

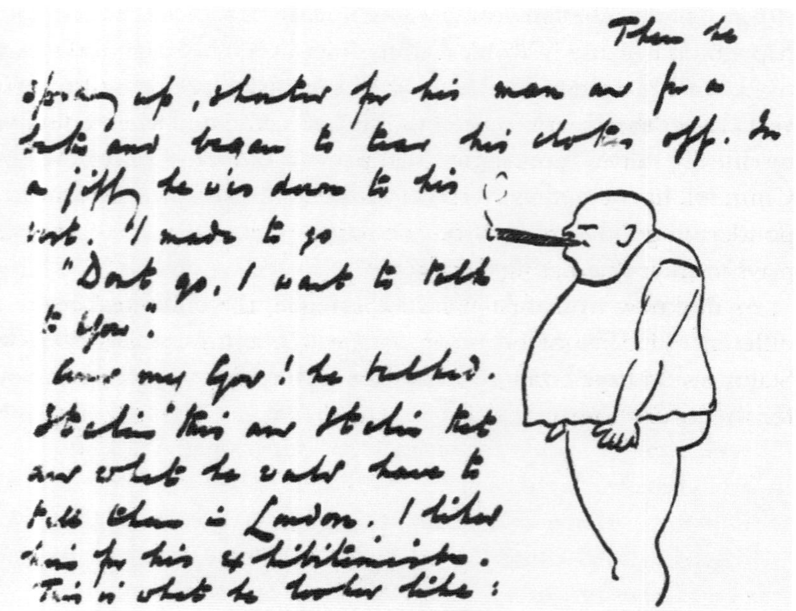
Then he
sprang up, shouted for his man and for a
bath and began to tear his clothes off. In
a jiffy he was down to his
shirt. I made to go
"Don't go, I want to talk
to you".
And my God! he babbled.
Stalin this and Stalin that
and what he would have to
tell them in London. I liked
him for his exhibitionism.
This is what he looked like:

Archie was rarely shocked, but he watched wide-eyed as Churchill stripped naked while debriefing him about his meeting with Stalin. He included this sketch in his memo to the Foreign Office, which delighted his colleagues in London.

No sooner had the prime minister's party left Moscow than journalist Larry LeSueur asked to see Ambassador Clark Kerr. He wanted insider gossip on the private meeting between Churchill and Stalin. Archie remained unusually tight-lipped. 'All I can say is that the meeting was epochal. And that is a word I use very infrequently.' LeSueur begged for more information, but Archie refused. 'If only I could tell you!' he said. 'It's on the tip of my tongue.'

Later that day, Arthur Birse was summoned to the still-damaged British Embassy, where he found a bare-chested Archie working from his deckchair. Together they pieced together an exact record of what had occurred during those tumultuous days in Moscow. It was good they did, for Churchill's own account of his time in the Soviet capital – written for publication in *The Hinge of Fate* – was crafted with great care. It made no mention of his angry exchanges with Stalin, nor of his own impetuous behaviour.

Sir Charles Wilson criticised Churchill for his version of what happened, because it avoided all the inconvenient parts of the narrative. 'As one reads of these now-distant days,' wrote Wilson many years later, 'they seem to be smoothed out, and as it were edited; the terrifically alive, pugnacious, impatient and impulsive Winston Churchill has been dressed up as a sagacious, tolerant elder statesman, pondering good-naturedly on the frailty of men and the part chance plays in their fluctuating fortunes.'[14]

As he knew from first-hand experience, the truth had been very different. Had it not been for Archie, Churchill's relationship with Stalin would have come to an abrupt end, with serious consequences for the future course of the war.

21

Stalin's Lifeline

STALIN'S ARMY WAS desperately short of weaponry at the time of Churchill's visit. Thousands of tanks had been lost in combat, along with aircraft and heavy motors, and very few had been replaced. The crushing Red Army defeat at Rostov just a few days earlier was held to have been due, in part, to an acute lack of munitions.

The ongoing evacuation of factories to the east had led to a catastrophic fall in arms production, while the Germans had captured all the heavy plants in Kharkov, the most important industrial city in Ukraine. They had also seized the Donets Basin, which produced huge quantities of coal, steel, and power, along with vital oil resources. The massive Maikop refineries were captured at the very moment Churchill was in Moscow.[1]

Stalin had been promised impressive quantities of weaponry, supplies, and raw materials from the West, but delivery had been curtailed by the repeated sinking of Arctic convoys during their perilous sea voyage to Archangel. Less than two million tons had so far been delivered to the Soviet Union, a fraction of what was required.

This was a serious problem, as Averell was quick to realise. On the long journey back to London from Moscow, he stopped off in Iran with the aim of investigating his idea of using the Iranian railway as a supply line to Stalin.

One of the principal lines began in the port of Bandar Shahpur, where summer temperatures regularly exceeded 120 degrees Fahrenheit. From here, it traversed lonely scrubland before climbing into the spectacular Elburz Mountains, where it skirted the snow-blasted peak of Mount Damavand. One short stretch of track had 135 tunnels and viaducts.

Averell made pages of notes about the railway's gradients and curves: '1.5% ruling grade all the way, 12 degrees curvature, 800-foot radius . . . 18-ton axle load said to be maximum.' It was an impressive piece of micro-research.

He also visited the repair workshops at Ahwaz, Bandar Shahpur, and Abadan, which he found poorly staffed and equipped: 'The worst mess I have ever seen.'[2] The British had shipped in large numbers of steam locomotives from India, but these were not powerful enough to climb the steep mountain gradients, nor could they be used in the waterless desert. Averell was hoping to supply Stalin with 6,000 tons of equipment each day – the equivalent of 230 tanks. This was impossible using steam trains.

Once his research was complete, Averell flew to Cairo to present his railway plan to Churchill, who had stopped off in the Egyptian capital on his way back to London. Aware of the prime minister's belief that 'anything worthwhile can be put on one side of paper', he prepared a concise memorandum stating why the Americans should take over the railroad.[3] Churchill didn't need much convincing. 'A good arrangement,' he said, and agreed to transfer the entire Trans-Iranian Railway into Averell's hands.

Averell Harriman flew back to London with Churchill but did not spend long in the capital. After just four days with Pamela and Kathy, he flew to Washington to put his sweeping railway plan into action. The PM supplied him with a letter to Roosevelt, formally requesting the Americans to take over the railway. 'Only in this way', he said, 'can we ensure an expanding flow of supplies to Russia.'[4]

Averell's first meeting in America was with Bill Jeffers, president of the Union Pacific Railroad. Jeffers lived, breathed, and dreamed railways. 'I'd rather be President of the Union Pacific', he once said, 'than President of the United States.'[5] Together, the two men now thrashed out a plan to get supplies to Stalin.

At Averell's suggestion, engineers at Union Pacific were set to work designing a new six-wheel diesel locomotive powerful enough to climb the steep gradients of the Elburz Mountains but light enough to cross the poorly constructed viaducts. Fifty-seven of these trains were rapidly built and shipped to Iran, along with 1,000 twenty-ton freight cars and 650 forty-ton wagons.

Averell had the idea of supplying the Soviet Union via Iran. One of the most challenging logistical triumphs of the war, it necessitated a 900-mile journey to the Soviet frontier across inhospitable terrain.

Railway men were recruited in huge numbers, along with engineers and drivers. To assist them, 28,000 American troops were to join the Iran-based supply chain. Averell got the greatest boost when President Roosevelt approved the appointment of Major General Donald Connolly, a military engineer, to run what was to be officially known as the Persian Gulf Service Command.

Connolly was a redneck bruiser. 'A very big, stern-looking man with an outthrust chin,' wrote journalist Quentin Reynolds. 'When you first meet Connolly, you say to yourself, "Don't get into any trouble with this guy, or you'll get your ears knocked off."' He was uncompromising and equipped with fists of steel – the ideal candidate for leading what was described as 'one of the most important military operations in the world'.[6]

He forged unusually close links with his Soviet counterparts in the north of Iran, for Connolly knew the way to Russian hearts: all-night drinking bouts and wild-boar-hunting expeditions in the mountains. These, he said, were for 'promoting a better understanding between Russians and Americans engaged in operating the world's longest supply line'.[7]

He was a blunt-spoken Yank when dealing with his Soviet opposite number, Colonel Nikolai Vorobey. 'We won't make any phony promises to you,' he said. 'But I am telling you we will give you fellows more every month – and you better be ready to take it away.'[8] Connolly's hard talking impressed even Stalin's trade commissar, Anastas Mikoyan. 'When the Americans undertake anything, it is done,' he said.[9]

This was just as well, for the mighty German offensive was grinding relentlessly eastwards. At Stalingrad, General Friedrich Paulus's Sixth Army had recently advanced to the west bank of the Volga. It was now fighting through the northern suburbs in preparation for a final assault on the city. Stalingrad's loss seemed inevitable.

Aware of this imminent catastrophe, Averell urged officials in Washington to redouble their efforts to get supplies to the Soviet Union – aluminium, nickel, trucks, tanks, medical supplies, and food. 'The whole course of the war depends on that,' he said. 'Every day the Russian armies are destroying some of the strength of our enemies. Therefore, battles on the Russian front have a direct bearing on the sacrifices we will have to make and on the length of the war itself.'[10]

In the first week of September, President Roosevelt invited Averell to join him at Shangri-La,* his retreat in the Catoctin Mountains of Maryland. It was a place of wistful beauty, a thickly forested wilderness alive with chipmunks, deer, and black bears.

The residence itself was Roosevelt's Chequers; what it lacked in Jacobean grandeur it made up for in comfort. A simple woodland lodge with four bedrooms, it had a staff of Filipino sailors from the presidential yacht, *Potomac*. 'The food was far better than in the White House,' noted one visitor.[11]

Roosevelt conducted much of his business on Shangri-La's shaded porch, where he also listened to briefings about the war. Now, on that same porch, he wanted to hear from Averell everything that had happened in Moscow.

Averell would later note that Roosevelt 'appeared to enjoy hearing all about Churchill's discomfiture in those long, reproach-filled sessions at the Kremlin'. Roosevelt still believed that *he*, not Churchill, was the leader whom Stalin would like and respect.

* Renamed Camp David by President Eisenhower in 1953 in honour of his father and grandson.

22

Uncle Joe

ON A DAMP and sultry September afternoon, some two weeks after his meeting with Stalin, Winston Churchill rose to his feet in the House of Commons. The chamber was crowded and anxious to hear what the prime minister had to say. It was not a moment for high rhetoric. Churchill's subject was Joseph Stalin, with whom (he gleefully told the MPs) he had cultivated a close personal relationship. Flush with success from his recent trip to Moscow, he wanted to give parliament a few insights into what made Stalin tick.

'A man of massive outstanding personality,' said Churchill, 'suited to the sombre and stormy times in which his life has been cast. A man of inexhaustible courage and will-power and a man direct and even blunt in speech.' No mention of the criminal purges, the millions of murders, the Gulag prison camps. Churchill portrayed Stalin in a wholly positive light and confessed to having found him likable and impressively frank. 'Stalin also left upon me the impression of a deep, cool wisdom and a complete absence of illusions of any kind.'[1] The Soviet leader knew exactly what he wanted: total victory over the Wehrmacht. He and Churchill were singing from the same hymn sheet.

Such effusive praise from Churchill was remarkable. For years he had hurled insults at the Soviet leader; now he was saying the exact opposite. There was good reason for this volte-face. It was vital to retain British public support for both Stalin and the embattled Soviet people. But some in the prime minister's entourage feared that Churchill was starting to believe his own rhetoric. He seemed genuinely convinced that he had struck up a friendship with Stalin, despite having spent precious little time, and that grudgingly, in the Soviet leader's company.

After that visit to Moscow, he grew increasingly animated whenever he received a letter from Stalin. In the aftermath of the Allied landings in North Africa, Ambassador Maisky called at 10 Downing Street to deliver a congratulatory letter from the Soviet leader. Maisky was taken aback by Churchill's reaction: 'He stopped, raised his eyes, thought for a moment, and then, with tears in his eyes, exclaimed in moved tones: "Oh Stalin, how grateful I am to you! You understand me so well!"'[2]

The ambassador had experienced Churchill's histrionics on many occasions, but even he was surprised. 'I knew that Churchill was a bit of an actor and could, in case of necessity, half consciously and half instinctively, bring tears to his eyes. But nevertheless, I could not doubt that at that moment he really was very moved.'[3]

Archie met Stalin with increasing regularity in the late autumn of 1942. He would fly from Kuibyshev to Moscow, where he was picked up at the airport and driven to the Kremlin in a chauffeur-driven ZIS. 'I was to see him constantly,' he would later write of this hectic period, 'for these were days of crises so acute that they called for direct discussions with Stalin.'[4]

He was also invited to carouse with his commissars, affording him a unique opportunity to study the Kremlin's boisterous hotheads at close quarters. At one of these vodka-soaked evenings, the conversation turned to the subject of Tommy guns. Archie claimed to be a Tommy gun expert, having been trained to kill while living in Shanghai. 'I was Japan's public enemy number one,' he told the assembled company, 'and had to keep a Tommy gun in my car.'

They were all discussing the best way to shoot when the unexpected occurred. 'From nowhere there appeared in my hands a real live Tommy gun.' It was Archie's moment to shine. 'I went on to demonstrate my technique, which is shooting from the hip.' In defiance of everything he had been taught about firearms when younger, he proceeded to rake the bellies of Stalin, Molotov, and the other commissars. Had the gun been loaded, he would have annihilated the entire Soviet government. 'Then Stalin seized it and fairly decimated his guests.' Archie was amused to see him aim quite deliberately at each of his commissars, picking them off one by one. 'This he seemed to enjoy immensely.'

A few weeks after that evening in the Kremlin, Archie received an unexpected visit from Stalin's interpreter. 'Pavlov arrived, borne down by the weight of an important looking box, almost as big as himself.' Archie removed the cover and peered inside. 'After some fumbling I came upon a highly polished oaken case, which opened with a snap, and there, snug in the lining of marmalade-coloured plush, was a Tommy gun.'[5] It was the two millionth Tommy gun produced in the Soviet Union and Stalin wanted Archie to have it, in memory of that rowdy Kremlin party.

Not all Archie's meetings with Stalin were so lighthearted. They discussed the ongoing battles in the Caucasus, Averell's supplies of American-made munitions, and the readiness of British and American troops for the assault on mainland Europe. They also exchanged ideas about history and strategy, two of Stalin's favourite subjects.

The more Archie got to know the Soviet leader, the more he came to respect the breadth and depth of his knowledge. 'There was always some kind of stimulus to be drawn from an hour or so spent with him,' he wrote. 'I was impressed by the commanding grasp that this son of a serf, who for years had hardly ever moved from out of the battlements of the Kremlin, had acquired of world affairs and military strategy.'[6]

Archie knew that much of this knowledge came from books, for Stalin was a voracious reader and had a personal library of twenty thousand volumes. He claimed to enjoy the Russian classics – Tolstoy, Gogol, Chekhov – but had also read Steinbeck, Hemingway, and Fenimore Cooper's *Last of the Mohicans*. He was also widely read in philosophy, political writings, and military studies and particularly admired the German military strategist General Carl von Clausewitz.

He was a compulsive annotator. 'Fool . . . Yes-yes . . . Spot on . . . Gibberish . . . Rubbish . . . Scumbag . . . Piss off.'[7] These were his favourite annotations, along with the ubiquitous scribble 'Ha-ha-ha'. Grammatical or spelling mistakes were corrected in red pencil.

In one of his many memos to the Foreign Office, Archie warned senior figures to stop treating Stalin and his commissars as illiterate peasants. He was the first to admit they were brutal and distasteful, but they were also astute. Deploying a carefully tailored metaphor, he wrote: 'We are still holding these people at an arms-length. We have not yet let them into the club. They are still scrutinised by the hall porter, stared at by the members and made to feel that they do not really belong.'

He urged the Eton-educated Whitehall mandarins to treat them with greater respect. 'Of course, it is a bore having country cousins hanging about our club, asking questions and wondering suspiciously why there are no spittoons . . . But we shall have to learn not to be snobs and still more not to be fools.'

Archie found it ironic that Stalin had been far better informed than Churchill during that first trip to Moscow. 'It was on occasions such as these that he seemed to shine and even to dominate, his thought a lap or two ahead of anyone else's, his mind and indeed his tongue moving swifter than a weaver's shuttle.'

Stalin's retorts were always pithy, 'often putting Mr Churchill out of countenance by the shrewdness and pungency of what he said'. Above all, the Soviet leader had a particular ability that was absent in his commissars. 'He seemed to be able to capture the smell of a political or military situation, while at the same time lacking all but a twilight understanding of the psychology of the West.'[8]

Archie had been fascinated to watch these two opposing personalities in action: the retiring dictator brusquely demanding weaponry, the ebullient aristocrat responding with rhetorical flourishes. 'It was instructive to see him and Mr Churchill together – two old hands, well-practised in the game of politics and strategy, the one pitting his wits against the other, each one with a thesis to propound, a point to win.'

He had long been intrigued by human relationships, and none was more bizarre than the rapport between Churchill and Stalin. Both men were needy, both sought reassurance. Archie felt their relationship was based 'upon a common desire on the part of each one to be liked by the other'.

It was an astute observation and almost certainly an accurate one. The future of the Allied partnership was to depend on whether the two leaders could maintain a genuine and lasting friendship.

Archie flew to London on Friday, 27 November, for his first leave in over five years. He met the most senior figures in Whitehall, who were impatient to hear his thoughts about Stalin. The most important of these meetings was held in the Cabinet War Room on Tuesday, 15 December, when Archie addressed the chiefs of staff.

He began by speaking about the much-discussed Second Front in Europe, reminding his audience that Stalin had been promised 'a considerable operation involving a million men, and with this promise he had been kept quiet'. If such an operation did not take place, Stalin would feel betrayed.

Lord Mountbatten interrupted him: 'Surely Stalin would understand that by mounting Torch [the invasion of North Africa], we had delayed the timing for any eventual return to the continent?'

Archie warned Mountbatten that Stalin regarded Operation Torch as being of little strategic importance. 'If now he failed to get what he expected,' he said, 'he would probably turn very sour.' The Allied relationship would be imperilled.

Sir Alan Brooke raised the possibility of a small-scale attack on the French coast. 'Would Stalin accept a limited operation, say, with the object of capturing the Cherbourg Peninsula?'

Archie warned that that would also be unacceptable.

Similar questions continued throughout the meeting, as each person probed Archie for information about the Soviet leader's probable reaction to a delay in launching the promised Second Front. Archie was dismayed by their refusal to believe that Stalin's military strategy was predicated upon the Allied landings in northern France. Nor did they believe his assertion that Stalin had a deep-seated paranoia about betrayal by the British and Americans. His greatest fear, Archie told them, 'was that we were building up a vast army which might one day turn round and compound with Germany against Russia'.[9]

His words fell on deaf ears. The chiefs of staff scoffed at his warnings, thinking him too pro-Soviet. They had no need for advice from an ambassador who gave every impression of having 'gone native'.

Their blinkered approach left Archie morose. He foresaw a world of troubles ahead.

On the eve of his return to the Soviet capital, Archie lunched with the prime minister at 10 Downing Street. Churchill was in a foul mood and took umbrage when Archie asked him how he should deal with Stalin over the months to come.

'You want a directive?' scowled Churchill as he collected his thoughts. 'All right. I don't mind kissing Stalin's bum, but I'm damned if I'll lick his arse.'

Archie's reply was beautifully succinct. 'Thank you, Prime Minister,' he said. 'Now I quite understand.'[10]

PART V

Storm Clouds

1943

23

Uncertain Allies

In the early hours of Monday, 12 January, Winston Churchill boarded a B-24 Liberator at Stanton Harcourt airfield, just a few miles from Chequers. He was travelling under the *nom de guerre* Commander Franklin, and his destination was code-named Symbol. Only a handful of insiders knew that he was flying to Casablanca to meet Roosevelt and Stalin. If all went according to plan, it was to be the first face-to-face meeting of the Big Three.

Roosevelt was adamant that it should be an intimate affair and that he didn't want any extras. He declined to bring his secretary of state and requested that Churchill leave behind his foreign secretary. 'No ringers,' he said to the prime minister. There was to be one exception: 'I hope you can bring Averell with you.'

Churchill cabled back: 'Delighted to bring Averell.'[1]

Roosevelt was looking forward to his first meeting with Stalin and hoping to build the same close relationship that Churchill had achieved during his visit to Moscow. The president's goal was simple: 'to talk Mr Stalin out of his shell, so to speak, away from his aloofness, secretiveness and suspiciousness, until he broadens his views, visualizes a more practical international cooperation in the future, and indicates Russia's intentions both in the East and in the West.'[2]

But Roosevelt was to be disappointed. Shortly before he and Churchill flew in to Casablanca, the Soviet leader sent a wire informing them that the Red Army's winter offensive was now under way. 'I must say that things are now so hot that it is impossible for me to absent myself for even a single day. The battle is developing on the Central Front, as well as Stalingrad. At Stalingrad we have surrounded a large group of German armies and we hope to achieve their final capitulation.'

The Soviet leader was correct in assessing the importance of the battle for Stalingrad. Hitler had vowed to capture at all costs the city that bore Stalin's name, while Stalin was equally determined to stop him. The military significance of the city was nothing in comparison to its psychological importance. Both dictators were prepared to sacrifice everything in their obsession with Stalingrad.

General von Paulus's Sixth Army had initially made rapid progress, seizing the city's western suburbs and attacking the Soviet defenders with aircraft, tanks, and mortars. By December 1942, central Stalingrad had been reduced to rubble. Stalin's defenders used this to their advantage, fighting a rearguard battle from wrecked buildings and concealed cellars. Hundreds of thousands of men lay dead in the ruins, and horrific atrocities were committed on those who had the misfortune to be captured alive. Stalingrad had become a brutal killing field in which hand grenades, machine guns, bayonets, knives, and even spades were used to despatch the enemy.

General von Paulus's Sixth Army was eventually encircled and trapped. By the beginning of 1943 it was out of both food and munitions, and resupply from the air proved impossible. There was no escape; defeat was now a certainty.

The final blow came soon enough. On Sunday, 31 January, Soviet troops attacked and entered the ruined Univermag building that was serving as Paulus's headquarters. Shortly afterwards, Paulus surrendered.

Hitler was stunned when he heard this news. He had just promoted Paulus to the rank of field marshal, reminding him that no German field marshal had ever surrendered. He expected Paulus to fight to the death.

Stalin ordered the Kremlin bells to ring out a victory peal. The battle of Stalingrad was the Soviet leader's first great triumph since the Nazi invasion a year and a half earlier. The battle had cost a million Russian and German lives, and tens of thousands more had been left with horrific injuries. But the mighty Sixth Army had been annihilated and Nazi Germany's reputation for invincibility had been shredded. At long last, the war was on the turn.

Among the important decisions struck at Casablanca was an agreement that Germany must surrender unconditionally, and that the

Western allies would liberate Sicily before undertaking their cross-channel invasion of occupied France. This would push Operation Overlord back to 1944, breaking Churchill's promise to Stalin just a few months earlier.

Stalin was not surprised when he learned of this decision, but he was bitterly disappointed and wrote a deeply hostile letter to Churchill, accusing him of backtracking on his commitments. Indeed he said he would no longer tolerate it. 'The Soviet Government cannot put up with such disregard of the most vital Soviet interests in the war against the common enemy.'[3]

Churchill feared a major rupture was now inevitable and sent a cable to Archie asking for advice. 'Personally, I feel that this is probably the end of the Churchill–Stalin correspondence,' he wrote dejectedly. 'As you were the first to suggest my visit to Moscow, I should be most glad to hear what you think.'[4]

Archie urged Churchill to show forbearance, just as he had done during his visit to Moscow the previous summer. 'It would be a mistake to take amiss such stuff as this when it comes from a man as rough and green and bad-mannered as Stalin . . . I can therefore only urge you to expend your much-tired patience with the old bear, and to deal with him as with the bear he is. Honey and bites of meat – and the stick when he deserves it.'

He reminded Churchill that the stakes were too high to allow any rupture in their relationship. 'It is melancholy to reflect that we must willy-nilly cooperate with this man, not only in the beating of Hitler, but in the years that will follow, and that upon this cooperation depend millions of lives and to a large extent the future of the world.'[5]

Churchill had more bad news for Stalin as winter gave way to spring, informing him that the Arctic convoys were to be suspended again because of near-perpetual daylight. 'We feel it only right to let you know at once that it will not be possible to continue convoys by the Northern route,' he wrote. 'It is a great disappointment.'[6] It was also a great disappointment for Stalin, especially as one of the cancelled convoys had a cargo of 650 much-needed fighter planes.

Ambassador Maisky was furious when told of the suspension and stormed round to 10 Downing Street. 'Simply astounded,' he told the prime minister. 'What does it mean? That there will definitely be no convoys until September?'[7]

Churchill became emotional when Maisky posed these questions. 'Yes, I know that this is a heavy blow for you,' he exclaimed. 'It's terrible! I consider it my duty to tell Stalin the truth. You mustn't deceive an ally.' Agitated and visibly upset, he began circling the Cabinet room. 'But what could I do? I had no alternative!'

He made another circuit of the room. 'Will it mean a split with Stalin, or won't it?'

Maisky shook his head. 'Your decision will arouse very strong feelings in Stalin.'

'I don't want a split! I don't!' said Churchill, the tears welling in his eyes. 'I want to work with Stalin, and I feel that I *can* work with him.'

The prime minister had only a few days to wait before hearing from Stalin himself, for the Soviet leader sent a telegram to Ambassador Maisky for immediate transmission to No. 10.

Churchill invited the ambassador back into the Cabinet room before pulling Stalin's note from its envelope. He then put on his glasses and began to read. Maisky watched him intently, noting that he was 'gloomy and beetle-browed'.[8] He was fascinated by what followed.

'Something strange happened to him. The prime minister's face was convulsed by a spasm, he shut his eyes for a moment, and when he opened them I could see tears.' Maisky felt sure the emotion was genuine, for Stalin's message was as unexpected as it was gracious. He had accepted the PM's decision to halt the convoys.

Churchill was indeed gleeful. 'He jumped up from his chair again, walked to the fireplace and exclaimed to the room at large: "The deepest thanks to Stalin! You have never brought me such a wonderful message before."'

Maisky was taken aback.

'Was all this genuine?' he asked his diary. 'Or was it an act? There was a bit of both, it seems to me.'[9]

Churchill's relationship with Stalin was constantly tested that spring. A major flashpoint arose on Tuesday, 13 April, when the Nazi regime announced it had unearthed a mass grave at Katyn, close to Smolensk.

This semi-excavated grave contained the bodies of nearly ten thousand Polish officers.

These were some of the officers who had disappeared in September 1939, shortly after the Red Army had swept into eastern Poland. The Nazis insisted they had been shot by the Soviets, prompting furious denials from Moscow. The Polish government-in-exile also held the Soviets culpable and demanded an immediate investigation by the Red Cross. Stalin's response was to break off relations with the Poles in London – a government-in-exile he had long hated. It was the first sign of a serious rift between Stalin and his Western partners.

In London, it was widely believed that the Soviets had indeed carried out the killings. Archie also thought so. 'In a horrible way, it seems to fit in with the Poles' story of the disappearance of 8,300 officers. The anger and unconvincing terms of Soviet denials suggest a sense of guilt.'[10]

As the arguments raged, Stalin composed a letter to Churchill that was a virtuoso example of the Soviet leader's evil chutzpah. He categorically denied any Soviet involvement in the executions – a massacre he had personally approved in the spring of 1940 – and accused the Polish government-in-exile of colluding with the Nazis. He then turned this false accusation to his own advantage by establishing a rival Polish government-in-exile based in Moscow and comprised entirely of Communists.

Ambassador Maisky received word of Stalin's rupture with the London-based Poles on Wednesday, 21 April, and drove down to Chartwell, Churchill's country house in Kent, where the PM was spending a few days.

The meeting began well, with Churchill greeting Maisky with a cordial handshake. But his mood changed abruptly when he began reading Stalin's letter. 'The further he read,' noted Maisky, 'the darker his face became.'[11]

When he reached the end, he turned to the ambassador.

'What does it mean, breaking off relations?'

Maisky explained that the Soviet leader was cutting all ties with the London-based Poles, adding that he wanted this news kept secret so it could not be exploited by the Nazis.

Churchill was appalled, aware that such a move threatened to destroy the alliance. 'This conflict must be resolved at all costs,' he said. 'Whose interest does it serve? Only the Germans.'[12]

He invited Maisky to stay for supper and the ambassador accepted, although not for the quality of the food. 'Milk soup (edible!), a piece of fried salmon and a bit of asparagus from Churchill's own plots.'

They remained at the table until midnight, with Churchill smoking his cigar and sipping a large whisky-and-soda. He assured Maisky he didn't believe the German 'lies' about the Soviets murdering 10,000 Polish officers. But neither did Maisky believe Churchill's assurances. He was convinced the prime minister thought Stalin was to blame but did not want to say so in public.

'Even if the German statements were proved true,' said Churchill at length, 'my attitude towards you would not change. You are a brave people, Stalin is a great warrior, and at the moment I approach everything primarily as a soldier who is interested in defeating the common enemy as quickly as possible.'[13]

But the Katyn revelations laid bare the problems of allying oneself to a murderous dictator: Churchill had very little option but to collude in the Soviet crimes. Seemingly uneasy with this thought, he absolved Stalin of any personal responsibility. 'Everything can happen in war,' he told Maisky. 'Lower-rank commanders, acting on their own initiative, are sometimes capable of doing terrible things.'

The rancour over Katyn did not prevent the exiled embassies from returning to Moscow, something that Stalin had long promised. Archie was delighted to be finally leaving Kuibyshev and threw himself into preparations for the move. Vehicles were his priority. 'Without adequate transport of our own, it will be quite impossible to get anything done, particularly in the early stages of setting up shop.'[14] But there were many other things to be arranged: petrol, servants, chauffeurs, cleaners, cooks, and maids.

The move to Moscow made it easier for Archie to pay visits on Stalin. It was at one of these meetings, while seated in the Soviet leader's study, that he noticed something unexpected. The twin portraits of Karl Marx and Friedrich Engels had been taken down and replaced by portraits of General Alexander Suvorov and Prince Mikhail Kutuzov, two of the great military heroes of the Napoleonic invasion.

In a note to the Foreign Office, Archie mused on what it might mean. 'Their presence is interesting, as a further symbol of the throw-back to the past, which has been manifesting itself all over the place.'

His observation was astute. Stalin was about to take the Soviet Union in a wholly new direction.

24
Ambassador Averell

A STIFF EASTERLY was blowing off the Atlantic when the *Queen Mary* sailed down the River Clyde and headed out to sea. It was Thursday, 5 August, and the ship was heading for Halifax, Nova Scotia, where its most illustrious passenger, Winston Churchill, was to have another meeting with President Roosevelt.

The prime minister was travelling with his chiefs of staff and dozens of other senior military figures, but his inner circle consisted of just four people: Clementine, his daughter Mary, Averell, and Kathy. These four would be with Churchill for much of the time during the four-day Atlantic crossing. For the Harrimans, father and daughter, the trip was to prove another life-changing experience.

President Roosevelt himself had asked Averell to join the voyage. 'Hope you can come with the Colonel,' he wrote, a reference to Churchill's new *nom de guerre*, Colonel Warden.[1] The president was hoping to pressure Averell into accepting the position of American ambassador to Moscow, now the most important diplomatic post in the world. If he accepted – and he had still not made up his mind – he would be working alongside his British counterpart, Archie Clark Kerr. It was unclear what would lie in store for Kathy.

Kathy wrote to her sister about life aboard the *Queen Mary*, especially the young marines accompanying the PM. 'They just lie in huddled bundles sleeping or reading. Walking anywhere, you have to pick your way over jumbled legs and bodies. The ones on deck look blue around the gills, and the ones below, equally physically unhappy.' They spent most of their time dozing, but soon came to life when Kathy was in sight. 'At first, I used to get embarrassed walking around. The language when a gal passes is unimaginable – actually, it's not! Going to dinner, the officers we dine with make bets with each other as to whose dinner-date will get the most number of cat-calls, hoots and whistles and obscene remarks.'

Each morning, exercise classes were held on deck. Kathy watched in bemusement as distinguished British officers did jumping jacks and stretches. 'Can you imagine US generals dressing up in slacks or shorts and sweaters and making figurative fools of themselves in front of their junior officers, staffs and little secretaries. I can't – but that's what the British do.'

As honoured guests of Churchill, Averell and Kathy always ate with the PM and his family. 'We, the privileged, have three meals a day,' she wrote. The lunchtime cocktails were served punctually at noon – 'I can't stand pink gin, but that's what you get offered' – and the food was excellent.[2] 'A diet of pre-war times', wrote an appreciative Churchill, whose only complaint came when the steward served water before pouring the champagne.[3] 'Stop pouring all that water out!' he roared. 'It is too depressing a sight.'[4]

Churchill's impressionable daughter, Mary, particularly looked forward to each mealtime. 'The food is UNBELIEVABLE!' she wrote in her diary. 'White rolls and masses of butter!' At breakfast, she was served fresh orange juice – 'ORANGE JUICE!' – an unobtainable luxury in wartime England.[5]

Each evening, Churchill would invite Averell and Kathy to join him for the screening of a few war films. These were almost always the same, with the prime minister's favourites being *Prelude to War* and *The Nazis Strike*. 'The PM has seen them three or four times each,' wrote Averell, who had noticed the same obsession with war films in Joseph Stalin. He also wrote of Churchill's enthusiasm for martial music, which would see him jump to his feet and start marching to and fro. 'He parades up and down what he calls his quarterdeck, the space between the entrance to his room and the big window.'

When it got late, the PM and Averell would retire to a quiet cabin and play cards. 'Although he is as intense as ever on the game, in playing bezique, his mind is always on the war. Out of a clear sky, Friday night, he said the single sentence: "We are going to win this war."'[6]

The strangest moment of the entire voyage came on the evening of Saturday, 7 August. The chiefs of staff had gathered in Churchill's cabin, where they were giving a demonstration of Operation Overlord – the invasion of northern France – now scheduled for 1944.

'If a stranger had visited his bathroom,' wrote General Ismay, 'he might have seen a stocky figure [Churchill] in a dressing-gown of many colours, sitting on a stool and surrounded by a number of what our American friends called Top Brass, while an Admiral flapped his hand in the water at one end of the bath in order to simulate a choppy sea, and a brigadier stretched a lilo across the middle to show how it broke up the waves. The stranger would've found it hard to believe that this was the British High Command studying the most stupendous and spectacular amphibious operation in the history of war.'[7]

The *Queen Mary* arrived in Halifax on Monday, 9 August, and Winston Churchill and company were whisked by train to Quebec, where they were to meet President Roosevelt and his advisers. Much of the ensuing conference, code-named Quadrant, was taken up with the planning of Operation Overlord, although they also discussed the war on the Eastern Front.

Averell became increasingly concerned by Roosevelt's naivety about Stalin. The president was convinced he could persuade the Soviet leader to behave decently once the war was over, and equally certain he could persuade him not to reoccupy territory he had gained under the Nazi-Soviet pact.

Averell was also disquieted by Roosevelt's idea of offering the people of the Baltic states a plebiscite on whether or not they wanted to be an independent country. 'He did not seem to realize that once the Russians occupied a territory, the plebiscite would almost certainly go their way.'[8] It was comments such as these that finally persuaded him to accept the post of American ambassador to the Soviet Union, a proposal first made by the president the previous spring. It would enable him to provide Roosevelt with unvarnished reports on Stalin's plans for the future of Europe and the world.

His acceptance led to a flurry of activity, with four weeks of consultation in Washington before returning to London. Kathy was already back in England, where she learned that she would be accompanying her father to Moscow. She was to be employed as his unofficial aide, as well as being the embassy hostess and public relations chief.

'I didn't have an inkling I'd be going with Ave until the passport department phoned,' she wrote. 'Everyone but me seemed to know my future.' Nor could she get any information as to what she would be doing, although she was told she would have to learn Russian.

She had previously found her reporting work in London to be the scariest thing in the world. 'Now,' she said, 'crashing London seems like chicken feed. All in all, I'm quite terrified.'[9]

25
The Deep End

THE WAR ON the Eastern Front had been transformed in the months since Stalingrad. The battle of Kursk, fought that summer, had begun as a sweeping Wehrmacht offensive. But the Red Army managed to seize the initiative, and the greatest tank battle in history ended in a Soviet victory.

The Kursk triumph was followed by a victorious assault on German-occupied Kharkov and strategic offensives against both Smolensk and Bryansk, occupied by the Germans since the autumn of 1941. These were also successful, with victory coming just a fortnight before the arrival in Moscow of Averell and Kathy.

Averell had accepted the post of ambassador on the condition that he would have total control over American-Soviet affairs, with a direct line to the White House. President Roosevelt agreed to this unusual arrangement, which meant bypassing the State Department. Never before had an ambassador been granted so much power.

Kathy's role as aide to her father was equally unusual, but it was welcomed by reporters who loved the idea of a society gal heading to Communist Moscow. 'Glamor Invades Yank Embassy' was the headline in the American *Herald* newspaper.

Their flight to Moscow was a thirty-three-hour ordeal in a four-engine propeller plane with a top speed of just 190 mph. The first leg of their flight, to Algiers, was bitterly cold, with the temperature in the plane plunging to far below freezing. 'Kathleen changed into her ski pants for the night,' wrote Meiklejohn, whose note-taking was becoming increasingly obsessive.[1] Thirteen hours later, they touched down in Algiers.

After meetings with General Eisenhower and his senior advisers, they headed on to Teheran, where they met General Donald Connolly, the redneck bruiser running Averell's trans-Iranian supply line into Russia. Connolly's team of Yankee workmen had dredged harbours in the Persian Gulf and constructed massive new dock facilities. Each dock was now discharging armoured trucks and cars at the rate of one every four minutes.

Connolly's drivers from the Pennsylvanian railway battled extremes of heat and cold as they pushed their supply trains across the desert and over the Elburz Mountains. 'The roughest, toughest railroading to be found anywhere in the world,' wrote *New York Times* journalist James Reston, in an article about Averell's Iranian operation. 'It snakes over straining grades and hairpin turns, crossing fearful chasms and boiling rivers and boring through the stony heart of mountain after mountain.'[2]

In the four weeks prior to Averell's arrival, General Connolly's men had despatched half a million tons of hardware to Stalin, the equivalent of 200,000 jeeps. When Bob Meiklejohn looked out of the window of his Teheran lodgings, he saw an endless procession of rail and truck convoys packed with American supplies.[3]

Averell and Kathy landed in the Soviet capital at three o'clock on Monday, 18 October, a crisp and sunlit afternoon with a hint of winter chill in the air. The Red Army guard of honour was dressed in stiff uniforms and gleaming helmets. 'Damned impressive', thought Kathy as she was greeted on the tarmac by Molotov, Vyshinsky, and other commissars. Bob Meiklejohn was meanwhile trying to manoeuvre himself into the newsreel shots so that his folks back home might see him. 'I don't think I succeeded,' he noted sadly in his diary.[4]

Molotov greeted Averell unsmilingly. 'We have found you a very tough man to deal with,' he said.

'I have come as a friend,' replied an indignant Averell.

'Oh, I know that,' said Molotov. 'I intended my remarks to be complimentary.'[5]

Averell, Kathy, and Bob Meiklejohn were taken straight to the ambassadorial residence, Spaso House. This was to be their home during their time in Moscow, as well as the nerve centre of American operations in the Soviet capital.

After two and a half years working alongside Churchill, Averell and Kathy were sent to Moscow to collaborate with Stalin. Averell dressed like a film star, while Kathy's elegance and intelligence made a deep impression on the Soviets.

Meiklejohn did a quick tour of the place and was astonished by the palatial luxury of his bedroom. 'I paced it off at twenty-seven feet by twenty feet, and the ceiling is easily fifteen feet high. No chance of getting claustrophobia here.' It was furnished with gilded antiques and giant wall mirrors.

He got an even greater surprise when Kathy showed him her suite of rooms. Even her bathtub was enormous. 'Long enough and deep enough to drown in without bending one's knees.'[6]

'The general theme is Regency,' wrote Kathy in a letter to her sister, Mary, 'with plenty of gold and black damask.' But Spaso House had been badly damaged during the bombing of Moscow, and its blown-out windows were still boarded up.

She found the massive vestibule particularly gloomy. And while the dining room was perfect for banquets, it was less ideal for breakfasts *à deux* with her father. 'He sits at one end of the table and I'm half a mile away at the other.' They had to shout to make themselves heard.

Averell and Kathy's arrival in the Soviet capital coincided with the Moscow Conference, a top-level meeting of the three foreign ministers – Soviet, American, and British. It was being touted as a major landmark in Soviet-Western relations, one in which the delegates could discuss increased collaboration in the fight against Nazi Germany. They also hoped to begin discussions on the architecture of the post-war world.

The conference began on Tuesday, 19 October, with a lavish luncheon in an old tsarist mansion replete with silks and damasks. This was followed by the first plenary session, at which the delegates debated the issues at a round table adorned with flags. Britain's representative was Anthony Eden, suave, urbane, and politically adroit. He managed to secure several meetings with Stalin and found him in remarkably good humour. The Soviet leader was particularly pleased with the Allied bombing of Germany. 'Hit the bastards hard, the harder the better!' he said to Eden, pounding his fist on the table for added emphasis.[7] But he remained bitter about the Western allies' lack of enthusiasm for the planned landings in northern France.

Stalin was right to be concerned about the landings, for unforeseen events were taking place offstage. In London, Winston Churchill was becoming increasingly lukewarm about Operation Overlord, the single most important issue for the Soviet delegates at the Moscow Conference. 'A very disturbing telegram from the PM, who has had second thoughts about the wisdom of Overlord,' wrote Eden's secretary, Oliver Harvey, on the fifth day of the conference. Churchill had also contacted Roosevelt, 'blurting out to the President all the doubts he had about Overlord'.

Eden was horrified when he heard this and threatened to resign if Churchill cancelled Overlord. Harvey was no less appalled. 'My God! The PM will lose us the war yet. His passionate and unscrupulous obstinacy is terrible, and he is as jealous as a ballerina.'[8]

British delegates had the unenviable task of informing Stalin of Churchill's conviction that the war in Southern Europe should take priority over Operation Overlord. They were fearful of the Soviet leader's reaction. 'We waited for the explosion,' wrote General Ismay. But it never came. 'On the contrary, there were no recriminations or veiled threats. Stalin appeared to comprehend our difficulties.' Everyone in the British team was hugely relieved. 'No harsh words were uttered,' wrote a surprised Oliver Harvey. 'Stalin was in benign mood.'[9]

What none of them knew was that even the Soviets were beginning to rethink their position about a Second Front. One of Molotov's heavy-drinking vice commissars, Alexander Korneichuk, let slip an alarming indiscretion when chatting with journalist Alexander Werth. 'Things are going so well on our front that it might even be better *not* to have the Second Front till next spring,' he said. 'If there were a Second Front right now, the Germans might allow Germany to be occupied by the Anglo-Americans.'

He intimated that the Soviet Foreign Ministry was worried that the Western allies might advance rapidly through Europe, liberating territory coveted by Stalin. 'It would make us look pretty silly,' said Korneichuk. 'Get the Red Army *right up* to Germany. And *then* start the Second Front.'[10] This would allow Stalin's forces to occupy Poland and Germany in advance of the Western allies.

Such a scenario was exactly what Averell had long feared. 'I gained the impression that Stalin wanted a pulverized Europe in which there would be no strong countries except for the Soviet Union. It seemed to me that the Russians were determined to control the smaller countries.'[11]

Archie's notes from the Moscow Conference are filled with snatched snippets of gossip and pencilled doodles: drawings of Molotov's shoulder pads; of a large-breasted woman; of naked figures hunched around a cooking pot.

At one point, he received a scribbled note from Averell, passed from hand to hand around the table. 'Archie,' it read, 'do you turn your shirt cuffs back when they are clean or when they are less clean?' Archie thought for a moment before jotting down his reply and sending it back. 'When they are clean.'[12]

Archie's notes about the Moscow Conference were enlivened by doodles. A shrewd reader of minds, he proved an invaluable adviser to Churchill.

The twelve days of discussions were hectic ones for Archie. Not only was he advising Anthony Eden, but he was also at the centre of a social circus. He hosted a dinner for Molotov on Wednesday, 20 October, had a meeting with Stalin the following afternoon, and then threw a cocktail party for notable Soviet figures.

The Moscow Conference ended in the third week of October and was widely held to have been a success. Most important, it had established a four-power structure that would shape the post-war world: the principal players were to be America, Britain, the Soviet Union, and China. It had also established the European Advisory Commission, tasked with finding solutions to the many problems that would face post-war Europe. And delegates also issued a Declaration on Atrocities, vowing to punish all who had committed 'atrocities, massacres and cold-blooded mass executions'. Stalin signed this without hesitation, because it only applied to atrocities committed by 'Hitlerite forces'.[13]

Before his departure for London, Anthony Eden thanked Archie for his hard work. 'I just can't find words to tell you adequately what a great help it was to me to have your wise counsel during the conference,' he wrote. 'We can be well satisfied with the result, which only your patience and masterly diplomacy has made possible.'[14]

Bob Meiklejohn had not participated directly in the conference because he had been too busy setting up Averell's new ambassadorial office. He had been forewarned that security would be a major headache. 'It is taken for granted that all the servants here are in the pay of the Russian secret service, the NKVD,' he wrote, 'and therefore we never leave any papers around loose. Even locked bags are not considered secure.'[15]

The security protocol was complex and exhaustive. State-of-the-art cryptographic equipment had been flown in from America: this enabled Averell to communicate directly and secretly with President Roosevelt without risk of the Soviets intercepting his messages. Meiklejohn was the only person allowed to handle super-cables to the president. 'It's rather pleasant that they figure I'm the man to trust with the high-powered stuff,' he wrote. 'The super-cables are in a locked briefcase in a locked cabinet in the safe' – an unbreakable steel strongbox installed in his Spaso House bedroom.

Meiklejohn was warned that even the cleaners were on the payroll of the NKVD. 'All the servants will turn anything they find over to the secret police.' He took it all in his stride. 'No hard feelings about the spying,' he wrote. 'That is the way they do business here.' But he nevertheless found it strange to be in a partnership with people that could not be trusted.

Averell proved extremely demanding in those first days in Moscow, and Meiklejohn again found himself working up to sixteen hours a day. 'I seldom get through before midnight,' he wrote. 'However, it is the most interesting work in the world – all about proposed peace terms for the Axis countries; strategic plans for the war in Europe; the details of the bombing offensive; and the plans for the forthcoming meeting of Stalin, Roosevelt, and Churchill.'[16]

He was at the epicentre of everything.

Stalin's decision to hang portraits of victorious tsarist generals in his study had been noticed by a number of the conference delegates, but Archie was the first to realise it was a conscious policy to turn back the clock.

The Soviet leader wanted to remind the Russian people of their splendid imperial heritage. This did not stop with the portraits. Just a few weeks earlier, in the gilded magnificence of Moscow's Epiphany Cathedral, the senior hierarch of the Russian Orthodox church, Sergius, had been enthroned as patriarch. As clouds of incense drifted heavenwards, the assembled bishops acclaimed their new spiritual leader.

When Archie next met Stalin, he expressed his surprise at this revival of the Church in a state that was officially atheist. The Soviet leader told him that 'in his own way, he also believed in God'. Archie almost chortled. 'I dare say he had his tongue in cheek when he said so,' he wrote, 'but it is surely interesting that he should have thought it politic to make such a remark to me!'[17]

Wherever Archie looked that autumn, it was as if the past was being resurrected. Tsarist heroes, imperial uniforms, and Suvorov military academies were all being revived – the latter named after the great martial hero, General Alexander Suvorov, whose portrait Stalin had installed in his study. When journalist Alexander Werth was taken to visit one of these newly opened academies, he was astonished by what he saw: 'Among the subjects the budding little officers were taught were English, fine manners and old-time ballroom dances (the waltz, the mazurka, the pas-de-quatre, etc.).'[18]

No less surprising was a string of newspaper articles in which venerable old generals spoke fondly of their days in the tsarist cadet schools. Stalin also commissioned the master filmmaker Sergei Eisenstein to make his epic *Ivan the Terrible*, in which the cruel but brilliant emperor was portrayed as the forerunner of Stalin. Alexander Werth labelled it 'Russian ultra-nationalism', a peculiarly Stalinist return to the heyday of the tsars.

This trend was to reach its apogee on the night of Sunday, 7 November, the anniversary of the 1917 revolution. The Soviet leader had already hosted a large dinner in honour of his Western allies at the end of the Moscow Conference. But this had been merely the precursor to a banquet of unparalleled extravagance.

The dress code was white tie and tails. This caused panic, for no one in the British or American embassies had brought formal attire to Moscow. Archie was to prove the exception. He borrowed a stiff dress shirt from a Swedish diplomat and acquired a jacket with tails.

'Together with his medals and big Knights Commander of the Bath red-and-blue ribbon worn horizontally across his chest and stomach,' wrote Kathy, 'he managed not to look insignificant next to a Russian. But he was the only one.'[19]

The guest list that night was stellar. 'Prominent Russian writers, artists and musicians', wrote Averell, 'including the composer Dmitri Shostakovich in full evening dress . . . it was as if the Russian elite had been commanded to make up, in a single night, for the studied boycott of foreigners that had been the iron rule of Moscow.' But the most important guests were the British and American ambassadors. 'The party might have been given for me and for Averell,' wrote Archie. 'Nobody else seemed to be of any account.'[20]

Molotov tried to play the genial host, but it did not come naturally. 'He was carrying a large tray of brimming glasses of champagne, going up to guests at random to offer a drink from the ministerial hand and exchange toasts. Wooden-faced, expressionless, his pince-nez glinting, he raised his own glass again and again: "To victory! To victory! To victory! To victory!" with each in turn.'[21] As he passed the ambassador of Sweden, he hissed, 'Weeee donnn't like neutrals!'[22]

Many of the guests were soon drunk, but the night was still young. Archie feared the worst. 'Molotov planted me at a table in the corner', he wrote, 'with the three toughest drinkers in the Soviet Union. Everything but sheer vodka and a bowl of apples was excluded from the table. They would not allow me to eat "because it would spoil the vodka".'

Averell was seated at the same table next to Anastas Mikoyan, Stalin's commissar for foreign trade, with whom he had had frequent discussions about the delivery of supplies and weaponry. 'Mikoyan is famous for his ability to put any guy under the table,' wrote Kathy, 'so I guess that's why he was picked. He and Averell drank bottoms-up after bottoms-up in toasts to all the obvious things, in vodka.'

She managed to escape the initial rounds of vodka. 'Fortunately for me, soon after I sat down the drink was changed from vodka to sour Caucasian white wine, but even it has a pretty high alcoholic content! It's hard to cheat at toast drinking as you have to turn the glass upside down at the end of it, and the drops of liquor that fall out are, according to the Russian custom, drops of misfortune you wish on the person you are drinking with.'

The perils of life in Moscow: Kathy and Averell were required to drink dozens of vodka toasts at the Kremlin banquets they attended. Glasses had to be emptied in one gulp.

As the clock struck midnight, Archie rose from the table to deliver a final toast to the assembled company. He looked spectacular in his white tie, medals, and fine silk sash: he could have stepped from the pages of *War and Peace*.

What happened next was to be remembered in Moscow for years to come: 'Sir Archibald Clark Kerr, GCMG, His Britannic Majesty's Ambassador Extraordinary and Plenipotentiary, teetered speechlessly in all his glittering regalia for one brief but splendid moment, before falling with an almighty crash onto the table in front.'[23]

Kathy gasped as Archie slid from the table, dragging the tablecloth with him. 'He fell flat on his face at Molotov's feet, bringing a goodly number of plates and glasses clattering down on top of him.' Bob Meiklejohn rushed over and found that Archie's head had ended up in a bowl of pickled fish. The floor was awash with vodka and champagne, along with smashed glass and shards of broken crockery.

Apart from a nasty gash on his forehead, Archie was fine. Those seated at the adjacent table helped the still-beaming ambassador to his feet. Like a stout galleon in troubled waters, he wobbled slightly before regaining the perpendicular. Then, after brushing down his dress shirt and jacket, he made his way to the exit. 'There were long halts and at one of these Molotov thumped me [Archie] in the chest and said: "Kerr is all right. He's the sort of chap we like!" Then at the next halt came another thump and: "If he was one of us, he would be a partisan."'[24]

Kathy had had enough. 'I turned to Averell and said, "Let's get the hell out of here!"'

She felt dreadful by the time they were back in Spaso House. 'When I got to bed, the room really started whirling . . . so I got up and drank three glasses of very strong soda bicarbonate.'

She was woken by her father late the following morning; he was desperate for Alka-Seltzer. 'And as none could be found he was not in particularly good shape.' Averell went back to bed, giving Bob Meiklejohn a rare day off work. 'He didn't get up till three o'clock,' noted Meiklejohn in the office diary, 'while Kathleen drank buckets of water all morning.'

Archie's day was to prove equally painful. He woke up fully dressed, lying on the floor of his bedroom with his head in the fireplace and his butler snoozing in the armchair. When he asked his footman why he was on the floor and his butler in the chair, the footman answered in his measured tone: 'Because, Your Excellency, you insisted.'

26

The Real Moscow

Kathy's presence in Moscow puzzled the Soviets. It was very unusual for an ambassador to bring his daughter along as his aide – a daughter, moreover, who was intelligent, accomplished, and more than able to hold her own in any company. Stalin's commissars couldn't pin her down, although they'd been impressed by her confident wit when they first met her at a Bolshoi ballet performance.

She had chatted with the ashen-faced Molotov, who melted in her presence and even cracked jokes, to everyone's astonishment. 'He's got a hell of a swell sense of humor,' wrote Kathy after that first meeting, 'and nice twinkling eyes.' She was also introduced to Andrey Vyshinsky and Alexander Korneichuk, one of Molotov's deputies, who likewise oozed with charm. 'I got stuck talking to Korneichuk for nearly the whole intermission. Youngish, nice looking and easy to talk to.'

Kathy wanted to make good use of her time in Moscow. 'I'm determined not to get into what seems to be a hell of a rut,' she wrote to her sister. 'There's plenty to keep me busy.'[1]

This was because she made herself busy. Within days of arriving, she had carved out an official role for herself. She first got employment with the embassy's Office of War Information, which liaised with its Soviet counterpart. This gave her insight into how society functioned in Stalin's Russia. She also set up her own news service, compiling a daily summary for all the embassies in Moscow. And she helped establish a glossy magazine, *Amerika*, whose aim was to inform Russians about American life. It would survive, on and off, until 1994.

Kathy was shocked by the diffidence of the Western journalists in the city. 'The American press boys are a pretty crummy bunch, taken as a whole. It's too bad, because a good corps of correspondents could get a lot more out of this country.' None had bothered to learn Russian, something she was working at day and night. 'It's a town where foreigners get depressed, because they can't become a part of the town.' She chatted with a group of them after a press trip to Kiev and was not impressed. 'They were struck by two things: the amount of food and the number of banquets they were given.'

She also found them deeply cynical. 'They were worried as to whether or not they should believe the atrocity story they were told: fifty thousand Jews killed and burned in a ravine just outside town.'[2] This was Babi Yar, the infamous site outside Kiev where 100,000 or more Jews and Soviet prisoners of war would be massacred during the course of the war.

Kathy was particularly keen to record the realities of daily life in Stalin's Moscow, which the press corps never wrote about. 'One of my favorite sports is just plain walking the streets, watching people. Going round with Averell is like traveling on the Union Pacific. His NKVD minders make everything smooth and easy. But me, on my own, operates much like any New Yorker in subway rush hour.'[3]

Her written observations were never intended for publication: hers was a sister-to-sister correspondence, filled with gossip and chatter. But her letters reveal a great deal about the realities of daily life in the Soviet Union.

She first explored the area where she lived, Spasopeskovskaya Square, where she found the tenement blocks in a sorry state of disrepair. The entire Soviet economy was focused on the war effort and there was no money available for state-owned housing. 'We live on a prettyish little square,' she wrote, 'but it has an air of frustration about it. The trees are half dead and the houses around it are a combination of brick factory-like apartment houses or smaller one-story cottages.' All had the same peculiar smell: 'Decaying cabbage and musty clothes and damp stone stairways . . . this really is the damnedest town.'[4]

Yet the people themselves struck her as being remarkably cheerful. 'I came here anticipating streets filled with unhappy, unsmiling people. T'ain't so! The streets are invariably crowded with mobs of men in uniform, women who all look old, and tiny kids. The smaller kids play on their sleds, slide on the icy spots and make snow figures and generally seem very happy and contented.'[5]

Everyone was visibly suffering, though, after two years of malnutrition. 'So far, I haven't seen one beautiful Russian. Hair is badly kempt, and through holey white long underwear you can see wool stockings or perhaps another layer of underwear.' Little wonder that all heads turned when she walked down the street. 'People stare at me so much due to my furs and silk stockings. There's no one around who dresses like me.'[6]

Kathy was particularly struck by Moscow's lack of traffic. The only vehicles on the streets were American imports: 'It seems slightly odd to see the familiar sight of countless jeeps and good old American trucks galloping down the avenues.'

One of Kathy's official duties was that of embassy hostess, in charge of food and entertainment. 'I've taken to mixing cocktails. Each day we experiment. Vodka with sherry. Vodka with wine. Vodka with synthetic fruit juice. The result is good' – she meant potent – 'but not the cocktails themselves.'

Averell also made her responsible for managing both the embassy and Spaso House. 'I think I run a reasonably successful boarding house,' she wrote, although her meals (produced in straitened circumstances) were not always welcomed. 'Slabs of Spam, very attractively arranged around a scalloped mound of mashed potatoes and ringed by hospital-green canned peas bring howls of displeasure from all boarders, Averell included.'[7]

Over the months that followed, Kathy was the hostess of countless functions at Spaso House. 'Our merchant-king's palace lends itself very well to a reception,' she wrote after one large party.[8] 'It will hold two hundred people comfortably, plus huge tables for food and drink.'[9] Whenever she was hosting an official soirée, she could order unlimited supplies from Burobin, the central office servicing Moscow's diplomatic community.

These evenings became far more absorbing when she was allowed to invite Russian guests. This was a major breakthrough, even though each person had to be vetted in advance. 'A list is sent to the protocol department at the Foreign Office, and they let us know which of the people are okay to invite.'

Kathy (seated on roof) was the official hostess for the American Embassy in Moscow, and her radiant presence transformed daily life. She and her colleagues are returning to the capital after a day in the countryside, with Bob Meiklejohn in the foreground, leaning against the truck.

The American naval officer Kemp Tolley noted that Kathy's parties were fun but never innocent. '[They] served a wholly useful and necessary function – that of gathering, pooling, and checking intelligence on the developments, mood, temper and direction in a country where normal sources did not exist.' Snippets of rumour and gossip could prove invaluable. 'In such a society, informal, sometimes wholly unexpected, sources turned up tiny clues, which when fitted in with other pieces of the jigsaw, produced a recognizable picture that was supposed to help fashion intelligent responses or countermeasures.'[10] Tolley's assessment was spot on: such parties enabled Kathy and her father to gather important information on Stalin's inner circle.

Many of Kathy's Soviet guests found themselves wondering what to make of this alluring young lady, whom they referred to as Garriman on account of being unable to pronounce the letter 'h'. They seemed unaware that she was using that allure to good effect, gathering intelligence on them.

'I spent a good bit of energy trying to get stiff generals and admirals to dance with me,' she wrote after one party. 'Some would, but some refused.' But with each dance – and each new conversation – she got a deeper insight into the Soviet regime.

This would prove invaluable for the future.

27

In the Ruins of Stalingrad

IN THE THIRD week of November, Averell, Archie, and a small group of advisers set off by plane for Cairo. Their task was to finalise plans for the first 'Big Three' meeting of Roosevelt, Churchill, and Stalin, due to take place in Teheran.

As they neared Stalingrad, the plane began to behave in erratic fashion. 'We were beginning to lose height,' noted Arthur Birse, 'and one of the engines seemed to be behaving badly.' The next thing they knew, they were plunging to earth, with the pilot struggling to make an emergency landing in a field littered with burned-out vehicles.

'We are landing at Stalingrad,' he announced with impressive calm as they thudded heavily into the mud. The airfield was so badly damaged that it was unrecognisable. 'We bumped along till we drew up within a few yards of a Soviet sentry who stared at our plane in amazement.'[1] So wrote Birse, who added that the sentry ran off to his guard-hut to telephone for instructions.

Everyone alighted from the plane and shivered in the winter chill. As Averell and Archie discussed their predicament, they were told that Stalingrad's mayor, Dmitri Pegalov, was coming to meet them. He had been tasked with looking after them during their unintended stay.

Pegalov arrived shortly after and greeted them warmly before driving them to the only intact building on the ruined outskirts of Stalingrad. Here, a small army of waiters was busily loading food onto a rough wooden table. 'Not the delicacies we had been served at official functions in Moscow,' wrote General Deane, Averell's military adviser. 'There were big chunks of black bread, cheese, sausages and coleslaw, and, of course, bottles of vodka.'[2]

Among the assembled Soviet officials was Alexey Semenovich Zhadov, who had helped organise the defence of Stalingrad. He told them that 91,000 German soldiers had been captured after the initial surrender but said that a further 10,000 had subsequently emerged from cellars and hiding places. Debilitated by dysentery, most had died during the short march to the nearby prison camp. Zhadov said their corpses, 'partially decomposed and in a horrible state', still littered the roadsides.

He also told them how he had witnessed bitter recriminations from the Romanian soldiers fighting in Stalingrad, who had turned on their German allies as soon as the battle was lost. At one point, 18,000 Romanians were being transported across the Volga, along with a small detachment of Germans: 'The Romanians pounced on the Germans, took all their clothes off, threw them in the river, and drowned them, saying, "You wanted to reach the Volga. Now you can have it." '[3]

The Soviet officials who joined Averell, Archie, and company for the lunchtime meal were very different from the commissars they had met in Moscow. 'Unpolished and unprepossessing', thought Arthur Birse, although he soon realised that appearances can be deceptive. 'Often the round, shaven heads, the high cheek bones, the almost Mongol features, hide unexpected qualities and talent. There was no trace of good breeding or gentility in them; none was of the class known as "intelligentsia". But their very roughness was probably the quality required for the job of management and restoration.'[4]

They certainly didn't wear the gilded uniforms so recently seen in Moscow. 'Most of the men wore high boots, into which their trousers were tucked, dark jackets or tunics, dark well-worn overcoats . . . and the familiar black peaked caps.'[5]

Bob Meiklejohn watched everyone relax as the alcohol took its effect. 'Very genial', he thought. 'Mr Harriman trading his cigarette lighter with Semenovich, with much vodka and toasts to everything under the sun.'

Archie's military adviser, General Giffard Martel, was rather too enthusiastic when downing his vodka, forgetting there would be toasts throughout the meal. It was to prove his undoing. 'He got trapped with half a tumbler of vodka,' said Meiklejohn, 'and he had to down it at one gulp. He never quite got over it, being glassy-eyed all the rest of the day.'[6]

★

When lunch finally came to an end, Mayor Pegalov proposed a tour of the ruins. This was eagerly accepted by everyone, for it was a rare chance to see a Soviet battlefield. As they drove towards what had once been the centre of Stalingrad, Averell was staggered by the scale of the destruction. 'As far as the eye could scan, streets and squares, houses and shops, had been erased in the house-to-house fighting. Nothing remained but a desert of broken brick and rubble, the survivors huddling in cellars or tar-paper shanties.'[7] Not one house in fifty thousand was left intact.

Meiklejohn had never seen such destruction. 'We passed one stretch of eighty wrecked German tanks, and dumps of airplane wings and fuselages, apparently stretching for miles along the railway tracks.' One dump contained the skeletal remains of 2,500 Luftwaffe planes.

They were given a tour of the battlefield's most significant buildings, including the wrecked Red October Tank Factory and the city's shattered grain elevator. 'It looked like a colander, it had so many holes in it,' wrote Meiklejohn.[8]

Averell, Archie, and company made an unscheduled stop in Stalingrad while en route to Cairo and Teheran. They were staggered by the devastation. 'Nothing remained but a desert of broken brick and rubble.'

Their plane was taking much longer than expected to repair, requiring the group to spend the night in what remained of Stalingrad's Intourist Hotel. 'A small army of men and women were carrying beds and bedding into a hut which was to be our common dormitory,' wrote Arthur Birse, 'while others were bringing tables and chairs, food and wine, into the adjoining premises.'[9]

The ensuing feast was enjoyed by everyone, especially Averell. 'Toasts were raised in Russian and English as if at a Kremlin banquet,' he wrote, 'but this was a highly informal party, producing a flow of songs, war stories and dances that no official entertainment could rival.'[10] Even the serving staff joined in the fun.

Averell was known to all the Soviets as 'the father of Lend-Lease' and was showered with gifts in recognition of his work. These included German watches and sabres, all trophies of the battle for Stalingrad. Both he and Archie were also presented with the ultimate Soviet souvenir, a captured German Luger pistol.

Averell's interpreter, Charles Bohlen, spent the next hour or so knocking back the vodka with impressive efficiency. 'Thoroughly oiled', noted Meiklejohn, who was watching him out of the corner of one eye. But it was to everyone's benefit, for he began belting out the bawdy Russian folk songs he had learned as a student.

Eventually the party began to wind down. Averell asked General Deane to sing a final song, and he duly obliged with a heartfelt rendition of 'Show Me the Way to Go Home'.

Everyone was overcome with nostalgia and found themselves longing for happier times. Archie was almost in tears, telling General Deane that 'he had never heard the song rendered with such feeling'.[11]

The words had indeed tugged the heartstrings of everyone. All had been away from their loved ones for many months, and in Archie's case for several years. None of them wore their emotions on their sleeves, but touring the ruins of Stalingrad had hit them hard. An entire city had been destroyed, and it was but one of thousands. The old world had been pulverised and a new one had yet to rise from the ashes.

Arthur Birse stepped outside for some fresh air before going to bed. 'Night had fallen and there was a moon, in the light of which the maze of broken-down walls, bare chimney stacks and heaped up rubbish looked ghost-like. It was indeed a graveyard through which we moved.'[12]

Averell had placed Kathy in charge of the embassy and residence for the fortnight of his absence, a responsibility that led her to write a mock letter of protest to her sister. 'Averell the skunk is about to go off and leave me in the clutches of the esteemed members of the Soviet Foreign Service. That's just a little better than leaving me in solitary confinement in Lubyanka' – headquarters of the NKVD. But she was secretly looking forward to her father's absence. 'I anticipate an amusing time.'[13]

For the first few days, she focused on improving her Russian. She was having lessons six days a week and had made impressive progress since first arriving in the country. 'Now I can ask for anything from the servants,' she wrote, 'and get along with an atrocious American accent, regularly slaughtering the grammar. I talk using the nominative, accusative and dative cases and say to hell with the other three.' The language no longer seemed so daunting. In a letter to Pamela Churchill, she said she could already read Chekhov novellas in Russian. 'It's amazing how few words you need to know to get the gist of a story.'[14]

Six days after her father left Moscow, Kathy decided to throw open the doors of Spaso House. Thursday, 25 November, was Thanksgiving Day, and she wanted to host a dinner for all the Americans in Moscow. 'When you add the military, navy, embassy staffs to the aircraft missions, the press and a Catholic priest, it came to damn near a hundred.' Kathy broke the diplomatic norms by also inviting the junior clerks, who were never normally welcomed at anything. The festivities were a roaring success, with generous supplies coming from the embassy's provision store. In this way, Kathy managed to provide a traditional Thanksgiving feast, including turkey and pumpkin pie. She also bought gallons of vodka, which the embassy's two Chinese butlers, Chin and Tung, transformed into a lethal punch. The junior embassy clerks had never had such fun. 'Most of them, up till the party, were inclined to be suspicious of me,' wrote Kathy. 'But now, that's all straightened out.'

She loved playing the society hostess in such a setting; never had her father's absence been so enjoyable. 'The best damned thing that could have happened to me was to have Averell leave me alone in this place!'[15]

Kathy's unique position in the American Embassy gave her the opportunity to visit places that no other westerner had been allowed to see, including schools, orphanages, and one of Moscow's larger maternity hospitals. This latter institution was taking Soviet collectivisation to new extremes. Its birthing room could accommodate twenty women simultaneously, in various stages of labour. But the place had few painkillers and even less anaesthetic, rendering a visit here an unappealing ordeal. Moscow that autumn was so short of medicines that all operations, including amputations, were being done under local anaesthetic, or none at all.

Kathy was also allowed to visit a children's hospital, housed in a *fin-de-siècle* villa with a marble staircase. 'Very swell,' she wrote. The youngsters being nursed here were a stark reminder of the Nazis' contempt for human life, for most had been saved from areas previously occupied by the Wehrmacht. These were the fortunate survivors. Hitler's call for a war of extermination in the Soviet Union had been heeded by both generals and soldiers, but most especially by the sinister Nazi *Einsatzgruppen*, or death squads. These had liquidated vast numbers of innocent victims in the occupied territories. 'The most pathetic was a little three-year-old girl who had been evacuated from the Kiev area,' wrote Kathy. 'Her mother and father were both in the army and during the two years of German occupation of Kiev, she'd lived with her grandmother.'

That grandmother told Kathy of their desperate struggle to stay alive, for the Germans had stolen every item of foodstuff and left them with nothing. 'They'd had to walk six miles for black bread, their only food, and now the child is still suffering from starvation.' She was pathetically thin, with huge swollen joints and a distended stomach.

Nurses told her that the girl was being given regular blood transfusions, which seemed to be working, for she was suffering less than before. 'Lord only knows what she was like when she first was hospitalized,'[16] wrote Kathy.

★

Averell's Stalingrad group were woken at 5 a.m. for breakfast. Most had aching heads and several were a sickly shade of green. Charles Bohlen had last been sighted two hours earlier wandering around the ruined hotel in his underpants. According to his own vague recollection, he was coaxed back to bed by an elderly Russian maid.

General Martel was in a particularly foul mood that morning. 'Most of us felt like death,' he said, 'and we looked a very sorry party.'[17] Breakfast was a particular ordeal: steak, mutton chops, ham and eggs, caviar, raw fish, vodka, and red and white wine. Several of the group had to dash outside to avoid being sick.

The group flew from Stalingrad to Cairo, where Churchill, Roosevelt, and the leader of the Chinese Nationalists, Chiang Kai-shek, were holding discussions about the Far East. Then, on Saturday, 27 November, everyone headed to Teheran for the first meeting of the Big Three wartime leaders. For the next four days, Churchill, Roosevelt, and Stalin would plan the future of the world.

28

The Big Three

THE TEHERAN CONFERENCE was a cause of both excitement and anguish for those involved in the planning. It was the first meeting of the Big Three; the first occasion on which Churchill, Roosevelt, and Stalin would get a chance to discuss vital issues face to face.

No one knew how the human dynamics would unfold, nor whether the three leaders would be able to compromise and reach agreement. Stalin's unpredictability was the principal cause for concern. It was impossible to know how he would react to any given situation. But Roosevelt's manner could also cause offence. He had made it abundantly clear that he wanted a closer relationship with Stalin than was already enjoyed by Churchill.

Five months earlier, he had told Averell that he intended to get to know Stalin, break down the barriers of suspicion and 'talk him out of his shell'. Now he said to his advisers that he wanted 'to develop an intimate personal relationship with Stalin, to allay Stalin's suspicions', and – in his own striking phrase – 'convert the wary Communist tiger into a pussycat amenable to Western persuasions as to the shape of the post-war world'.[1] He even told Harry Hopkins that he was by far the best-placed person to befriend the Soviet leader. 'After all,' he said, 'he had spent his life managing men, and Stalin could not be so very different from other people.'[2] Many in Roosevelt's inner circle found the president's approach worryingly naive.

One of the principal subjects on the Teheran agenda was the much-discussed opening of a Second Front against Nazi Germany. This had the potential to be explosive: Roosevelt did not see eye-to-eye with Churchill on the timing of Operation Overlord, but nor was he in agreement with Stalin, who wanted it launched immediately.

Other matters for discussion included the military situation in Turkey and Iran, and support for Marshal Josip Tito's Yugoslav partisans. There were also political issues to be debated. The fate of Poland and the Baltic states had yet to be resolved.

The three leaders arrived in Teheran on the same day, Saturday, 27 November. They brought a host of advisers. Roosevelt's Soviet expert was Ambassador Averell, but he had also travelled with Harry Hopkins and a number of military officials.

Winston Churchill was to rely on Ambassador Archie for advice about the Soviet Union, but he had brought a veritable entourage of senior military personnel. Stalin, by contrast, was accompanied by just two other senior figures, Molotov and Voroshilov.

Teheran had never seen such tight security arrangements, with a ring of steel protecting the three most important leaders in the world. Churchill's lodgings at the British Legation were guarded by an impenetrable cordon of Sikh soldiers shipped in from British India, while Stalin's adjacent compound was swarming with NKVD officers. Roosevelt's lodgings were equally secure. When Bob Meiklejohn arrived at the American Legation, he found the place awash with sentries. 'Armored cars, Tommy guns and God knows what else.'[3]

That afternoon, Averell and Archie received an urgent summons to the Soviet compound, where Molotov gave them some alarming news: 'Soviet intelligence had discovered the existence of a plot among Nazi-orientated Iranians and Nazi agents, to assassinate some or all three participants in this conference.'[4] He proposed that President Roosevelt move into a villa within the Soviet compound. This would enable security to be focused on one small area of the city, since all three leaders would be adjacent to each other. It would also enable the Soviets – though he did not admit this – to bug the president's bedroom.

Averell was sceptical about Molotov's alleged assassination plot. 'I pressed him to within the limits of civility for details,' he said, but Molotov refused to reveal anything more.[5] Roosevelt himself took the threat at face value and agreed to move into the Soviet compound, along with his Filipino servants and Secret Service bodyguards.

'Do they know we are listening to them?' Stalin would later ask the apparatchik in charge of eavesdropping on the president. They did.

Roosevelt had assumed his room would be bugged and used this knowledge to good effect, making utterances designed to win Stalin's confidence.

Stalin's first meeting with President Roosevelt took place on the day after their arrival, Sunday, 28 November. It was a sparkling day, mild and sunny, with a clear blue sky. To several observers, it was as if the weather had cast a benign spell over the conference.

Only four people were present at the initial tête-à-tête between Roosevelt and Stalin – the two leaders themselves and their interpreters, both of whom were feeling unusually nervous. A weight of responsibility was hanging on their shoulders. Roosevelt's interpreter, Charles Bohlen, was intending to keep a close eye on the Big Three over the days that followed, aware that the future of the world depended to a large extent on the personal relationships between them. Their meetings, he said, 'provided me with an opportunity to size up the three leaders, to understand their views of important problems, to feel the force of their personalities, to watch the interplay of one on the other'.[6]

From the very outset, Bohlen was alarmed by Roosevelt's naivety, especially when he spoke with Stalin about the Soviet system. The president referred to the Bolshevik Revolution as a mass uprising rather than a brutal power grab, and he didn't seem to appreciate that the Soviet Union was led by a band of ruthless revolutionaries. Stalin, by contrast, displayed the same impressive familiarity with international affairs. He even explained to Roosevelt the complexities of the caste system in rural India.

Averell was not surprised that Stalin was better briefed than Roosevelt. 'In my own talks with him, I was struck time and again by the extent of his knowledge of other countries, which I found remarkable in view of the fact he had done so little traveling.'[7]

The Big Three met together for the first time at the plenary session that Sunday afternoon. Everyone was watching intently, keenly aware of the significance of the event. Bob Meiklejohn was particularly excited to see the trio of leaders in the same room. 'I've seen quite a mess of bigwigs in my time,' he wrote, 'but I must confess I got quite a kick out of seeing that particular gang all together.'[8] Bohlen agreed:

'The three most powerful men in the world were about to make decisions involving the lives and fortunes of millions of people.'[9]

Stalin had spent time and effort rehearsing for the conference; he'd even practised his arrival in the conference hall. 'I am going to sit here, to one side,' he told his deputy interpreter. 'Roosevelt will be brought in in his wheelchair. Let him position himself to the left of his chair, where you [the deputy interpreter] will be seated.'[10] The Soviet leader wanted to be master of every situation, just as he was already master of his brief.

Winston Churchill gave a warm greeting to Stalin before shaking hands with Roosevelt, who was already seated at the table in his wheelchair. 'In that position,' wrote Arthur Birse, 'with his broad shoulders and fine head, he had the appearance of a tall strong man, and it was only that chair which gave away his infirmity. He beamed on all around the table and looked very much like the kind, rich uncle paying a visit to his poorer relations.'[11]

Bohlen was impressed by Stalin's qualities as a negotiator. The Soviet leader was confident and artful in the way he spoke. There was a subtlety to his performance that was lost on anyone not fluent in Russian.

'Stalin used phrases like "in my opinion", "I could be wrong, but I think", and "I believe", with no hint of the arbitrary dictator,' said Bohlen. But he only used such accommodating language when dealing with his Western partners. 'With Russians he never smiled and was rough and abusive in his language.'

On one occasion, Bohlen approached Stalin from behind with a request from Roosevelt. 'Without turning, he snarled, "For God's sake, allow us to finish this work." Then he turned and saw that the interruption came not from a Russian but from an emissary of the President of the United States. This was the only time I ever saw Stalin embarrassed.'[12]

Roosevelt's performance during that first session was less impressive than Stalin's, but those observing felt it was nonetheless satisfactory. He repeatedly removed his pince-nez in order to emphasise what he was saying, and he 'spoke firmly, as if sure of his ground'. He was always ready to listen to suggestions from his advisers.

Churchill was the least accommodating of the three. Grumpy on account of a sore throat, he feared that Roosevelt and Stalin were going to take sides against him. When Sir Charles Wilson spoke to him at the end of the session, he was very downbeat. '[I] asked him outright whether anything had gone wrong. He answered shortly: "A bloody lot has gone wrong." '[13]

The conference soon settled into a routine, with plenary sessions every afternoon and a dinner each evening. At Roosevelt's insistence there was no formal agenda, and the discussions were wide-ranging. The three leaders spoke about the future of Germany, Poland, and France, and also of the Far East and Japan. In addition, there were discussions around the vexed issue of the Second Front, with Stalin pressing for a specific date. Recent setbacks on the battle-front had convinced him of the need for Operation Overlord in the near future.

Churchill spoke enthusiastically of operations in the Mediterranean but did his best to avoid the subject of Overlord. Stalin's response was to lean forward in his chair and ask the prime minister an awkward question. 'Do the British really believe in Overlord,' he said, 'or are you only saying so to reassure the Russians?'

Churchill glowered and told Stalin it was the duty of the British government 'to hurl every scrap of strength across the Channel', but only when conditions were right.[14] The Soviet leader next asked who was to command Overlord, another tricky question. Roosevelt said that no commander had yet been appointed, an answer that disappointed Stalin. 'He made it plain that until the Supreme Commander was announced, he could not take seriously the promise of a cross-channel invasion.'[15] He also demanded a date. 'I don't care if it is the 1st, 15th or 20th,' he said tersely, 'but a definite date is important.'[16]

Churchill continued to prevaricate when talking about Operation Overlord, but much was happening behind the scenes. Harry Hopkins paid a private visit to the prime minister and told him of the American determination to launch Overlord the following spring. He added that Roosevelt refused to be deflected and advised the prime minister 'to yield with grace'.[17]

Churchill's response to Hopkins's advice was a masterclass in bravado. At the next plenary session, he informed the conference delegates that he had some good news to announce: the great offensive against Hitler would be launched no later than the following May. Archie was astonished by the PM's performance: 'The Prime Minister proceeded to read these decisions, which he had opposed to the very last, as if they were his own chosen strategy. It is at such moments that you get a whiff of greatness from this strange creature.'[18]

In private, Churchill was dismayed by the manner in which Roosevelt and Stalin were setting the agenda. 'There I sat with the great Russian bear on one side of me, with paws outstretched, and on the other side the great American buffalo, and between the two sat the poor little English donkey.'[19]

To many of those attending that Big Three conference, the human dynamics between the wartime leaders made for compelling viewing. Their ever-shifting relationships were at their most visible at mealtimes when they ate together.

The first of these dinners ended in spectacular fashion when Roosevelt was taken ill after eating a steak-and-potato dinner prepared by his Filipino mess boys. Bohlen was watching him when he noticed an alarming transformation. 'In the flick of an eye, he turned green and great drops of sweat began to bead off his face; he put a shaky hand to his forehead.'[20] Some in the room feared he had been poisoned. The president was wheeled back to his room and examined by his personal physician, who was adamant that it was merely an attack of indigestion.

At the following day's luncheon it was flatulence, not indigestion, that caught everyone's attention. One member of the lunch party broke wind in quite spectacular fashion, causing Archie to chortle loudly. Churchill sternly admonished him. 'Do not let the heat imparted by someone else's buttocks detract you from the discipline of a solemn matter.'[21]

Stalin was in an obstreperous mood at the conference dinner he hosted, taking every possible opportunity to deride Churchill. He even mocked him for having failed to destroy the Bolsheviks after the First World War. 'I can't understand you at all,' he said caustically. 'In 1919 you were so keen to fight, and now you don't seem to be at all. What happened? Is it advancing age?'[22]

Archie was amused by how effective the Soviet leader was in needling the prime minister. 'In superb form,' he said. 'Pulling the PM's leg all the evening.'

At one point Stalin declared that he wanted a bloodbath of German officers after the war. 'Fifty thousand Germans must be killed. Their General Staff must go.'[23] Archie thought he was merely making mischief, but Churchill took his words at face value. 'I will not be a party to any butchery in cold blood,' he fumed, jumping to his feet in outrage. 'I would rather be taken out into the garden here and now and be shot myself than sully my own and my country's honour by such infamy.'[24]

President Roosevelt shocked many by brazenly siding with Stalin. 'I have a compromise to propose,' he said mockingly. 'Not fifty thousand, but only forty-nine thousand should be shot.' Churchill was so disgusted that he stormed out of the room.

It was a taunt that risked ending in disaster. Even Stalin feared he had overstepped the mark and scurried after the prime minister, saying that his comment was intended as a joke. The two leaders eventually came back into the room together, 'Stalin with a broad grin on his face'.[25]

The interpreter, Charles Bohlen, thought it one more example of an unfortunate misunderstanding. 'To this day there are those who believe that Stalin was serious when he suggested that some 50,000 or possibly 100,000 German military officers should be liquidated. Actually, Stalin made the remark in quasi-jocular fashion, with a sardonic smile and wave of the hand, and meant this as a gibe at Churchill.'

Bohlen was particularly disappointed by Roosevelt's response. 'I did not like the attitude of the President, who not only backed Stalin but seemed to enjoy the Churchill-Stalin exchanges. Roosevelt should have come to the defense of a close friend and ally, who was really being put upon by Stalin. In his rather transparent attempt to dissociate himself from Churchill, the President was not fooling anybody and, in all probability, aroused the secret amusement of Stalin.'[26]

But Churchill could also be adept in his relations with Stalin. On Monday, 29 November, he arranged for a unique and moving ceremony, the presentation to the Soviet leader of the Sword of Stalingrad, King George VI's gift 'to the steel-hearted citizens of Stalingrad'.[27]

The sword was a superb piece of craftsmanship with a four-foot blade of tempered steel. The hilt was silver and adorned with leopards' heads, while the scabbard was covered with crimson lambskin. The ceremony was held in the conference room of the Soviet Embassy, and everyone was present, including the Big Three.

Churchill and Stalin stood with their right hands in a salute as the band struck up 'The Internationale', followed by 'God Save the King'. A British lieutenant then handed the sword to Churchill, who addressed Stalin with a message from King George VI. Birse was standing close to the Soviet leader and saw that he had tears in his eyes. He was not the only one to remark on this unusual display of emotion. 'For the first time in my dealings with the USSR,' wrote Sir Charles Wilson, 'this hard-boiled Asiatic thawed and seemed to feel the emotions of ordinary people. For a moment, it seemed that we were meeting as friends.'[28]

As the conference entered its fourth and final day, there was widespread relief that the three leaders had come to an agreement on the most pressing issues. A date had been set for Operation Overlord, a welcome development, and Stalin had also agreed to join the war against Japan as soon as it was feasible. By the final evening, the mood of the conference had been transformed. Against all the odds, the Big Three had cemented a friendship of sorts.

The final dinner fell on Churchill's sixty-ninth birthday. The prime minister had previously said he would insist on only one thing in Teheran, 'which was that he should be allowed to give a dinner party on the 30th . . . He said he would get thoroughly drunk and be prepared to leave the following day.'[29]

The dinner was held at the British Legation, where security was paramount. 'The NKVD insisted on searching the British Legation from top to bottom,' wrote Churchill, 'looking behind every door and every cushion before Stalin appeared; and about fifty armed Russian policemen, under their own general, posted themselves near all the doors and windows.'[30]

President Roosevelt was beaming as he was wheeled in by his security staff and Stalin was also in a good mood. As he entered the room, he turned to Arthur Birse and asked what he should drink. A flummoxed Birse suggested a shot of whisky. 'He drank it neat, saying it was good, but he thought ordinary vodka was better.'[31]

The drinks reception was followed by a gala dinner, at which table etiquette was scrupulously observed. Birse felt that the Soviet leader looked nervous, as if daunted by the Old World formality of it all. 'Stalin, who sat uncomfortably on the edge of his chair, looked with anxiety at the display of different-sized knives and forks before him, turned to me and said: "This is a fine collection of cutlery! It is a problem which to use. You will have to tell me, and also when I can begin to eat. I am unused to your customs."'[32]

Kathy took photographs of the historic events she attended. Here, from her scrapbook, is a picture of Churchill's sixty-ninth birthday dinner at the Teheran Conference. Left to right: American interpreter Charles 'Chip' Bohlen, Roosevelt, Churchill, Uncle Joe (Stalin), and British interpreter Arthur Birse.

That night's banter was very different from the simmering resentment of the previous dinners. The PM toasted Roosevelt and Stalin in turn, drinking to 'Roosevelt the Man' and 'Stalin the Great'. Gushing with goodwill, and perhaps not entirely sober, he told Stalin that 'he would be ranked with the great heroes of Russian history'.[33]

President Roosevelt was the next to make a toast, speaking of his joy at being a close friend of the prime minister.

Stalin gave an altogether different address, aiming his generous compliments at Averell. 'He stressed the role of motors in this war, whose native land was the United States. He said that without the United States as a source of motors, this war would have been lost.'[34]

Churchill was by now so jovial that he told Stalin how the political complexion of Britain was becoming 'a trifle pinker'.[35] The Soviet leader welcomed this, saying it was a sign of good health. Churchill agreed, 'provided the process was not carried so far as to induce indigestion'.[36]

The festive dessert was wheeled in as soon as the speeches were over. It was a spectacular tower of ice cream, known locally as a 'Persian Lantern', and its base was a huge block of ice. The waiter serving this *chef-d'oeuvre* was listening rather too attentively to Stalin's speech and didn't realise that the tower was rapidly melting and had begun to tilt.

'By the time he reached Pavlov, the Russian interpreter, the laws of gravity could be denied no longer,' wrote General Ismay. 'The pudding descended like an avalanche on [Pavlov's] unfortunate head. In a moment, ice-cream was oozing out of his hair, his ears, his shirt, even his shoes.'

But Pavlov never once stopped translating. 'Mr Stalin says that the Red Army is worthy of the Soviet people . . .'[37]

The conference ended on Wednesday, 1 December, with a joint declaration focused on the future course of the war. Operation Overlord was scheduled for the following May and all three leaders agreed that Germany should be divided once the war was won. They also agreed that an international organisation should be established, with America, Great Britain, the Soviet Union, and China playing the role of global policemen.

The declaration contained a noteworthy phrase that committed the Big Three to 'the elimination of tyranny and slavery, oppression and intolerance'. Several delegates were surprised that Stalin should have signed such a statement, but Averell knew that the Soviet leader's view of tyranny was radically different from that of Churchill and Roosevelt. For Stalin, tyranny did not exist in the Soviet Union. 'It was capitalism exploiting the downtrodden.'[38]

As the three leaders prepared to leave Teheran, those on the sidelines evaluated their performance. There was widespread agreement that Roosevelt had been staggeringly naive. This was particularly apparent in his discussions about the future fate of the Baltic states, which Stalin was clearly intending to annex. Roosevelt proposed that the three states should hold plebiscites but added that he had no intention of intervening 'when the Red Army reoccupied these areas'.[39]

The president also said he did not wish to involve himself in the contentious issue of Poland's post-war government. There were some six to seven million Americans of Polish extraction, he told Stalin, and he did not wish to lose their votes. The Soviet leader assumed that Roosevelt was giving him carte blanche to intervene in Poland and went so far as to thank him for clarifying his position. Charles Bohlen was deeply shocked by what he was translating. 'A great mistake,' he wrote. 'Roosevelt dismayed me.'[40]

Bob Meiklejohn made considerable efforts to discover what had taken place at the private meetings between Roosevelt and Stalin. He was appalled to learn that the president had repeatedly undermined Churchill.

'It is sad and disillusioning to note how these private meetings were used by Roosevelt, in his conceited and naive quest to curry Stalin's trust and goodwill, to work against the interests of his other allies.' At one point, Roosevelt had even suggested that he and Stalin should thrash out a solution to the future of India, which was to be done without Churchill's involvement.

Most observers of the conference agreed that Stalin had been by far the most impressive performer. He knew what he wanted and was ruthless about getting it. As one commentator put it, 'Churchill employed all the debater's arts, the brilliant locutions and circumlocutions, of which he was a master . . . while Roosevelt sat in the middle, by common consent, the moderator, arbitrator and final authority.' But it was the third member of the Big Three who emerged as the clear victor: 'Stalin wielded his bludgeon with relentless indifference to all the dodges and feints of his practiced adversary.'[41]

The Soviet leader had captivated everyone. He had none of Churchill's rhetorical flourishes and never made rambling digressions like Roosevelt. 'He spoke extemporaneously,' noted Bohlen, 'doodling wolf heads on a pad with a red pencil and pausing considerately so that the interpreter could translate. He never showed any agitation and rarely gestured.'

Charles Bohlen jotted a note to Averell expressing his alarm about the post-war world if Stalin's conference goals were realised. 'The result would be that the Soviet Union would be the only important military and political force on the continent of Europe. The rest of Europe would be reduced to military and political impotence.'[42]

Averell agreed. Stalin looked set to be the only real winner of the Second World War.

29

Christmas in Moscow

By the end of 1943, the allies were on the offensive in every theatre of war. On the Eastern Front, the Red Army continued to advance after inflicting major defeats on the Wehrmacht around Orel and Kharkov. In the Mediterranean, the Western allies were rapidly advancing up the Italian mainland after their landings in Sicily. Their successes had led to the collapse of Mussolini's Fascist regime. There had also been significant victories in Southeast Asia, with major offensives in Burma and landings on many of the Japanese-occupied islands. Although the war was far from over, both Archie and the other Teheran delegates were confident that the Allied partnership was heading towards victory.

Archie had appeared as jovial as ever during his time in the Iranian capital. He had been genial company at the dinners and made typically risqué witticisms. No one would have known that he was in a state of emotional turmoil. This was because he had still received no news from his darling Tita, his 'rose in an icy climate'.

He had written scores of letters, always finding excuses to pen another missive. One of these letters was prompted by news that the American government was considering rationing basic supplies. 'I hope, darling, that rationing or no rationing, there will still be enough red meat for you to get those pretty teeth of yours into.'[1] His correspondence was to no avail. Tita never replied.

Now, in the aftermath of the Teheran Conference, Archie decided to act. Instead of returning directly to Moscow, he made a whistle-stop trip to New York – flying via Cairo, Algiers, and Puerto Rico. If Tita would not answer his letters from Moscow, then he would go to New York and find out why.

He arrived in the city shortly before Christmas, and soon discovered that his hope of reviving their marriage was futile. Tita at first refused to meet him at all. She later relented but only on condition that another person be present. Even then, she showed no desire to repair their relationship.

Did she know about rumours, never fully substantiated, that Archie had been having an affair with Chiang Kai-shek's wife during his time in China? Had she overheard gossip about his being bisexual? Or did the problem lie with her? A long time later she would write him a letter explaining that she had been suffering from some sort of malaise. 'I've been a little sick, both mentally and physically . . . I have had such a lot of headaches, such a lot of worries and upsets that finally my doctor decided the best thing was to put me in a nursing home . . . I believe it is called a nervous breakdown.'[2]

Whatever the truth, there was to be no repairing their marriage for the foreseeable future, and Archie returned to Moscow lonelier than he had ever been. 'A nervous wreck,' wrote embassy staffer Thomas Barman.[3]

Tita, it seemed, had been lost for ever.

Back in Moscow, Kathy started to notice big changes taking place whenever she ventured outside. 'There's a lot of superficial bomb-damage repair going on day and night,' she wrote. 'Camouflage is being taken off, which in view of the supposed shortage of materials and labor, seems strange. It's all apparently just part of the general "Victory is in Sight" program to bolster morale.'[4]

Victory was indeed in sight, a development that had lifted everyone's spirits. But the smiles at the Teheran Conference had been concealing an altogether more devious battle that was already under way: the battle to win the peace.

PART VI

Darkness and Light

January–August 1944

30
Into the Forest

On Thursday, 20 January 1944, a group of reporters was meeting with Averell at the American Embassy when there was a phone call from the Soviet Foreign Ministry. The ministry was organising a press trip to Katyn Forest, on the eastern bank of the River Dnieper, to show reporters the mass graves of Polish officers found in the wake of the Wehrmacht's retreat. The Soviets claimed to have evidence that the Nazis had committed this atrocity, thereby disproving the allegation that it had been perpetrated by the NKVD.

The selected reporters were told they would be travelling by automobile and that each individual should bring enough food for three days. But this was changed as soon as Kathy requested to accompany the trip, a request accepted with alacrity by the Soviet Foreign Ministry. As daughter of the American ambassador, she warranted first-class treatment. The authorities shelved the plan to travel by car and organised, instead, a four-carriage wagon-lit train that was warm, well lit, and stocked with food and drink. 'Everything was superswell,' wrote Kathy. 'I don't think even Averell could have gotten more for nothing.'[1]

The reporters were delighted to be accorded such regal treatment. 'One of the most plush outfits I saw in Russia,' wrote William Lawrence of the *New York Times*. 'The newspapermen were delighted with the results of Miss Harriman's presence.'[2] The train even had a cheerful dining car newly decorated in pastel green.

The press group left Moscow Station on Friday, 21 January, for the 130-mile journey to Smolensk, the nearest city to Katyn Forest. 'Our speed at best was not more than 30 mph,' wrote Kathy, 'and we spent hours in various sidings while priority supply trains passed en route for the front.' The journalists kept themselves amused by playing cards.

As they drew in to Smolensk Station the following morning, they found a city of ghosts. 'The railroad yards in Smolensk were a complete shambles only having been rebuilt enough to keep operations going.' So wrote John Melby, second secretary at the American Embassy, who had joined the trip.

The group were met by a guide and given a walking tour of the city's ruins. 'Compared to bombed English towns, it gave the feeling of being completely dead and deserted,' wrote Kathy. She was told that just sixty-four buildings in the city were habitable, while 8,000 were in total rubble. Every bridge over the River Dnieper had been blown up, and the city's infrastructure had been dynamited by the retreating Germans.

When the guide launched into a dull monologue about Smolensk's Lenin Library, Kathy and one of the Russian-speaking journalists slipped away and headed to the market, where they interviewed a few of the locals who had survived the horror of the previous two years.

'We discovered that during the German occupation those who worked got 200 grammes of bread a day; those who didn't work, and children, got only 75 grammes, which is sort of starvation ration. They told us that the Germans took everything of any value away with them and destroyed the rest and killed thousands of people.'

This had been the work of Hitler's paramilitary death squads, the SS *Einsatzgruppen*, whose diabolical task was to liquidate entire communities – especially of Jews – in the territories conquered by the Wehrmacht.

Kathy eventually rejoined the group and was introduced to a local official who called himself the Secretary of the Special Commission to Establish and Investigate the Circumstances of the Shooting by the German Fascist Invaders of Captive Polish Officers in the Katyn Forest. Despite this heavily weighted title, he claimed to be an impartial judge of what had taken place.

A fleet of vehicles took the press group ten miles west of Smolensk, along the ruined Vitebsk highway. When they arrived, a large group of photographers was waiting for them. Most of the cameras were focused on Kathy, immaculately dressed in plaid skirt, orange pullover, and her trademark red nail varnish. The journalists were introduced to the surgeon in charge of examining the exhumed Polish corpses. Seven hundred had already been dug from the high ground above the River Dnieper and he estimated another twelve to fifteen thousand remained buried in the soft, sandy loam.

After this short introduction, Kathy and the others were led into the forest. A light snow began to fall, powdering the birch trees and pines and settling on the mounds of frozen earth.

'Katyn Forest turned out to be a small, measly-treed pine wood,' wrote Kathy. 'We were shown the works by a big-bug Soviet doctor who looked like a chef, in white peaked cap, white apron and rubber gloves.' This was Dr Victor Prozorovsky, senior medical expert on the Atrocity Commission. Black-haired and of medium height, he had a sharp goatee.

Dr Prozorovsky led them to the excavated graves, some twenty-five-foot square in size. 'We must have seen a good many thousand corpses,' wrote Kathy, 'or parts of corpses, all in varying stages of decomposition, but smelling about as bad.' They smelled of rotting meat and old drains, pungent and deeply unpleasant. 'Luckily, I had a cold, so was less bothered by the stench than others.'

The *New York Times* reporter was impressed by Kathy's fortitude. 'It was the first time Miss Harriman had seen mass graves, but she didn't flinch . . . [she] joined the reporters in taking notes.'[3]

The bodies were partially frozen, mildewed, and clad in faded grey-blue uniforms with tarnished brass buttons. The Polish eagle was still recognisable on many of them. Kathy noted that some of the bodies had been buried with care, 'laid in neat orderly rows, from six to eight bodies deep'. But others looked to have been buried in haste, 'tossed in every which way'. The manner of execution had been the same for each one. 'Every Pole had been shot thru the back of the head with a single bullet [and] some of the bodies had their hands behind their backs.'

The tour through the forest was stomach-churning, but it was just the beginning of what was to prove a grimly memorable day. 'Next on the program, we were taken into the post-mortem tents,' wrote Kathy. This was an ordeal for everyone, for the stench of rotting corpses was overpowering inside the heated canvas shelters. 'They were hot and stuffy and smelled to high heaven.' Hundreds of rotting corpses, severed heads, and dismembered limbs were stacked up on trestles and benches.

One of the journalists, Richard Lauterbach, wrote a striking description of the scene: 'Dr Prozorovsky ripped open a corpse numbered 808, sliced chunks off the brain like cold meat, knifed through the chest and pulled out an atrophied organ. "Heart", he said, holding it out to Kathy. Then he slit a leg muscle. "Look how well preserved the meat is."' He explained that the loamy soil had slowed the rate of decomposition.

Kathy was curious and couldn't help taking a closer look at the cadavers. 'I was amazed at how whole the corpses were,' she wrote. 'Most still had hair. Even I could recognize their internal organs and they still had a goodly quantity of red-colored "firm" meat on their thighs – attractive, isn't it! The internal organs, though considerably flattened and shrunken, were only partly decayed and the liver and spleen were green.'

The eleven Soviet experts working on the post-mortems said they were undertaking 160 each day. They said the decomposition was consistent with corpses that had been in the ground since the summer of 1941, when the Germans were in control of Katyn Forest.

'So ended the first section of the tour,' wrote Kathy. 'All feeling as though our clothes still retained the smell, we trooped back to our train for a hearty meal.' They were then taken back into Smolensk for a meeting with the Atrocity Commission, which had been examining the evidence collected by Dr Prozorovsky and his team.

The commission's members included distinguished personalities whose presence was clearly intended to give an air of authority to the proceedings. Among them were Metropolitan Nikolai of Kiev, a senior church hierarch, and Alexei Tolstoy, a well-known novelist and relative of Leo Tolstoy. But neither they nor any of the others had any expertise in evaluating the evidence of atrocities.

Kathy kept detailed notes of everything they saw and heard that afternoon. 'The committee room was warm and stuffy and I was very sleepy. Being scared of falling asleep, I kept verbatim notes – and thus kept from disgracing myself.'

Among the several witnesses she met was a young woman named Anna Alexeyeva, a tall, sharp-featured brunette with hair styled into a boyish bob. Miss Alexeyeva nervously explained how she and a few other locals had been hired as servants for the thirty German officers stationed in a nearby dacha.

Speaking rapidly but fluently, she gave a vivid testimony of what she claimed to have witnessed. 'Towards the end of August 1941,' she told Kathy, 'she and the other girls noted that cars and trucks could be heard turning off the highway at the Goat Hill entrance. When this happened, invariably the Germans in the dacha would go out into the forest. About ten minutes later, single shots, fired at regular intervals, would be heard.'

Alexeyeva said this routine happened on numerous occasions. 'Always on these days, the bath house water was heated. The men went directly to the baths and returned to be served a particularly tasty meal, plus double the usual hard liquor ration.' On one occasion, she said, 'she was asked to wash off fresh blood from one of the non-commissioned officers' sleeves.'

Kathy and the reporters heard from many witnesses that afternoon. The local Orthodox priest, Father Alexander Oblobin, described how his parishioners had seen groups of twenty to thirty Poles being led into the forest. The local burgomaster, Boris Bazilevsky, said he had been warned by a German collaborator that 'the Polish prisoners were going to be liquidated . . . liquidated in the most precise and literal meaning of the word.'

The group was even shown pages of old German notebooks containing written evidence of the atrocities. Yet more evidence was said to have been found in the pockets of the murdered Polish officers. 'One hundred and forty-six items have been found,' wrote Kathy. These were mainly letters, written in the summer of 1941, when the Germans controlled Katyn Forest.

The letters looked genuine enough. Kathy was shown one written by an officer named Kuchinski, and addressed to his wife, Irena. 'My dear little Sunbeam', it began, and instructed her to sell any of their belongings if she needed money to buy food.

'We were shown all these documents and trinkets and the most important and significant ones were translated for us. They included letters from Warsaw and Moscow dated in the winter of 1940, receipts for valuables dated in the spring of 1941, and numerous newspaper clippings dated from early 1940 through early 1941.' Most of the letters were written by left-leaning or Communist Polish officers. 'The Atrocity Commission inferred that the Polish prisoners-of-war had pro-Soviet rather than pro-Polish leanings.'

One sharp-eyed reporter noticed that many corpses were wearing fur-lined coats. He wanted to know why this was the case, given the Soviet claims that the massacre had taken place in midsummer. The Soviet experts had a ready reply. 'Nights were cold in Smolensk', they said, 'and the prisoners probably had no other outer garments.' Journalist Richard Lauterbach allowed himself a wry smile. 'A none too convincing reply,' he noted.

The purpose of the press trip was to convince Kathy and the reporters that the Germans – not the Soviets – had murdered the Poles in Katyn Forest. But determining who was guilty was not easy, as Kathy explained in her report on the visit. 'As no member [of the press group] was in a position to evaluate the scientific evidence given, it had to be accepted at face value.' Nor could the testimonial evidence be corroborated. 'We were expected to accept the statements of the high-ranking Soviet officials as true, because they said it was true.' They were also expected to accept that the documents found on the corpses were genuine.

Those Soviet officials had certainly put on a convincing show, and Kathy reluctantly concluded that the Germans had indeed committed the Katyn Forest massacre. 'It is my opinion that the Poles were murdered by the Germans,' she wrote.

The journalists agreed. 'As far as most of us were concerned,' wrote Richard Lauterbach, 'the Germans had slaughtered the Poles.' Even John Melby, the diplomat from the American Embassy, concurred with this assessment. 'On balance, and despite loopholes, the Russian case is convincing.'

What no one yet knew was that Stalin himself had ordered the massacre in March 1940 and that it had been undertaken in the greatest secrecy by officers of the NKVD. The chief executioner, Vasily Blokhin, had personally shot 7,000 prisoners, earning him the dubious reputation of being the most prolific official executioner in history.

The ensuing cover-up was elaborate. All the documents shown to Kathy and the journalists – the diaries, handwritten notes, and letters to loved ones – were fake. They had been planted in the jacket pockets of the corpses as 'evidence' that the Nazis had committed the atrocity.

The conclusions of the journalists, though wrong, suited both the Soviets and their Western partners. The British and Americans were frantically trying to restore diplomatic relations between Moscow and the Polish government-in-exile in London. The very last thing they wanted was a rift over the mass graves in Katyn Forest.

Many in Washington and Whitehall remained convinced that the Soviets had committed the atrocity and felt deeply uncomfortable at having to collude in Stalin's crimes in order to keep the Allied relationship on track. Such collusion seemed unsustainable over the long term. At some point, the West's marriage of convenience with the Soviet leader looked certain to end in divorce. And divorce would inevitably lead to an angry wrangle over who got what from the lucrative spoils of war.

31

Behind the Soviet Curtain

STALIN'S SOVIET UNION had always been secretive, and few westerners had ever been allowed to see behind the scenes. But the Allied wartime relationship with the country was changing all that: by the beginning of 1944, the doors to the regime stood ajar, and Kathy's work at the Office of War Information allowed her a unique glimpse behind the Soviet curtain.

She continued to marvel at her fellow Americans' lack of curiosity about life in the Soviet Union. Bob Meiklejohn was particularly uninterested. 'Dear Bob, I've gotten very fond of him,' wrote Kathy. 'Unfortunately he doesn't have enough initiative to go sightseeing. He'll probably leave Moscow without seeing anything of the town at all – gathering statistics about the place is all he seems interested in.' She teased him mercilessly about his obsessive note taking. 'He loves life only when it's ordered and to schedule.'[1]

Kathy had been forbidden from becoming acquainted with any local Muscovites during her first months in the country. 'It's sort of sad that we can't really get to know any Russians informally,' she had written to her sister soon after arriving. But her work inevitably brought her into contact with local officials and her increasing fluency in Russian enabled her to communicate without an interpreter.

The greatest change came with the newly warm relations between the Soviet regime and the West. As news from the battle-front grew evermore optimistic, Kathy was allowed to mix with locals in a way that would have been unthinkable two years earlier.

She jumped at the opportunity to meet distinguished intellectuals, aware that she was being given a once-in-a-lifetime chance to gather information on the private lives of the Soviet elite. When her father staged a screening of *Casablanca* at Spaso House, Kathy invited Alexei

Tolstoy. She had heard a great deal about this chimerical individual and was delighted, finally, to meet him. 'An enormous roly-poly man, about sixty, with long hair on the sides but bald on top. He prides himself as being "the most glorious drunk" in Russia and he certainly is a very pleasant one.'[2]

He was also disreputable. In his earlier years, Tolstoy had been an outspoken critic of the Bolshevik regime, living in exile in Paris and penning vitriolic diatribes against the country's new rulers. But he missed the motherland and began planning his homecoming. 'His longing for Russia got the better of him and he returned,' wrote Averell after chatting with him at the screening of *Casablanca*. 'He said that he got along with the authorities because he wrote within the prescribed limits. In the historical field, he found enough leeway to write without offending party sensibilities.'[3]

This was an understatement. Tolstoy wrote a string of fiercely pro-Soviet novels and plays that won him plaudits from the regime, especially when he laced them with anti-German propaganda. Feted by Stalin and showered with riches, he became known as the Red Count on account of his highly indulgent lifestyle.

'Alone among Russians, Tolstoy lived in baronial style in a rambling many-roomed mansion stocked with rich antiques,' wrote journalist Eugene Lyons, who had met him some years earlier. 'The whole atmosphere of ripe old-world culture seemed like a throwback to a nearly forgotten period.'[4] Tolstoy's wife – 'his fourth', noted Kathy – was the same age as her. 'Pretty, in a solid sort of way, and very earnest.'

Kathy never suspected that Tolstoy had helped to fabricate the Katyn evidence, writing fake Polish letters and documents in order to dupe the Western journalists into thinking the Germans had committed the atrocity. Nor did she realise he was as cynical as he was gifted. Tolstoy had placed his remarkable literary talents at the service of Stalin, and in return he lived a life of wine-soaked indulgence.

He never sought to hide his willingness to collaborate with the Soviet regime. Indeed, he told Kathy (in fluent French) that it was characteristic of the Russian soul: 'An idealist and, at the same time, a complete scoundrel when dealing with everyday life.' He warned her that such a mix was peculiarly Russian, and familiar to anyone acquainted with the novels of Dostoyevsky. Averell found him a most interesting character – witty, urbane, and charming. Like Kathy, he never suspected him of being a manipulator of the truth.

What made Tolstoy so unusual was his candour when talking about the Soviet regime: 'To understand the Kremlin today', he said, 'you must understand the Kremlin of Ivan the Terrible and Peter the Great.' He went on to explain how 'terror in the Kremlin did not begin with Stalin, nor was it the Communist Party that initiated the suspicion of foreigners and foreign ideas.' Russia had long been a brutal and inward-looking country.

Tolstoy enjoyed Averell and Kathy's company as much as they enjoyed his. A week after the *Casablanca* screening, he reciprocated their hospitality by inviting them both to his country residence. 'Our first unofficial Russian dinner party,' noted Kathy, 'and quite an event.'

The old wooden dacha was half an hour from Moscow and seemed like a throwback to tsarist Russia. 'Shostakovich and his wife were there, a very nice theater director, an architect and another couple.' There was also Tolstoy's secretary, who spoke excellent English and acted as interpreter.

Tolstoy first gave them a tour of the house. The rooms were large and furnished with the latest accessories. 'Very swell,' wrote Kathy. 'It was given to him by the government about ten years ago as a reward for a book he wrote – the last of a trilogy – in which he saw the light.' *The Road to Calvary* had so impressed the Soviet authorities that he had been awarded the Stalin Prize.

Kathy had a long conversation with Dmitri Shostakovich over the pre-dinner cocktails. 'He looked about twenty-one years old (he's over thirty) with very heavy glasses and more concentrated nervousness than I've ever seen in any man. He continually wiped his face, rattled his fingers or squinted his eyes.' She liked him, 'but very definitely an introverted genius type. For instance, a couple of times he suddenly got up and went and sat alone on the stairs, for no particular reason that I could see.' His wife stood meekly in his shadow, 'a young little thing, and like a goodly number of Russian gals, didn't look too clean'.

Cocktails were followed by a two-hour dinner. 'Hors d'oeuvres alone, in quantity, were equal to a big meal by our standards. And after them came a special meat-and-cabbage pastry, soup, fish, and finally a huge roast pork with vegetables; and finally ice cream.'

There were endless toasts, 'mostly sentimental in variety', and the party grew increasingly merry. The exception was Shostakovich, who drank heavily and became increasingly maudlin at the thought of having to perform on the piano. 'He decided he didn't feel like playing for us after dinner – something I didn't blame him for in the least – but finally he did; part of a concerto, second movement of his eighth.* I can't say I get anything out of his things (my loss) and his eighth is worse than the others.'

After this impromptu concert, the little party adjourned upstairs for coffee and brandy. Tolstoy was thoroughly enjoying himself. 'He spent his time sitting or lying on the floor on his stomach' – which was huge – 'expounding on any subject that happened to come into his mind. He really is a lovable soul.'

Kathy was particularly drawn to his secretary, a refined lady who had learned English from a governess when still a young child in pre-revolutionary Petrograd. 'A lovely person with a nice sense of humor and a complete lady – something very rare for us to have the privilege to see.' It made a refreshing change. 'It's really stupid that the only Russian girls I see are the girlfriends of the Americans. I don't mean to be snobbish, but it would be nice to get to know some gal who wasn't just one of the girls around town.'

As winter gave way to spring, the Soviet regime opened up yet further. Hitherto, many of Stalin's senior officials had only been glimpsed at banquets and parties. Now they stepped from the shadows. Among them was Alexander Poskrebyshev, head of Stalin's personal secretariat, who also served as his watchdog and messenger in chief.

Archie Clark Kerr and Arthur Birse first got acquainted with him on one of their many visits to the Kremlin. 'About five foot tall, tubby, with broad shoulders, a bent back and a large head, heavy jowl, long crooked nose, and eyes like those of a bird of prey.'[5] Poskrebyshev was always dressed in a khaki jacket with a high collar and long khaki trousers. He looked like a thug and had a reputation to match.

* She meant Shostakovich's eighth symphony.

'According to local gossip', said Birse, 'he was the dreaded rod in Stalin's hands that carried into effect the more ferocious comments of the master. No one was allowed to enter Stalin's room without first passing this man's scrutiny.'[6] Meeting him gave Archie a glimpse into the malevolent hinterland of the Kremlin, staffed by a small army of criminal bruisers. Outwardly courteous and even charming, they were driven by a deep-seated fear of Stalin. Kathy said they all fell into one of two categories: 'The educated fine-looking variety – usually with tiny beards and all in uniform – and the big fat sinister type, with pig eyes and pince nez.'[7]

Another open door led to the offices of Anastas Mikoyan, the Armenian-born commissar for foreign trade, whose trademark black moustache made him an instantly recognisable figure among the Soviet elite. Mikoyan was in charge of negotiating all the weaponry, machinery, vehicles, food, and medicines being brought in from the United States. He was also overseeing the delivery of these supplies to the Soviet Union, via Iran, Murmansk, Archangel, and the Pacific port of Vladivostok. This required him to meet Averell and Archie on a regular basis.

In 1943 (including the early months of 1944), Averell had orchestrated the delivery of six million tons of supplies from America. Britain was also delivering large quantities. Between June 1941 and spring 1944, more than a million tons had been shipped, including 5,800 planes and 4,300 tanks.

Archie had met Mikoyan at many of the drunken Kremlin dinners and had come to know him well. Now he introduced others to this wily negotiator extraordinaire. 'He had all the *savoir-faire* of a super salesman,' wrote the embassy's first secretary, Thomas Barman. 'He could have made a highly successful career for himself in any country, under any kind of social system. He could have made a fortune as a Wall Street operator; or as a manipulator of markets; or as a commercial traveller. He was a superb fixer . . . but always, it seems, a lone wolf.'[8]

The most sinister of Stalin's henchmen was also the most secretive: Lavrentiy Beria was the rotund and bespectacled head of the NKVD. Archie had met him at several Kremlin banquets and found him deeply malignant. Beria had been the architect of the Katyn Forest massacre and had also undertaken the bloody Red Army purge which had ended just months before the German invasion. Sexually depraved, he was a serial rapist who was said to kill the women who refused to submit to his depredations.*

Beria kept a distance from the British and Americans in Moscow, with one notable exception. George Hill had been sent from London as a representative of the Special Operations Executive (SOE), the clandestine guerrilla outfit tasked with operating behind enemy lines. His job was to liaise with Soviet guerrilla commanders.

Hill's lodging happened to be just a few doors away from that of Commissar Beria and it was not long before their paths crossed. 'Returning from my afternoon walk I saw, coming out of the gates of the next house but one to mine, six NKVD soldiers with Tommy guns at the ready. They spread out to each pavement, walking in file, with about three yards between them. Then came the People's Commissar of the Interior, Lavrentiy Beria, who lives in the villa, well away from the street, in a cage of barbed wire.'

Hill found him unremarkable. 'He wore a black fur cap, black leather coat, black jackboots, and had his hands deep in the coat pockets. A plump, small, dark, bespectacled creature, with a sallow complexion and sullen countenance. Following him were a further six guards with Tommy guns, who similarly spread out in file behind Beria. Lordy! Twelve armed bandits to guard one commissar taking an afternoon stroll.'[9]

One of Hill's missions was to open a dialogue with the NKVD, for it had been suggested that SOE and NKVD agents might run joint operations behind enemy lines. It was only natural, therefore, that he should meet Commissar Beria. This was eventually arranged by a senior NKVD official named General Ossipov, who drove Hill to Beria's Lubyanka headquarters.

It was an extraordinary moment for Hill. Twenty-five years earlier, he had been working as an undercover British spy in post-revolutionary Russia. Operating under the *nom de guerre* Georg Bergmann and posing

* When plumbers installed water pipes in the garden of Beria's former villa in 1998 (by then the Tunisian Embassy), they unearthed the remains of five young women.

as a Baltic businessman, he lived incognito for many months as he gathered intelligence on the new regime. He was hunted by the authorities and had a price of 50,000 roubles on his head, but he always kept one step ahead and eventually slipped out of the country unseen. Now he was back, only this time he was working with the Russians rather than against them.*

He was led through endless corridors of the Lubyanka building towards a large double door guarded by two NKVD officers, both carrying Tommy guns. He was then escorted into an anteroom, where he was met by an NKVD colonel who took him into Beria's private study. 'A large room, thickly carpeted, with heavy curtains at the three big windows. The walls were bare, except for an enormous framed painting of Stalin in uniform, about life-size; a conventional, rather flattering portrait.

'Beria rose from his desk as we came in and, having greeted us, motioned to the easy chairs and we sat down. We talked trivialities suitable for the occasion. I found Beria's Russian slurred and very guttural, with odd turns of phrase.'

Beria became suddenly alive when Hill told him that he had known Lenin in 1918, prior to his work as a spy. 'For a few moments he was really animated, and his sallow sour looks seemed to vanish.' The meeting became more convivial. 'After a few minutes a Mongolian-faced orderly, with a pistol on his belt, brought in a tray with glasses of hot tea, Caucasian brandy and Russian liqueurs.'

As Hill sipped the hot tea, he grew less and less impressed by Beria. 'He was badly briefed, he knew little about the SOE-NKVD set up, and he did not know the name of my opposite NKVD number in London.' But he did ask a lot of questions. 'I was quizzed on poisons and silent firearms. How silent could an automatic pistol really be? Knowing a good deal about both subjects, and not wanting to be drawn, I gave noncommittal, vague answers.'

At one point Beria, without warning, turned menacing, asking Hill if SOE would help to drop NKVD agents behind enemy lines. 'As he put the question, all his ruthlessness came to the fore, and I

* The story of George Hill's undercover adventures in post-revolutionary Russia is recounted in the author's book, *Russian Roulette* (2013).

realised the power that he had within him. A power that has brought him to, and kept him at, the top.'

Hill thought him a personification of the darkness at the heart of the Soviet regime. 'The more I saw of him, the less I liked him,' he said. 'An evil sinister creature.'[10] He was increasingly disturbed by the idea of being allies of such odious individuals and foresaw a world of future troubles. If and when the rupture finally came, it was likely to be violent.

32

Sunshine in Moscow

Soviet forces made huge advances in the early months of 1944. In January they broke the 900-day siege of Leningrad, whose emaciated citizens had suffered appalling deprivation. Some 800,000 had died of hypothermia and starvation, and the city's infrastructure had sustained serious damage, but this was nevertheless a moment to be savoured. A celebratory 324-gun salute was fired in honour of the historic victory.

The Red Army followed up this success with a major military offensive that sent the Wehrmacht into retreat all along the Baltic Front, abandoning enormous quantities of munitions and equipment. In February and March, Marshal Ivan Konev's troops were equally successful in Ukraine, encircling several large German divisions at Korsun-Cherkasy. Victory followed victory that spring. By the first week of April, triumphant Soviet troops had crossed the Bug, Dniester, and Prut rivers and were advancing headlong into Romania.

Moscow announced that the River Prut marked the frontier between the Soviet Union and Romania. The significance of this official statement was lost on no one: it meant that Stalin now considered Bessarabia and Bukovina, first seized by the Red Army in the summer of 1940, to be Soviet territory. Averell was shocked by the Soviet leader's newly assertive policy, noting that it was 'startling in its aggressiveness, determination and readiness to take independent action'.[1] He feared for the future.

Whenever Averell saw Stalin in the Kremlin, he found him in the best possible humour. Indeed, the Soviet leader did everything possible to be conciliatory. One of their most important discussions concerned the possibility of American bombers using Soviet air bases, an issue first raised at the Teheran Conference. This was deemed essential if daylight bombing raids on Germany were to be increased. Averell reminded Stalin that the loss of planes and crews would be greatly reduced if they were allowed to fly onwards to Soviet bases after their raids, rather than heading back to England through swarms of German fighters.

Many of the discussions between Averell and Stalin were interpreted by the diminutive Vladimir Pavlov (second right). On the left is Mikhail Kalinin, the semi-senile official head of state.

Stalin had previously refused to permit American planes to land and refuel on Soviet soil, a refusal that had cost many hundreds of American lives. But he was now more amenable, asking Averell how many planes he was envisaging. Averell suggested 360, flying in three formations of 120 each.

Stalin asked if the Soviets would have to supply the fuel.

'No,' said Averell. 'Fuel, bombs and spare parts would be supplied by the United States.'

'What about ground crews?' Stalin wanted to know if they would be American or Russian.

'A number of Americans would have to be brought in,' said Averell. 'Men who were specialists in servicing the B-17 and B-24 bombers.'[2]

Stalin even asked about the octane rating of the fuel needed for the bombers, a grasp of detail that came as no surprise to Averell. The Soviet leader then thought for a moment before giving his consent.

Bob Meiklejohn noticed that Averell was rather chirpy that evening. 'The ambassador came back to Spaso House as we were at dinner, looking like the cat that swallowed the mouse. In other words, things went well!'[3]

Within days, three airfields in Ukraine had been selected and a monumental logistical exercise was under way. Everything needed for the three air bases had to be shipped from America to Archangel, then transported by train to the bases – at Poltava, Mirgorod, and Pyryatin, all of which lay some fifty miles northwest of Kiev.

The airfields had been destroyed by the retreating Germans. There were no hangars, control towers, or maintenance facilities. In addition, the runways were too short and the concrete too thin. It took 534 freight cars to transport the 26,000 tons of supplies to the bases, including steel mat runways, aviation fuel, bombs, and aircraft spare parts.

Stalin had agreed to having 1,200 Americans stationed on Soviet soil, many of them specialist construction engineers. They were helped in their work by a small army of Russians, mainly women, who proved impressively tough when laying the runways. 'When they heard that American engineers habitually lay ten yards of matting per day, per man,' wrote one American officer, 'these great, brawny exuberant wenches went out and laid twelve.'[4] If all went to schedule, the first fleet of bombers was due to arrive on Friday, 2 June.

In the first week of May, Averell and Kathy flew to London for discussions with Churchill. Averell found the PM in anxious mood, 'oppressed by the dangers and disasters that could flow from Operation Overlord if the landings should fail'. Churchill was indeed torn by doubt. 'He told me that if Overlord failed, the United States would have lost a battle. But for the British, it would mean the end of their military capability.'[5] Averell and Kathy were among the few to have first-hand experience of this vulnerable side to Churchill. In public the prime minister was decisive, often bombastic, and always self-assured, but behind closed doors, he was a great deal more troubled.

Averell flew on to Washington for meetings with President Roosevelt before returning to London in the last week of May. He was relieved to find Churchill's mood completely transformed. 'Much better in spirit, and physically, than he was when I saw him several weeks ago. Although conscious of the risks, he is confident and determined. He speaks with respect and enthusiasm of Eisenhower and the other United States officers on the team.'[6]

The PM invited Averell and Kathy to Chequers for that last weekend in May, an offer they accepted with alacrity. 'I'm sitting in wonderful un-English sunshine,' wrote Kathy, 'watching Averell get beat at croquet by Mrs Churchill.' She was delighted to be back at Chequers, even though it was a flying visit. 'The PM is on fine form, as he always is when battles are raging well.'[7]

The two of them flew back to Moscow on 1 June, then took an onward flight to Poltava air base to see the arrival of the first American bombers. The transformation of the place was remarkable. Just a few weeks earlier it had been a bombed-out ruin. Now it was a fully functioning air base.

There was great excitement the following morning when it was announced that the American planes had left their bases in Italy and were now en route. This was a momentous chapter in America's relationship with the Soviet Union, the first time they stood side by side in a military operation. Those based at Poltava hoped it would bode well for the future.

'We were driving out to the field when the first bombers appeared as specks off in the horizon,' wrote Kathy. 'It looked like thousands, then suddenly the First Squadron was overhead with its welcome roar. Jesus – it was exciting; more so than anything I ever saw in England.'

Equally excited was General Aleksandr Perminov, the Soviet commander of Poltava. 'He bubbled over with joy and apparently started to throw his arms around Averell and kiss him, when he restrained himself and instead let out a few more Russian equivalents of cowboy hoots.'

Kathy caused a sensation wherever she went. Here she receives a large bouquet of flowers from General Perminov, Soviet commander of the American-run air base at Poltava.

It was indeed an exhilarating sight. 'The first three Fortresses were flying in a perfect V-shaped wedge,' wrote one observer. 'They were followed by seventy more, flying in perfect formation. They circled the field at an elevation of about 1,000 feet. The sky was filled with them, and huge as they were, they seemed much bigger with their silver wings silhouetted against the black sky above. For an American standing on the field below it was a thrill beyond description.'[8]

First on the ground was Lieutenant General Ira Eaker, whom Kathy had interviewed in London almost two years earlier. Eaker decorated General Perminov with the Legion of Merit and proudly introduced his American pilots. The Soviet commander responded by presenting Kathy with an enormous bunch of flowers. 'Most of all, the Russians were impressed by our bombers being in formation after a long bombing mission,' she wrote. 'Apparently, theirs never are, and they appreciated the skill of our pilots.'

Kathy felt that the day had been a triumphant success. 'All in all, the shuttle-bombing has made a great impression on them and it's certainly a big step forward to proving that – god dammit – we can all do a job of working together.'[9] She felt optimistic about the future.

Three days later, in Moscow, Archie received top-secret news that required an immediate four-word note to Stalin:

'We are off tonight.'[10]

D-Day was finally taking place.

33
D-Day

KATHY WAS AT Moscow airport on the morning of Tuesday, 6 June, when an American military aide rushed up to her with news of the Allied landings in Normandy. 'All hell broke loose in France!' she wrote later that day. 'Whoopee!' She rushed back to Spaso House and spent the morning listening to different radio broadcasts. 'Gosh it was exciting!'

That afternoon, she walked over to the Soviet Cultural Centre to discuss a photographic exhibition with Russian friends who worked there. They were ecstatic about news of the landings. 'We did little work that afternoon. Three of us – two Russians and me – consumed the better part of two bottles of cherry brandy – all drunk in toasts, bottoms up! I don't like having a hangover come 5 p.m., but that day it was worth it.'

Everyone was discussing the invasion and poring over the limited information available. 'My Russian friends said that their phones had been ringing all day – people swapping rumor-stories of where the landings were; how big, etcetera. They were all out in their enthusiasm, and being the first American they'd come across, I got the brunt of their hospitality.'[1]

Bob Meiklejohn was at Spaso House when he first heard the news announced on German radio. 'Early this morning, the expected Anglo-American invasion began when airborne forces were landed in the area of the Seine estuary . . . German naval forces are engaged in fighting with landing craft.'[2]

Was it true? Meiklejohn noted that none of the local staff at the embassy believed it, but he was later given confirmation by Averell. 'His nibs confirmed that this was the real thing.'

It was a good day to be American in Moscow, for the Soviets viewed them as the principal players on D-Day, with the British believed to be playing a smaller supporting role. The American Embassy's second secretary, Eddie Page, was eating in a newly opened restaurant when he found himself toasted by Russians he had never met. 'Are you an American?' he was asked. 'You're sure not British. Well then, sit down and have a drink with us!' Page later told Kathy he'd been treated like a celebrity. 'It's funny the way the public gives us complete credit for the invasion, not the British or Canadians. No one toasted them at all.'[3]

Averell first discussed the landings with Stalin during a two-hour meeting on the evening of Saturday, 10 June. He gave him an overview of the five-beach assault and explained how the Allied troops had succeeded in avoiding the underwater obstacles and mines by landing at low tide.

Stalin was filled with admiration at what had been achieved and told Averell that 'he considered the cross-channel operation unparalleled in history.' He used superlative after superlative. It was a 'grandiose operation' and 'an unheard-of achievement'. He personally inscribed a photograph of himself to President Roosevelt, writing, ' "From his friend", in honour of the occasion.' Obsessed with military strategy, he spoke at length about how the British and Americans should create a defendable beachhead on the Normandy coastline. 'He believed it was sufficient to seize eight kilometers in depth and then build up.'

More than anything else, he was delighted that the Second Front was finally under way. 'We are going along a good road,' he said. 'Napoleon himself never attempted it. Hitler envisaged it, but he was a fool for never having attempted it.'[4] Stalin viewed D-Day as one of the greatest military endeavours of all time.

Shortly after this meeting, an American colonel named Anatole Litvak flew in to Moscow, bringing with him several short films which had been shot from landing craft on D-Day itself. General Deane organised a screening for the Red Army General Staff. All were stunned by the scale of Operation Overlord. 'Their eyes were on their cheeks with amazement at the magnitude of the invasion,' wrote Deane. 'The pictures definitely changed their previous attitude, that crossing the English Channel was only a little more difficult than crossing the Volga.'[5]

Litvak had been a Hollywood director before the war. He was also of Russian origin and spoke the language fluently, to the delight of everyone at the screening. They wanted to know every detail of the landings.

'They sat around Litvak in a circle, like children, and plied him with questions,' wrote Kathy in a letter to Pamela Churchill. 'The Russians were spellbound.'

The uppermost question on her mind, and on everyone else's, was how long it would be before the Allied forces broke out of their Normandy beachhead and began heading for the German frontier. The capture of Berlin remained the ultimate prize for both the Soviets and the Western allies, but there was a real fear that Stalin's Red Army would reach the German capital before the Americans and British.

If that were to be the case, Stalin would be the master of Germany's destiny.

34
Poles Apart

MOSCOW WAS TRANSFORMED by the arrival of summer. The last heaps of slush finally melted and there was a welcome warmth in the air. Kathy's spirits were lifted by the sunshine. 'The trees and parks are green. The people are out of their sacking winter clothes and felt boots. Now they look more human – almost gay.'

Throughout the city, workmen were taking down the last of the huge canvas camouflage screens erected to disguise the most important buildings. It was a tangible sign that Moscow was now beyond the reach of the Luftwaffe. At the American Embassy and Spaso House, the shattered windows were finally being reglazed. 'Before there were no windows at all – just beaver-boarded blank holes. The downstairs hall now gets sunlight for the first time.'[1]

Relations between the Soviet regime and Averell were equally sunny. Just eight days after the Normandy landings – and in celebration of the second anniversary of the Lend-Lease Act granting American aid to the Soviet Union – Stalin's commissar for foreign trade, Anastas Mikoyan, sent generous gifts to Averell and Kathy. 'Mine was enough baby karakul (thirty sheepskins) for a size 40 coat. My fur expert friends say it's the cat's whiskers of karakul!'

Averell got an even more extravagant gift: a massive thousand-pound stuffed polar bear. 'The biggest thing I've ever seen,' wrote Kathy. 'It's so huge that it takes up nearly the entire floor-space of our upstairs sitting room. The skin's outlined with a frill of shocking pink felt. We figure it will be just the thing for Sun Valley.'[2]

More presents were offered in celebration of American Independence Day on Tuesday, 4 July: 'A huge bear rug, a fur coat, a piece of monstrosity china, a valuable ikon and an old silver box.' The latter was a gift from Kathy's Russian friends in the Society of Cultural Relations, with whom she liaised on a regular basis. They had inscribed the box, as she would later write, 'from friends who sincerely and earnestly love her' and had painted an American flag on the lid alongside the date. 'A nice touch, but they got the date wrong! It had 14 July painted instead!'[3]

Two parties were held to mark the Independence Day celebrations. While Averell hosted a celebratory luncheon at Spaso House for Molotov, Vyshinsky, and Archie, Kathy was in charge of festivities at the embassy dacha. She had invited more than 150 guests, all American, to the day-long party. It got off to a shaky start when the promised barrels of beer failed to arrive. 'I had to start people off drinking vodka punch', she wrote, 'which adds up to dynamite.'[4] It certainly got everyone in the party mood. They played baseball and swam in the nearby river and Kathy got the 'navy boys' to rig up a makeshift raft made of empty petrol canisters. Soon after, the beer finally arrived. There was a general feeling that life was changing for the better, with the Allies now sniffing at victory. Even the ever-present NKVD agents were in good humour, especially when offered beer by the embassy juniors.

The warm relations were not to last. Over the course of that summer, Averell and Archie were to find themselves in and out of the Kremlin as Stalin's goodwill began to dissipate.

A presage of the mounting tensions came on Tuesday, 12 July. The American Embassy's newly arrived electrician was checking the telephone switchboard when he made an unpleasant discovery: 'a connection through which the Soviets were recording all conversations to and from both the Embassy and the Military Mission'. Bob Meiklejohn was outraged. 'A hell of a way for allies to treat each other,' he wrote, 'but the Soviets don't know any better.' Averell was irritated but not surprised, telling Meiklejohn, 'If they expect really to play a part in world affairs, they will have sometime to learn to stop eating with their knives.'[5]

More serious than the eavesdropping was a radical change in Stalin's attitude towards the two ambassadors. The touchstone was Poland, a vital issue for each of the Big Three leaders. For Churchill, the Nazi invasion of Poland had been the *casus belli*. It was unthinkable for him to consider anything other than an independent and democratic post-war Poland.

Averell forged a close working relationship with Stalin, yet found it impossible to reconcile his charm and courtesy with his deviousness and murderous brutality.

Poland was an equally pressing concern for Roosevelt. The presidential election was fast approaching and between six and seven million Polish Americans were about to cast their votes. He needed their support if he was to be reelected.

Stalin's approach was dictated by military strategy. He viewed Poland as the country through which any would-be invader of the Soviet Union had to pass. He was determined to install a Soviet-friendly government. In heated arguments that summer, Archie and Averell gained troubling insight into Stalin's vision for the future. He seemed intent on dominating all the territories newly liberated by the Red Army. 'No argument was of any avail,' wrote Archie after one angry meeting. 'Not a pleasant talk.'[6]

Stalin was equally stubborn during his meetings with Averell. 'Again the Poles!' he growled during a particularly fractious meeting in the Kremlin. He said he could never trust a Polish government-in-exile that had blamed the Soviets (quite correctly) for the Katyn massacre. Nor did he trust any émigré Polish activists. He reached for a bulging briefcase on his desk and pulled out a six-month-old copy of *Niepodległość*, an underground Polish newspaper. The headline, in Polish, read 'Hitler and Stalin: Two Faces of the Same Evil'. Stalin told Averell it was impossible to deal with people who could produce such a rag.

The fate of Poland soon became a pressing issue, for the advancing Red Army was rapidly approaching the Polish frontier. Soviet troops captured Lubin on Sunday, 23 July. They took Brest-Litovsk three days later.

Averell's chief military adviser, General John Deane, had been allowed to accompany the Red Army as it swept westwards into Poland. 'Suddenly everything was going forward,' he said. 'When a truck broke down, the Russians would commandeer a team of horses or oxen, reload as much of the stuff as the wagons could hold, and move on. The Germans had broken. Their divisions had been obliterated by death or by capture. There was nothing to stop the Russians – until they hit the Vistula.'

Averell realised that unless the Americans and British acted quickly, the situation would be beyond their grasp. 'The solution to the Polish question', he said, 'would be a completely Soviet one.'

His fears were compounded by the revelation that Stalin had been holding secret meetings with a Moscow-based group of Poles known as the Polish National Council. They claimed to represent the interests of Poles inside Poland, unlike the London-based Polish government-in-exile. 'Living people,' said Stalin pointedly, 'not émigrés.'[7]

Archie made it his business to get to know these Moscow-based Poles, inviting their leading members to the British Embassy. 'The meeting took place in the ambassador's study in the fading light of a July evening,' wrote Arthur Birse, one of several interpreters working that night.

The president of the Polish National Council was Bolesław Bierut, an unsavoury Communist agent. 'I sat opposite Bierut, who did most of the talking,' wrote Birse. 'He looked comparatively young, was thickset and had an interesting lifeless face, neither good-looking nor ugly, with a cynical expression. His manner of speaking was that of an automaton repeating set phrases. I disliked his thick, cruel-looking hands.'

His comrade was Eduard Osubka-Morawski, a former journalist who shared Bierut's Communist beliefs. 'Ascetic and fanatical,' wrote Birse, 'and was inclined to be dramatic.' He also spoke incessantly. 'There was no means of stopping him.'

Both men told Archie a string of untruths about the London-based government-in-exile, claiming it was secretly working for Hitler. 'The boasting and half-truths were nauseating,' said Birse. 'The impression they made could not have been worse.'[8]

Both Archie and Averell warned their respective governments that Stalin was intent on installing the Polish National Council as the new pro-Soviet government of Poland. 'We will be faced with a fait accompli,' Averell told the State Department.[9] He received no answer.

The first Soviet forces reached the east bank of the River Vistula on Saturday, 29 July. They were now within sight of Warsaw. At 8.15 p.m. that same day, the population of Nazi-occupied Warsaw was encouraged to tune in to a broadcast on Radio Kosciusko, a Polish-language station based in Moscow. It was a message from the Stalin-backed Poles, and it called for an immediate uprising against the Nazis.

'The Germans will no doubt try to defend themselves in Warsaw and add new destruction and thousands of victims,' said the message. 'Our houses and our parks, our bridges and railway stations, our factories and public buildings will be turned into defence positions.' It was incumbent on every inhabitant of Warsaw to play their part in the uprising.

'All is lost that is not saved by active effort; that by direct, active struggle in the streets of Warsaw, in its houses, factories and stores, we not only hasten the moment of final liberation, but also save a nation's property and the lives of our brothers.' The broadcast ended with a rallying cry. 'Poles, the time of liberation is at hand! Poles, to arms! There is not a moment to lose!'[10]

The Moscow-based Poles were not alone in broadcasting a call to arms. The London-based Poles were also determined that the population of Warsaw should liberate their own capital and had instructed the commander of the underground Home Army, General Tadeusz Bór-Komorowski, to proclaim an uprising at the most propitious moment. With the Red Army on the east bank of the River Vistula, that moment seemed to have arrived. The reassuring boom of nearby Soviet guns only served to encourage Warsaw's inhabitants. The general assumption was that these Soviet soldiers would come to their aid, especially as Stalin had given his blessing to the broadcast of the Moscow-based Poles.

The uprising began at 5 p.m. on Tuesday, 1 August. General Bór-Komorowski had rallied a makeshift army of 35,000 Poles equipped with meagre supplies of weaponry and ammunition. They faced the 11,000-strong German garrison of Warsaw, commanded by General Rainer Stahel, with numerous other heavily armed units on standby. It was a very unequal contest.

The Polish forces fought heroically for the first few days of the uprising and made significant gains, driving the Germans from large parts of the city. Four battalions of Polish troops, fighting alongside the Soviets, managed to cross the River Vistula and establish a small bridgehead on the west bank. Led by the Polish commander, General Zygmunt Berling, they fought with steely determination.

On Friday, 4 August, the notorious SS commander General Erich von dem Bach was placed in charge of all German forces fighting against the uprising. The tide of battle began to turn as the Germans sent Tiger tanks into the streets to mow down the insurgents.

Archie and Averell were frequent visitors to the Kremlin in that first week of August, and they pressed Stalin to intervene. The Polish resistance urgently required weaponry and reinforcements, both of which were available on the east bank of the Vistula. But Stalin prevaricated for more than five days. On Wednesday, 9 August, he promised to drop a Soviet communications officer into Warsaw by parachute. This officer was to liaise with Polish underground leaders and plan an airdrop of supplies. But Stalin's promise never materialised.

As the situation inside Warsaw grew ever more desperate, the RAF attempted to drop munitions under the cover of darkness, using planes based in Italy. But most of these supplies missed their intended recipients and ended up in German hands. 'Forlorn and inadequate,' wrote a despondent Churchill when told of what had happened.[11]

On Monday, 14 August, Averell sent an urgent message to Molotov requesting Soviet approval for a massive American airdrop to Warsaw: he wanted to use the planes stationed at Poltava air base. Molotov didn't reply. Instead, Averell received a terse note from his deputy, Commissar Vyshinsky, refusing to let the Americans use any planes based on Soviet soil. He described the Warsaw uprising as 'a purely adventuristic affair to which the Soviet government could not lend its hand'.

The following day, Archie and Averell headed together to the Kremlin in the hope of seeing either Stalin or Molotov. Neither man was available. They were eventually taken to see Vyshinsky, whose continual refusal to help the Poles incensed the two ambassadors. They insisted on aid and supplies being given to the brave Polish fighters and added that Moscow's current stance would have serious ramifications in both London and Washington.

'The toughest talk I ever had with a Soviet official,' wrote Averell after the meeting. But it did little good. Vyshinsky astonished them by belittling the tumultuous events in Warsaw. 'Not worthy of assistance,' he said, before adding that 'the Soviet government does not wish to associate itself directly or indirectly with the adventure in Warsaw.'[12]

Not until Saturday, 23 September, did Stalin deign to see the two ambassadors. He was frank but nonchalant, admitting to have misjudged the motives of the Polish resistance. He claimed to have been inaccurately informed about the situation on the ground, despite the fact that both ambassadors had repeatedly warned of the desperate scenes taking place inside Warsaw.

'To me,' wrote Averell, 'nothing could excuse his outrageous denial of help for so very long.'[13] He displayed no contrition for his lack of action, claiming that the River Vistula was a huge obstacle that had halted the advance of the Red Army. 'It was impossible to get tanks across the river because of continual heavy German shelling, and it was difficult to carry on operations without tanks.' This may have been true, but the shelling had not prevented General Zygmunt Berling and his four Polish battalions from crossing the Vistula.

Averell didn't believe a word Stalin told him. 'I can only draw the conclusion that this action was taken out of ruthless political considerations, in order that the underground may get no credit for the liberation of Warsaw and that its leaders be killed by the Germans.'

He thought Stalin was delighted that so many Polish partisans had been slaughtered by the Wehrmacht. 'If the Germans should now get rid of them,' noted a dejected Averell, 'they would not be a thorn in his side later on.'[14]

The ongoing uprising continued throughout September but looked increasingly doomed. After sixty-two days of front-line fighting, the Polish resistance was finally crushed, and the last remaining insurgents laid down their arms. Averell was later told that a quarter of the city's population (some 250,000 fighting men, women, and children) had been killed or wounded. The 35,000-strong underground army had lost at least 1,500 fighters. The once-glorious Polish capital was in ruins and thousands of corpses were trapped under the rubble. Stalin had achieved his goal: the Polish resistance had been wiped out.

Archie was deeply shaken by Stalin's refusal to support an uprising he had actively encouraged. He was no less appalled by the way in which Stalin had treated his Western partners. 'Our scrupulously honest intentions were constantly misinterpreted and frustrated to the point of exasperation. Again and again we were baffled and enraged by the handfuls of grit that found their way into our benevolent oil.'[15]

Archie foresaw a troubled future. Stalin seemed determined to impose a Soviet vision on the post-war world, one that was 'divorced from the restraining influence of enlightened public opinion, and hyper-sensitive in all matters affecting national prestige'.[16]

Averell had reached a similar conclusion. 'Unless we take issue with the present policy,' he said, 'there is every indication the Soviet Union will become a world bully.'[17] Stalin viewed the generosity of spirit displayed by his Western partners as a sign of weakness.

Someone, somewhere, needed to fight back.

PART VII

The Reckoning

Autumn 1944–Spring 1945

35
The Face of War

KATHY'S WORK AT the Office of War Information was taking up an increasing amount of her time in the summer of 1944. As the Red Army advanced towards the German frontier and victory seemed a certainty, the Soviet press was clamouring for information about America. Kathy was their principal contact. As a Russian speaker, she was the link between the American Embassy and Moscow's American press agency.

'Oh dear,' she wrote to Mary. 'This office is a madhouse and there's so damned much work to do. I don't know if I'm coming or going, so I'm giving up and writing to you. Thanks to the shuttle bombing and the landings in Normandy, the Soviet press is using a lot of our pictures. All very nice, but it means I have to keep on my toes.'[1]

Kathy wrote another letter a few days later, revealing that she had just witnessed something extraordinary. Sixty thousand German prisoners, all captured at Minsk, were being paraded through the streets of Moscow.

'They walked in batches of about a thousand and were headed by horse-ridden militia and flanked by foot militia with rifles and bayonets.' She and Bob Meiklejohn rushed to the outside balcony of Tchaikovsky Hall, which afforded a panorama of the march-past below.

'The people had been warned by radio throughout the early morning that they must be orderly, not to jeer or try to get to the prisoners, so they were actually on their best behavior . . . They just stared at the Germans and the Germans stared back.'[2]

Meiklejohn had heard a great deal about the professionalism of the Wehrmacht over the previous four years. Now, seeing Hitler's soldiers close up, he was not impressed. 'A rather seedy lot,' he wrote. 'The ones I saw didn't look starved, neither did they look like the so-called Aryan Nazi Master Race. Many runts and dark-featured people.' He was nevertheless troubled by the parade. 'The large gray-green masses of moving men seemed to roll up the street like a dirty stream or a flock of sheep, very somber and sinister in appearance.'

Kathy and Meiklejohn went down into the street to get a closer look. Most of the prisoners were between eighteen and thirty-five and were in remarkably good physical shape. 'Their uniforms were complete and, aside from being dusty, in good condition. Those walking barefoot carried their shoes or boots. Some looked glassy-eyed and shell-shocked, some were glum and refused to look at the sights of Moscow. But the great majority walked along quite unconcernedly, chatting among themselves and pointing out things of interest.'

A photo from Kathy's scrapbook. In summer 1944 she witnessed thousands of German prisoners of war being paraded through Moscow, and correctly surmised that their future would be grim.

Staff at the British Embassy had also made their way outside. Interpreter Arthur Birse was as fascinated as Meiklejohn to see the vanquished master race, 'a pitiful rabble of soldiery, evidently straight from the trenches, unshaven, unkempt, their clothes bedraggled and torn'. Birse tried to persuade Archie to witness the spectacle, but he declined. 'He said he could not bear inhuman sights, and it might look too much like a parade of human captives in ancient Rome.'

Both Meiklejohn and Kathy pondered their eventual fate. 'Watching these prisoners, we speculated on how many would ever get home again, see their families,' wrote Kathy, who had been told that the Soviet regime was expecting its prisoners of war to rebuild everything they had destroyed. 'Perhaps none of them realized just how grisly their future is. It's not particularly nice to think about.'

Meiklejohn reckoned that none would make it home alive. 'My guess is that when the time comes to send them back to Germany, the Russians will have conveniently lost the records of where they are.'[3]

The two of them were to prove correct in predicting their grim future. Of the three million Germans captured by the Soviets, more than a million were to die in captivity. The rest finally made it back to Germany, but only after years of hard labour. The last prisoners were not released until 1956.

Ten days after the parade, Kathy was offered the chance to join an unnamed American general on a flying visit to the Italian battle-front. The purpose of the trip was to question a large number of German prisoners of war captured in and around Monte Cassino. 'Doubly interesting for me,' wrote Kathy, 'having just seen the sixty thousand Germans captured at Minsk.'

The low-level flight across southern Italy took them over Naples, Cassino and Anzio and afforded Kathy a panoramic view of the war-scarred landscape. 'Completely pock-marked with shell holes,' she wrote. 'Piles of ammunition still lie around – the area is a maze of slit-trenches and tank emplacements.' As they flew over Cassino, she blinked in disbelief. 'I didn't recognize it as the remains of a town. It bore no resemblance to anything living . . . like a deadly disease of yellow callous, the rubble spreads upward as though trying to meet the rubble of the monastery on the top.' It was the first time she got a sense of the scale of destruction across vast areas of Europe.

Finally they arrived at Caserta, where the largest group of prisoners was being held. In a letter to Pamela Churchill, Kathy compared them to the ones she had seen in Moscow. 'Every type of uniform,' she wrote, 'bits and pieces, and they were a straggly lot. They looked far worse physical specimens than the ones on the Russian front.' On questioning them, she found that a third were unrepentant Nazis while the rest were sick of the war.

In the same compound was a second group of prisoners, dishevelled and in rags. 'They looked like scarecrows.' Kathy soon discovered they were Russian and had been captured at the River Don more than two years earlier.

'They beamed with joy when I started to talk to them in my lousy Russian. One blond thirty-year-old man acted as their spokesman.' He told Kathy they had been forced to work for the Organisation Todt – Nazi Germany's military engineering company – but had managed to escape a month earlier. They had subsequently been fighting alongside partisans in the hills around Florence, before turning themselves over to the Americans. The spokesman said they were appalled at having been locked up with the hated Germans and begged Kathy to tell the camp commandant 'that they were fighting the same war as us'.

Kathy promised to see what she could do and then asked them if they wanted to return home. 'They hesitated and then said, "Yes, if it was possible."' Kathy understood the reason why they demurred. Stalin had vowed to execute any prisoner of war returning to the Soviet Union on the grounds that Red Army soldiers were supposed to fight to the death.

Kathy knew several senior military figures in Italy and was therefore well looked after. She was taken to Capri, where she was invited to the sprawling villa, Il Fortino, owned by the American multimillionaire Harrison Williams. He was there with his young wife, Mona, a famous American socialite.

Kathy's wartime life had thrown up so many surprises that she was almost unfazed when another familiar-looking figure appeared for dinner. It was Marshal Josip Tito, celebrated leader of the Yugoslav partisans, who had been fighting a spectacular guerrilla war against the Nazis since the spring of 1941. 'Tito turned up', wrote Kathy, 'with three staff officers plus a lovely looking young female interpreter.' This was Olga Huma, Tito's personal secretary, who was tall and graceful, and had a pistol casually hanging from her belt.

'Tito himself is small and heavy set,' she wrote. 'Very handsome with a strong face. Slit steel-blue eyes that were cruel and hard-looking, but when he smiled or laughed, as he frequently did, his whole face lit up and made him appear less foreboding.'

The strangest thing about him was his hands. 'Smooth and well-kept, the hands of a pampered politician rather than a guerrilla chieftain.' On his wedding finger, he wore a platinum ring set with a huge cut crystal.

Kathy was delighted to discover she could follow much of his conversation. 'Jug [Yugoslav] and Russian aren't too far apart.' She realised that this was a unique opportunity to probe for information from a war leader, 'so I gulped down an extra sherry, to give me the lacking courage'.

She certainly found Tito easy to talk to. 'A good answerer of questions,' she wrote, 'and does it directly, without hedging, but seemed to lack the creative imagination to expand. He's very literal, with a good sense of humor and likes the same kind of joke a Russian would.'

Security was tight that evening, with two loyal guards constantly at his side. 'They form a very essential part of the Tito set-up. They go where he does in the same room and presumably even the can [toilet]. Each is armed with a revolver, plenty of ammunition belts hung every which way, and a sub-machine gun held most of the time at the hip.'

Kathy was still chatting with Tito when into the room walked the celebrated adventurer Fitzroy Maclean, a pre-war employee of the British Embassy in Moscow. He was now head of the British Maclean Mission, fighting a guerrilla war in the Yugoslav mountains alongside Tito and his partisans. Kathy knew all about Maclean from Pamela Churchill and was delighted to meet him in the flesh. 'Absolutely charming', she wrote, 'and lots of fun.' He was sharp, smooth, and good-looking. Better still, he was a guerrilla.

Tito and Maclean were just two of the many unexpected guests to pitch up that weekend. Among the new arrivals were two of Kathy's old friends, the glamorous Hollywood actress Bebe Daniels and her actor husband, Ben Lyon. They had travelled to Italy to entertain the troops. They all dined together that night, along with Olga Huma. 'Bebe and I both felt rather stupid in our silk frocks and red fingernails,' wrote Kathy. 'Olga's partisan uniform seemed so much more appropriate.'

Kathy was having coffee with Tito and Maclean the following afternoon when one of the smaller dogs at the villa attacked Tito's huge mongrel, Tigr. Within seconds, a violent dogfight was under way. 'Soon Tito himself joined in the fray, trying to separate them,' wrote Kathy. 'He succeeded only at the expense of a goodly number of coffee cups and plates.' Once he had regained control of Tigr, he removed his lead and began to thrash him with terrifying violence. In that moment, Kathy glimpsed a far more brutal side to Tito.

Kathy spent a few more days in Italy, travelling to Naples by boat with Tito and his son, Zharko, who had joined them at the villa. 'Naples harbor was filled with every type and kind of warship, troop ship and landing craft,' she wrote. 'Headquarters people were flying all over the countryside, inspecting everything.' Although she could not speak about it in her letters, she was witnessing the troops and ships being prepared for Operation Dragoon, the Allied landings in southern France, scheduled for Tuesday, 15 August.

'D-minus-one', she wrote on the eve of the landings. She clearly knew all about them and had possibly learned the details from an unlikely source. Winston Churchill was on a whistle-stop tour of Italy when he heard that Kathy was staying nearby. He insisted she join him for lunch at the Villa Rivalta, overlooking the Bay of Naples.

Churchill was in good humour that morning. He had swum in the sea, smoked a large cigar, and drunk an early pre-luncheon cocktail. Now he had an entertaining diversion to look forward to.

Kathy had to negotiate her way through a tight security cordon when she arrived at the Villa Rivalta. 'As I walked into the vestibule (having successfully overcome the British and American Military Police guarding the villa), four very sour British naval officers and strange-looking civilians greeted me with stony glares.'

Kathy was uncharacteristically daunted. 'I felt like crawling under the table. A little sergeant finally appeared and asked what I wanted. When I said I was invited for lunch, he didn't believe me.'

Nor did anyone else. A private secretary was summoned, but he didn't believe her either. The prime minister lunched with senior generals and military personnel, not vivacious American girls in their twenties. 'I was left once more with hostile glares descending upon me. One came from a British full admiral, who later admitted he was on the verge of throwing me out.' But help was at hand. 'The PM appeared and most cordially kissed me, thereby establishing my right to be there.'

Kathy had got to know Churchill well during her two and a half years in England and was adept at reading his moods. 'The PM is always at his best on the eve of great battles, or when things are going well,' she wrote. 'The Falaise Gap [in Normandy] was beginning to be closed, Southern France about to be invaded, so he was on top form, intermixing the past with the present and refusing to be troubled by dark or unpleasant thoughts.'

He jokingly accused Kathy of trying to 'pull a Virginia Cowles trick' in coming to Italy at such a critical moment in the war. (Virginia Cowles, an American journalist, had been arrested when trying to enter Normandy illegally just before the D-Day landings.) 'When I said I'd arrived in complete innocence, he still didn't believe me!'

Kathy knew that Churchill's daughters, Sarah and Mary, often travelled with their father and hoped they would join the two of them for lunch. 'But he said they were both too busy – Mary's now on the coast in an ack-ack battery.'[4]

When Kathy eventually arrived back in Moscow, she found her father in bad shape and exhausted from overwork. 'Ave has almost nightly excursions to the Kremlin,' she wrote on the evening of her return. 'The last one at 2 a.m. . . . It all adds up to a very bloody time. God knows, it has been difficult before, but I gather the last bit has topped all, both unpleasant and worrisome. Adding to his work troubles, Ave's ulcers have cropped up again.'[5] He was also painfully thin, having lost a lot of weight.

He told Kathy about his bitter wrangles with Stalin over the future of Poland and expressed his very real fears for the future. The Soviet leader looked set to dominate everything. Just as victory was on the horizon, the world seemed to be once again tipping into darkness.

36

Churchill's Naughty Document

THE FIRST SIGN that something unusual was about to happen went unnoticed by almost everyone. Quietly, and without any fuss, Archie Clark Kerr cancelled his planned leave in England. He had been due to head home for a few weeks in October but changed his intentions at short notice. One of the Moscow-based reporters, Alaric Jacob, was convinced that something big was in the offing. He just didn't know what.

The answer came on the afternoon of Monday, 9 October, when Winston Churchill flew in to Moscow on his second visit to Stalin, accompanied by his doctor, a team of advisers, and his excitable young secretary, Elizabeth Layton. 'Moscow!' she wrote. '*Heavens – Moscow!*'[1]

The PM's flight had almost ended in catastrophe. He fell asleep with a lit cigar in one hand and an oxygen mask over his face. The mask slipped from his face and fanned the burning cigar into a fiery disaster in the making. Thankfully, his ever-vigilant doctor, Charles Wilson, was on hand to extinguish the cigar. 'One day, we shall all go up in flames,' he wrote in his diary.[2]

Churchill's arrival in Moscow came in the wake of another meeting with President Roosevelt, at Quebec, where the two leaders discussed arrangements for a second gathering of the Big Three. Roosevelt suggested they should meet in the Mediterranean, but Stalin could not be persuaded. 'Old age was creeping up on him,' he told Averell, adding that his doctors refused to let him travel.[3] This may have been true, but he also wanted Churchill and Roosevelt to come to him. It was a way of showing the world that he, and the Soviet Union, were indispensable in the fight against Hitler.

Churchill was so alarmed by the Red Army's breakneck advance into Eastern Europe that he felt the need for face-to-face discussions with Stalin. Roosevelt was incensed by the PM's solo voyage, venting his anger in a letter to Averell. 'Quite frankly, I can tell *you*, but only for you and not to be communicated under any circumstances to the British or Russians, that I would have preferred very much to have the next conference between the three of us.' Roosevelt insisted that Averell be present at every meeting between Churchill and Stalin, fearing that the prime minister might try to strike a deal behind his back. 'In this global war,' he said, 'there is literally no question, military or political, in which the United States is not interested.'[4] The future of the world was at stake and Roosevelt was insistent that America would play a leading role when it came to dividing the spoils.

Averell was intending to be present at every meeting, but Churchill ensured that he knew nothing about his secretive opening discussions with Stalin, which took place on his first evening in Moscow, Monday, 9 October. The only other people in attendance were the two foreign secretaries, Eden and Molotov, and the two interpreters, Arthur Birse and Vladimir Pavlov. Birse kept verbatim notes of what happened that night, and they reveal exactly why Churchill didn't want Averell to be there.

The PM and Stalin began their discussions in cordial fashion, with a caustic joke about Poland. 'Where there were two Poles, there was one quarrel,' said Churchill. Stalin chuckled and added a rejoinder: 'Where there was one Pole, he would begin to quarrel with himself through sheer boredom.'[5]

Churchill was about to tell Stalin the reason for his visit to Moscow when the Soviet leader stopped him mid-sentence and said he had received a message from President Roosevelt: 'The president wanted Mr Harriman to attend their talks.'

Churchill nodded and said he would welcome Averell to the rest of their discussions, 'but he did not want this to prevent intimate talk between Marshal Stalin and himself'.[6]

These words were the cue for a proposal so stunning and cynical that it took everyone by surprise, not least Arthur Birse. 'The Prime Minister then produced what he called a "naughty document".' This was an understatement. It contained a list of five countries – Greece, Romania, Bulgaria, Yugoslavia, and Hungary – with a percentage written next to each one. These denoted the extent of influence that Britain and the Soviet Union were to have in each country. 'How would it do for you to have ninety per cent predominance in Romania,' Churchill asked Stalin, 'and for us to have ninety per cent of the say in Greece?' He added that they should have equal shares in Hungary and Yugoslavia – fifty-fifty – with Stalin getting seventy-five per cent of Bulgaria.

Birse's private notes about the naughty document were later struck through with a cross, a sign that they were to be redacted from the official account of the meeting. '[Churchill] said that the Americans would be shocked if they saw how crudely he had put it,' before adding that 'Marshal Stalin was a realist' and that 'he himself was not sentimental'. He wanted to carve up Europe there and then, dividing the spoils between himself and his Soviet comrade-in-arms. Churchill's percentages note was written in pencil on a small sheet of paper. He waited for Pavlov to finish translating his words before pushing it across the table. 'There was a slight pause. Then he [Stalin] took his blue pencil and made a large tick upon it and passed it back to us. It was all settled in no more time than it takes to set down.'[7]

PRIME MINISTER then produced what he called a 'naughty document' showing a list of Balkan countries and the proportion ix of interest in them of the Great Powers. He said that the Americans would be shocked if they saw how crudely he had put it. Marshal Stalin was a realist. He himself was not sentimental while Mr Eden was a bad man. He had not consulted his cabinet or Parliament. The Prime Minister declared that Britain had been much offended by Bulgaria. In the last war the Bulgarians hade beaten back and had cruelly attacked the Roumanians. In this war they had done the same to the Yugoslavs and Greece

An example of how history gets edited: interpreter Arthur Birse's note about Churchill's 'naughty document' is redacted from the official record.

Churchill was correct to call it a naughty document. Neither the people nor parliaments of Central or Eastern Europe had been consulted about such a sweeping proposition. Nor, indeed, had the PM discussed it with his Cabinet. And Roosevelt himself was completely oblivious to Churchill's extraordinary proposition. With that one small slip of paper, and in barely any time at all, he was sealing the fate of millions of newly liberated people.

Churchill downplayed the incident when he later wrote about it in his memoirs, saying it was intended as a short-term solution that would have been overridden by any future settlement. But he didn't say this to Stalin at the time.

Aware of the sensitivity of what he was suggesting, he now proposed that they burn his sheet of paper. 'Might it not be thought rather cynical if it seemed we had disposed of these issues, so fateful to millions of people, in such an offhand manner?'

Stalin pushed the sheet back across the table.

'No, you keep it,' he said.[8]

It was some days before Averell learned about the events of that evening. 'I vividly recall Churchill's being in bed, where it was his custom to dictate letters and memoranda,' wrote Averell. 'He read me a letter he had drafted for Stalin, giving his interpretation of the percentages agreed to at their first meeting.' Averell expressed his shock at such an agreement – even if it was only intended to be temporary – and told Churchill there was no way Roosevelt would agree to such terms. 'I don't understand now, and I do not believe I understood at the time, just what Churchill thought he was accomplishing by these percentages.'[9] It was an outlandish deal to have struck with Stalin, and one that would only serve to infuriate President Roosevelt.

The vexed issue of Poland dominated the next few days of discussions. The head of the London Poles, Stanisław Mikołajczyk, was summoned to Moscow on Thursday, 12 October. At a Kremlin meeting with Churchill, Stalin, Averell, and Archie, he came under heavy pressure to accept the proposed new frontiers of Poland, already decided upon by Churchill and Stalin. These shifted the country a hundred miles to the west, handing the cities of Lvov and Brest to the Soviet Union. Mikołajczyk was also urged to team up with the Polish politicians backed by Stalin.

The Polish leader proved stubbornly inflexible, infuriating Churchill. 'We are not going to wreck the peace of Europe because of quarrels between Poles,' he said sternly. 'Unless you accept the frontier, you are out of business for ever. The Russians will sweep through your country and your people will be liquidated. You are on the verge of annihilation.'

He warned Mikołajczyk that the future of Poland was entirely dependent on his trusting Stalin and his Polish Communists. 'You hate the Russians,' he said. 'I know you hate them. We are very friendly with them, more friendly than we have ever been. I mean to keep things like that.'[10]

But Churchill was himself frustrated when he met Stalin's Poles, who displayed a disturbing willingness to cede large parts of their country to the Soviet Union. 'Stalin kept looking at Churchill and smiling mischievously,' noted Birse, 'and Churchill's face was growing darker.' He sensed that he was being duped. 'Suddenly he got up, pushing back his chair noisily and muttering under his breath.'[11] He moved to a side table and clattered the glasses to drown out the voices of Stalin's Polish stooges. Stalin laughed, seemingly delighted at having got the better of Churchill over the vexed question of Poland.

Stalin had never been so cordial as he was during Churchill's ten days in Moscow, perhaps because he was so close to achieving his territorial goals. The Red Army was advancing westwards on every front. Within days, Soviet troops would launch their all-out attack on East Prussia. Berlin was already in their sights.

One of the high points of the PM's stay was an evening at the Bolshoi with Stalin himself in attendance – an unprecedented event. Averell and Kathy were invited to join the two leaders, an event that Kathy described in a letter to Pamela:

'Averell and I were invited to sit in the royal box. The PM arrived late, with Uncle Joe coming in some minutes afterwards, so the audience didn't realise they were there till the lights went on after the first act. A cheer went up (something that I've never seen happen here) and Uncle Joe ducked out so that the PM could have all the applause for himself, which was a very nice gesture.

'But the PM sent Vyshinsky out to get Uncle Joe back, and they stood together while the applause went on for many minutes. It was most, most impressive – the sound like a cloudburst on a tin roof. It came from below, on all sides, and above, and the people down in the audience said they were thrilled seeing the two men standing together.'

Churchill was interested in neither the ballet nor the opera, but he came to life when Cossack dancers appeared on stage and the Red Army sang rousing martial songs. 'Are they going to sing the Volga Boat Song?' he asked hopefully.

The greatest moment of Churchill's ten-day visit came on Wednesday, 11 October, when Stalin made history by accepting Archie's invitation to dine at the British Embassy. The dinner was kept secret until that very evening. Journalist Alaric Jacob realised something was afoot only when he noticed that the electric beacons atop the embassy gates had been lit, casting a flood of light over the building's ornate facade.

Jacob was the only journalist allowed in the building that evening, a unique privilege accorded him because his cousin, General Ian Jacob, was in Churchill's Moscow entourage. He described the embassy as being in a fever-pitch of excitement. 'A little knot of embassy secretaries were peering through the doorways in the hope of catching a glimpse of Stalin.'

Much was also happening behind the scenes. In the embassy kitchens, Archie's Greek chef, Timoleon, had been working since dawn on preparations for the banquet. Archie had asked him to cook a meal that was as English as possible. By early evening, Timoleon was putting the finishing touches to a substantial feast: melon, tomato soup with sour cream, white fish poached in wine, cold suckling pig and mayonnaise, roast chicken and green peas, cream pudding, mushroom savoury, and dessert. The vegetables had been grown by Archie himself, in the embassy potager, while the mushrooms had been cultivated from spores he had scattered over the long-disused tennis court.

'Not quite a Kremlin banquet perhaps,' noted Archie as he did a final tour of the kitchens, 'but we've done our best and I think it's going to take us a good couple of hours to get through.'[12]

A few hours before Stalin's arrival, the embassy was searched by the NKVD. Arthur Birse had witnessed the security precautions that surrounded Stalin's visit to Teheran, but these were now taken to a whole new level. 'The garden, outhouses, cellars, and attic were subjected to a thorough search . . . the servants were interrogated. A searchlight was placed on the roof over the main entrance.' That evening, scores of guards were drafted in to secure the building. They were dressed in smart blue caps and wore pristine white gloves and highly polished boots. Each was armed with a loaded revolver.

Winston Churchill arrived first, having been driven from his dacha. He was beaming and in excellent spirits. Foreign Secretary Eden arrived a few minutes later, closely followed by Stalin and Molotov. Stalin was wearing his marshal's uniform with a single gold star on his breast.

Birse helped him out of his greatcoat. 'I could not help noticing that though he looked smart, the sleeves of his tunic were too long and came down to the knuckles of his hands.'[13]

Molotov scanned the room suspiciously, as if half expecting an assassin to jump from the shadows. When Vyshinsky arrived, he pointed to the many Soviet guards and cried out merrily, 'I see that the Red Army has had another victory. It has occupied the British Embassy.'[14]

Averell and Kathy arrived shortly after Stalin. In a letter to Pamela, Kathy said that Stalin had a far-away look in his eyes, something she had not noticed before. 'He seemed like a man in a daze, not much expression at all on his face. Very cold and distant.'

Archie served cocktails in the embassy's white and gold drawing room before leading his thirty guests into the dining room. Kathy was surprised to see Stalin's expression suddenly change. 'He smiled by squinting his eyes and seemed quite like a human being.'[15]

Arthur Birse, as interpreter, was seated next to the Soviet leader. 'This time there was no need to instruct him in the use of knives and forks. He was relaxed and evidently out to enjoy himself.' He told Birse he liked the British custom of serving cocktails and sherry before the meal, 'but could not understand why we weakened our whisky by putting water into it'.

The British Embassy dining room was oppressive and mired in old-world grandeur. On the walls hung life-size portraits of the royal family, with pride of place reserved for King George V and Queen Mary. Stalin gazed at them incredulously and then remarked, 'Is that our Nicholas II?' Birse gently reminded him of the close family relationship between the British and Russian royal families, steering clear of the latter's brutal murder by the Bolsheviks.

Stalin and Churchill were in the best possible mood throughout the meal, with Stalin directing a generous toast towards Averell. 'There was a time when Russia and England together could handle European affairs,' he said. 'In the First World War, American help was needed to beat Germany. But in this war, there was needed the full weight and strength of the United States.' To everyone's surprise, he went on to say that 'he doubted whether Germany could have been beaten without the full participation of America, both economically and militarily.'[16]

When one of the guests toasted the Big Three as the Holy Trinity, Stalin quipped: 'If that is so, Churchill must be the Holy Ghost, he flies around so much.'[17]

The next toast was made by Kathy herself, who somewhat nervously rose to her feet and delivered it in faultless Russian, to Stalin's great delight. 'The PM's interpreter coached me,' she later admitted to Pamela, 'so I'd be sure to get all the right words in their proper tenses.'

At one point, she overheard Maxim Litvinov, former Soviet ambassador to Washington, ask General Deane if it was true (as reported in *Look* magazine) that Averell had a personal fortune of $100 million. Deane confessed to not knowing, prompting another question from Litvinov: 'How could a man who had a hundred million dollars look so sad!'[18]

There was a surprise after dinner. The street loudspeakers outside the embassy announced a big-gun salute to celebrate the Red Army's capture of Cluj in Romania. The curtains of the dining room were drawn aside and Churchill and Stalin went out onto the balcony to see the domes and towers of the Kremlin illuminated by gun flashes.

This was followed by an intimate chat in the small embassy drawing room, which enabled Churchill and Stalin to discuss the state of the world with Averell, Archie, and Eden. Stalin sat in a grandfather chair next to the log fire, while Churchill, Averell, and Eden perched on the adjoining sofa. Archie himself sat on the floor, getting up only occasionally to serve whisky, cigarettes, and cigars.

They spoke of partisan warfare and of affairs in Yugoslavia, Italy, and Poland. They even discussed the forthcoming general election in Great Britain. Stalin dismissed the Labour Party as being like the Mensheviks at the time of the 1917 revolution and said that Churchill's Conservatives were certain to win. Churchill was not so sure. 'It is even harder to understand the politics of other countries than those of your own,' he said.[19]

Churchill felt his ten days in Moscow had cemented his friendship with the Soviet leader. Although the future of Poland still hung in the balance, the PM was more optimistic than ever about dealing with Stalin in the post-war period. He took particular delight in having held conspiratorial discussions behind Roosevelt's back. 'We are seeing a great deal of Averell,' he wrote in a disingenuous letter to Washington. 'He is sitting in on the military discussions and on the future of Germany talks, as well, of course as the Polish conversations.'

Averell himself remained appalled by the prime minister's 'naughty' proposition to Stalin, which had been made quite deliberately behind Roosevelt's back. 'President Roosevelt insisted on keeping a free hand,' said Averell, 'and wanted any decisions deferred until the three could meet together.'

Churchill knew that, but chose to ignore it.

Churchill fell ill after breakfast on Sunday, 15 October.

'Diarrhoea,' wrote his doctor, Charles Wilson, who noted that the prime minister was also running a temperature. He summoned extra medics and nurses from Cairo, just to be on the safe side, and also notified Clementine.

A bedridden Churchill called for his secretary, Elizabeth Layton, and asked her to read to him. It was a painful experience for her. 'For an hour and a half, therefore, I sat by his bedside reading a perfectly dreadful book called *A Primer of the Coming World*, about the influence of capitalism on wars, feeling how inadequate was my brain since I could understand not a word of what I was reading.'

Churchill lay prostrate with a black bandage over his eyes, 'concentrating, occasionally saying, "A wee bit faster" or "slacken off a little" to show he was not asleep'.[20] His fever soon passed and by the following day he was once again in rude health.

Stalin hosted a final dinner at the Kremlin on Tuesday, 17 October. It was a far smaller group than was usually invited to these occasions and it was to have a happy ending when Stalin once again invited Churchill back to his private study.

Churchill would later recount to Charles Wilson the events of the evening, which provided more insight into Stalin's private life. 'We got back at four-thirty this morning,' he said. 'But it was worth it. All very friendly.'

Stalin had led Churchill to his apartment, where yet more food had been set out on the table. 'Stalin ate heartily, pork mainly. I picked at things. He dines at 1 a.m., as a rule, goes to bed at four and rises between noon and one o'clock, a relic of the days when it was safer for him to lie low during the day.' The Soviet leader was in an unusually ebullient mood, opening up about his early life as a revolutionary.

'He told me stories of his exile in Siberia; he was a political prisoner with nothing to do in a forlorn place, with eight roubles a day to live on. He was there for four years before the 1914 war.' Stalin told Churchill how he had caught fish during his time as a prisoner. 'I floated logs down the river with a hundred hooks on them,' he said, 'and with this contrivance I caught a big sturgeon.' He confessed to having been a devious prisoner who infuriated the local police colonel.

Churchill found Stalin's dry sense of humour to be his most endearing characteristic. The Soviet leader even made a provocative joke about Churchill's attempt to destroy the Bolshevik revolutionary government back in 1919. Churchill turned suddenly wistful as the past came flooding back. 'I'm glad now that I did not kill you,' he said. 'I hope you are glad that you did not kill me.'

Stalin nodded and quoted an old Russian proverb. 'A man's eyes should be torn out if he can only see the past.'[21] His own eyes were very much fixed on the future.

The weather was filthy on the morning of Thursday, 19 October, the day on which Churchill and his entourage were due to leave Moscow. The sky was full of drizzle and there was a biting chill in the air.

Archie and Eden travelled together to the aerodrome and were surprised to learn that Stalin had come to say a personal farewell to the PM, something he had never done before.

Churchill himself had not yet arrived. 'We went on standing in the rain,' wrote General Alan Brooke, 'wondering how late Winston would be, and whether he was still possibly drying himself after his morning bath.' But his car rolled up soon afterwards and he delivered an impromptu speech in front of a hastily installed microphone.

'We have worked very hard,' he said. 'We have been a council of workers and soldiers.' Alaric Jacob was certain that Churchill had chosen the word 'council' quite deliberately, knowing it would be translated as 'soviet'.

The PM was swept with emotion as he spoke, perhaps because he already had an inkling that this would be his last meeting *à deux* with Stalin. Jacob recorded his words for posterity. 'Most of all it has been a pleasure for me, and an honour, to have so many long and intimate talks with my friend and war comrade, Marshal Stalin, and to deal with the many difficult questions inseparable from the united forward march of great nations through the many vicissitudes of war.' His great hope, he said, was that the three global powers – the Soviet Union, United States, and British Empire – would lead the world into 'the sunlight of a broader and happier age for all'.

Churchill invited Stalin into his giant Avro York aeroplane to show him all the gadgets. Then, once the Soviet leader was back on the tarmac, the PM settled himself into a window seat, lit a cigar, and offered a regal wave. Stalin replied with a military salute and then began rummaging in the depths of his pockets. 'He pulled out a handkerchief and began to wave it,' wrote Jacob. 'It looked a little ridiculous and a little charming . . . The immensely dignified figure in the marshal's topcoat stood fluttering his handkerchief. And as the machine did a rapid circle of the airport, Stalin stood following it around with his eyes. Only after it had vanished in the rainclouds did he walk back to his Packard.' Jacob thought the Soviet leader looked genuinely happy. 'You had the impression that Joseph Stalin had really enjoyed this visit.'[22]

The post-mortem began later that night when Archie invited the small Moscow-based press corps to a dinner in his embassy study.

Touchingly, he had his chef cook them the same meal he had served to Stalin. He then gave them a detailed debriefing and answered the reporters' questions. But the most pertinent question, concerning the strength of Churchill's friendship with Stalin, went unanswered.

The PM himself was sure he could now trust the Soviet leader. In a letter written to Stalin the day after his departure, he spoke of his optimism for the future. 'This memorable meeting in Moscow has shown that there are no matters that cannot be adjusted between us when we meet together in frank and intimate discussions . . . May we meet again soon.'[23]

As he wrote those words, the Red Army was sweeping into East Prussia.

37

Archie's Moscow Masseur

ARCHIE HAD HOPED to take some leave at the end of Churchill's visit, but seven weeks were to pass before he finally travelled to London. He used that time to write a lengthy despatch warning of the threat that Stalin posed to the post-war world. Unless Britain forged closer ties with the countries of Western Europe, he said, the Soviet leader would conclude that the country was no longer interested in playing a role in continental affairs. This posed a real danger, for Stalin and his commissars were certain to exploit the situation 'to their own exclusive advantage'.[1] A devious game of geopolitical roulette was already under way and Britain had not yet entered the casino.

Archie arrived in London on Thursday, 10 December. In the six weeks that followed, he had meetings at the Foreign Office, took a pleasure trip to Windsor and spent time at Inverchapel, his remote country home at the southern end of Loch Eck in western Scotland.

It was a holiday overlaid with sadness, for he had reluctantly concluded that his beloved Tita was not coming back. Shortly before Christmas, he began formal divorce proceedings. 'Our Envoy to Moscow Sues His Wife' was the headline in the *Sunday Dispatch*, which revelled in what it saw as a colourful scandal. 'Maria "Tita" Diaz Salas', it said, 'was once described as the most beautiful girl in Santiago . . . the president of Chile was best man at the wedding and there were fully 1,000 guests.'[2]

The divorce proceedings were a heavy blow to Archie, even though his reputed affair with Chiang Kai-shek's wife may well have caused Tita's flight from the marriage. Archie's legal advisers suggested that he change his will, but he declined to do so. Even when divorced, Tita was to remain the principal beneficiary of his estate.

Archie returned to Moscow at the end of January, flying to the Soviet capital via Stockholm. Although he did not yet know it, an exotic young Russian man was soon to enter his life. That man was Evgeni Yost, who had first joined the domestic staff of the British Embassy in 1938, serving as footman to the then ambassador, Sir William Seeds. Yost had arrived in Moscow with a grim back story, telling Sir William how his family had lived through terrible times in Ukraine.

His father was a prosperous grain merchant who had been arrested in 1925 and sent to a hard labour camp in Kazakhstan; the family's possessions had soon afterwards been confiscated. It was fortunate that Evgeni's older sister, Marguerite, had travelled to Moscow and secured a job as a maid in the British Embassy. She recommended her seventeen-year-old brother to the ambassador, who promptly hired Evgeni as well.

The security of embassy life did not last long for Evgeni. He was ethnically German, a descendant of the Volga Germans encouraged to settle in Russia during the reign of Catherine the Great. His ethnicity placed him under suspicion at the time of the Nazi invasion in 1941. Arrested and convicted on trumped-up charges, he was sentenced to seven years' hard labour in a camp east of the Urals. But he was released under a general amnesty and returned to the British Embassy, where his sister was still an employee, having managed to avoid arrest. Archie took an immediate shine to young Evgeni, whose broad smile and wide-eyed innocence were a magnetic attraction. He re-employed him as his personal footman-cum-valet.

The embassy attaché, Frank Giles, took a prurient interest in their budding relationship. 'In the weeks and months that followed,' he wrote, 'the sixty-three-year-old ambassador obviously took a liking to his young servant. He asked him to tell him the story of his experiences in the camp and showed great interest when Evgeni did so.'

Before long, rumours began to spread through the embassy, especially when it was discovered that Evgeni was giving Archie regular massages. Attaché Giles had the temerity to ask Evgeni if the two of them were having a homosexual affair, illegal in both Britain and the Soviet Union at the time. Evgeni vehemently denied they were in such a relationship and said that the ambassador 'never laid a finger on me'. Frank Giles had his doubts and would later express them publicly in a newspaper article filled with innuendo. 'The reverse could not have been exactly true', he wrote, 'for Evgeni was massaging his master several times a week.'

On one occasion, Archie showed Evgeni photos of his home in Argyllshire and asked if he would like to work there at some point in the future. Evgeni was deeply touched. 'I think he knew I'd had a hard life and that I'd never get on in the Soviet Union,' he said. 'He was very kind to me.'

There were even rumours that Evgeni was a Soviet plant who had been 'turned' by the regime in order to work as a spy inside the British Embassy. Frank Giles did not credit such stories. 'He presents himself (and the story of his early life gives strength to his claim) as an unrelenting opponent of the regime, who would not only not help it, but would do anything possible to encompass its downfall.'[3] In addition, Evgeni's German ethnicity meant he would not have been trusted by the NKVD.

The exact detail of Archie and Evgeni's relationship would matter little today, were it not for a sensational postscript that would involve Stalin himself.

38

The Future of the World

ARCHIE DID NOT remain long in Moscow. Within days of arriving back from London he was off again, this time heading to Yalta in the Crimea. He was travelling to the Black Sea resort for the second gathering of the Big Three. Churchill, Roosevelt, and Stalin were to meet once again. This time, their aim was little short of spectacular: to plan the architecture of the post-war world.

Archie travelled by air to Yalta, flying to Saki airfield in central Crimea before being driven across the vertiginous Roman-Kosh massif towards the coast. It was a tortuous six-hour drive along a treacherous slush-covered road.

Averell and Kathy headed to the conference by train, accompanied by Bob Meiklejohn and a few others from the American Embassy. Also joining them were Archie's interpreter, Arthur Birse, and Mrs Balfour, wife of the British Embassy's chargé d'affaires, John Balfour.

The journey was painfully slow. 'The train ambles along at about twenty-five miles an hour over the snow-covered landscape,' wrote Meiklejohn, 'about as monotonous as one could hope to find.'[1] They passed hundreds of freight trains laden with American trucks, most of which had entered the Soviet Union via Averell's Trans-Iranian Railway route.

There were stops at Orel and Kursk, both of which had been bustling cities before the war. Now they were in total ruin. 'Scenes of indescribable devastation,' wrote Arthur Birse as he stared blankly out of the window. 'Towns and villages had been practically wiped out, whole forests seemed to have been mown down by gunfire.'[2] The miserable weather did little to lift the mood – grey skies, the occasional snow flurry and relentless cold.

Kathy detected a change in the rural landscape as they travelled southwards through Ukraine. 'The Ukrainian peasants seem far more prosperous than those around Moscow,' she wrote. 'Their cottages are painted, with thatched roofs and quite picturesque. Some stations had vendors. At one we bought four fresh eggs (cheap, for $4) and made a nice punch – canned milk, bourbon and butter.'

They arrived in Yalta on Wednesday, 24 January. This resort city had once been the playground of the tsars and Kathy found it an enchanting place when seen from a distance. 'Really lovely – high mountains with snow-caps that border the sea, rather like Italy, with countless little villages perched on either side of the winding mountain roads.' But when she took a walking tour of the city itself, she was stunned by the scale of the damage. 'Hardly a house at all is standing. The needless destruction is something appalling. There wasn't much real fighting around here at all. The Germans and Romanians just burned and looted everything in sight.' The place was filled with Romanian prisoners of war, who were working around the clock to repair damaged buildings and roads.

It had been decided that the three delegations would be housed in separate palaces. Winston Churchill's British party were to stay in the Vorontsov Villa, some twelve miles down the coast, which Kathy visited with Bob Meiklejohn. It was an imposing structure, 'built in the style of an old English castle, complete with a Big Ben clock tower', perfect for the British contingent. It had previously served as the headquarters of the German commander, who had fled in such a hurry that all the original furnishings were still in situ. 'The main hall is full of paintings of the ancestral Vorontsovs and a great banqueting table with, at one end, an enormous sideboard.'

Stalin's delegation was staying at the Villa Koreis, modest in size but with an interesting history. 'Uncle Joe is living in the palace once owned by one of the men who killed Rasputin,' wrote Kathy. 'It adds up to quite a picture.' The villa was a light, pink-stoned edifice which dated from 1910. 'It overlooks the sea, with high snow-capped mountains behind.'

The Americans had been assigned the Livadia Palace, a rambling mansion set in lush botanical gardens. When Kathy and Meiklejohn stepped inside, they got a shock. 'The Germans had removed all the furniture and moveable fixtures and the Soviets have been frantically shipping furniture in ever since the decision to hold the conference here.' The place was in chaos. 'They are still hanging draperies, upholstering chairs, installing glass in windows, painting everywhere and making a very presentable job of it all.' They were racing against the clock, for President Roosevelt was due to arrive in less than a week.

When Kathy stepped into the presidential bedroom, she found it full of workmen. 'The rugs for the President's suite have been changed four times,' she wrote. 'Each time all the furniture had to be moved out – and it's big and heavy and Victorian. The Soviets just couldn't make up their minds which oriental colors looked best.'

The sanitation was far from satisfactory – 'washing facilities are practically nil' – and there were nowhere near enough bedrooms. 'Only full generals and admirals and chiefs of staff get rooms to themselves. The rest are packed in like sardines.' Meiklejohn thought this a recipe for disaster. 'We expect to have as many as thirty-five men using one toilet.'[3]

Every day saw the arrival of more furniture from the distant capital. 'All the Moscow hotels have been stripped to look after us,' wrote Kathy. 'Beside that, the country nearby is being scoured for such things as shaving mirrors, coat hangers and wash bowls. I guess things are just being requisitioned out of homes. We've found one ashtray that advertises a china factory, "by appointment to" five tsars.'

President Roosevelt flew in to Saki airfield on Saturday, 3 February. He arrived on his presidential plane, *The Sacred Cow*, accompanied by five P-38 fighters. Winston Churchill landed a short time after. Twenty American Skymasters and five British Avro Yorks transported everyone else, a huge delegation of 700 advisers.

Saki airfield was a bleak point of arrival. 'A sea of mud,' wrote Bob Meiklejohn. Churchill was first onto the tarmac. Braving the chill in a military greatcoat, he was grinning mischievously and chomping on an eight-inch cigar. He had brought along his second daughter, Sarah.

President Roosevelt took longer to alight: his wheelchair had to be lowered from the fuselage in a specially constructed cage. He, too, had brought his daughter, Anna.

Both men were greeted by Molotov, and then the Red Army band played 'The Star-Spangled Banner', 'God Save the King', and 'The

Internationale'. There were the usual refreshments: vodka, champagne, caviar, smoked sturgeon, and black bread. The president and prime minister were then driven to Yalta in separate limousines, enduring the gruelling six-hour drive along the mountainous Route Romanov. 'Christ,' said Churchill to Sarah after an hour on the road. 'Five more of this.'[4]

Stalin had ordered the entire eighty-mile route to be lined with troops – two Soviet divisions – who each stood in sight of the next one. 'As the presidential car passed', noted Roosevelt's interpreter, Charles Bohlen, 'the soldiers, many of them girls, snapped to the Russian salute . . . repeated thousands of times, the salute was most impressive.'[5]

As hostess for her father, it was Kathy's duty to receive President Roosevelt on his arrival at Livadia Palace. 'Well I've at last had my wish and met the President,' she wrote to Mary in New York. 'It seems kind of odd it would be in Russia. He's absolutely charming, easy to talk to, with a lovely sense of humor.'

Roosevelt kept up his smiling facade during those introductions at Yalta, but he was hiding a terrible secret: he was being treated for an enlarged heart and congestive heart failure. His doctors took care to ensure that his health condition remained under wraps, but those who knew him well were in no doubt that the president had a life-threatening illness.

'I was terribly shocked at the change since our talks in Washington,' wrote Averell. 'The signs of deterioration seemed to me unmistakable.'[6] He was concerned that Roosevelt wouldn't have the stamina to negotiate effectively when dealing with Stalin. Arthur Birse felt the same, having seen the president at close quarters during the Teheran Conference. 'A man weary in spirit,' he wrote. 'The good-humoured, benevolent uncle had become a shadow of his former self.'[7]

Many felt that Winston Churchill was also below par. War-weary and now in his seventies, he was increasingly prone to deliver rambling monologues. He was also drinking heavily. 'Buckets of Caucasian champagne which would undermine the health of any ordinary man,' noted one of his senior advisers.[8]

Averell had a long chat with the prime minister on the night of his arrival and found him in a particularly black mood. He told Averell he was 'all set for the worst'.[9]

★

Stalin arrived in Yalta on the morning of Sunday, 4 February, and called on Churchill that same afternoon, arriving at the Villa Vorontsov dressed in a khaki tunic, with a marshal's gold star embroidered onto the shoulder straps. Arthur Birse felt there was a genuine warmth in their greeting. 'Both seemed glad to meet again,' he wrote, 'and they talked like old friends.'[10]

The Soviet leader next paid a visit on Roosevelt, who had dressed for the occasion in a pale suit and flowered tie. 'The President grasped Stalin by the hand and shook it warmly,' wrote Charles Bohlen. 'Stalin, his face cracked into one of his rare if slight smiles, expressed pleasure at seeing the President again.'

Prior to their meeting, Roosevelt had told Averell that he didn't want Stalin to think that he and Churchill had a joint agenda. Nor did he want him to think they were close friends. To reinforce this point, he reminded the Soviet leader of one of his toasts at Teheran, about executing 50,000 German officers – an off-colour jest that had appalled Churchill. '[Roosevelt] expressed the hope that he would offer the toast again,' said Bohlen. He followed this with a criticism of the British for always wanting to 'have their cake and eat it too'.[11]

Averell kept a close eye on the president during those opening days, especially when he was in Stalin's presence. 'Roosevelt held fast to his belief that he personally could accomplish more in man-to-man talks with Stalin than Churchill,' he said. The president had decided that the best way to win Stalin's trust was to keep a distance from Churchill, whom he did not see alone until the fifth day of the conference. 'In his private meetings with Stalin, Roosevelt talked openly about his difficulties with Churchill, and on more than one occasion, poked a little fun at the Prime Minister for his old-fashioned attachment to Empire.'[12]

The two leaders chatted for an hour at that first private meeting, drinking martini cocktails mixed by Roosevelt himself. They then moved to the ballroom of the Livadia Palace for the first plenary session of the conference. Their work was about to begin.

Each of the Big Three had his own goals. Churchill's overriding concern was to prevent Europe from being dominated by the Soviet

Union; he was determined therefore to oppose the dismemberment of Germany. He also wanted France to have a major role in post-war Europe and would fight hard to achieve it. Churchill's third cause was Poland: he did not want a Polish government subservient to Stalin.

Roosevelt's main goal was to secure Stalin's help in the final battle against Japan, which was proving extremely costly in American lives. He also wanted to persuade Stalin to sign up to a new body, the United Nations, which he hoped would act as global policeman in the post-war world.

Stalin's primary goal was to prevent a resurgent Germany from ever again attacking the Soviet Union. To Charles Bohlen, Roosevelt's interpreter for every major session of the conference, it was crystal clear how he intended to achieve this. '[It] meant the establishment of satellite governments all through Eastern Europe.'[13] Stalin was intent on creating an empire in all but name.

The Big Three at Yalta with their advisers. Left to right: Stalin, Molotov, Averell, Archie, Roosevelt, Sarah Churchill, Eden, Churchill.

Each afternoon, the Big Three and their advisers filed into the Grand Ballroom of the Livadia Palace, simply furnished with a large round table. A fire crackled in the conical hearth, for it was near freezing outside, and a low winter sun filtered weakly through the six arched windows. There was much to be discussed, with Roosevelt saying they would 'range over the map of the whole world'.[14] It was a prospect both terrifying and exhilarating.

Kathy was to see Roosevelt constantly over the days that followed. She dined with him the night he arrived from Malta and had an intimate lunch with him the following day. 'Absolutely sweet,' she wrote in a letter to Pamela. 'Very easy to make conversation to. Amusing and generally on great form.'[15]

Her meals with the president usually included her father and five or six carefully selected guests. The conference itself was seldom mentioned at these informal get-togethers. 'In the main, it's politics, friends, with everyone swapping amusing stories.' Roosevelt was clearly delighted that Stalin had nominated him, not Churchill, to be chairman of the conference, for he mentioned it on several occasions. 'The president is getting a big kick out of presiding over the meetings,' wrote Kathy.

Among the guests at those intimate dinners was Harry Hopkins, the sickly 'half-man' who had been the first to visit Stalin back in the summer of 1941. The intervening years had not improved his health. 'Harry arrived not very well', wrote Kathy, 'and went straight to bed with dia – (can't spell it) – anyway, gypie tummy. He got up two days later for lunch: the doctors ordered him to eat nothing but cereal, but the fool had two huge helpings of caviar, cabbage soup with sour cream – and then the cereal. This brought his pains back.'

Roosevelt was also taken ill at one point and had to retire to his sickbed, from where he continued to hold discussions. It was clear to everyone that he was not on form.

As the conference progressed, each of the three leaders felt he was winning concessions. Roosevelt persuaded Stalin to join the war against Japan, although at a price. In return, large tracts of land in the Far East were to be ceded to the Soviet Union.

Roosevelt shares a joke with Stalin. His advisers disliked the way in which he sought to befriend the Soviet leader, at Churchill's expense.

Churchill scored two notable victories: he argued successfully against the dismemberment of Germany and also succeeded in getting France a zone of occupation in Germany. But Poland was to prove a sticking point, for Stalin was adamant that the country should be ruled by a Soviet-backed government. When Churchill reminded Stalin that Poland's post-war frontiers were, for him, a question of honour, the Soviet leader had a perfectly poised rebuff. 'If Poland was a question of honour for the British,' he said, 'it was for the Russians a question of life or death.'

Churchill next suggested that a new Polish government satisfactory to everyone should be formed at Yalta. Stalin's response was equally sharp. 'I am called a dictator and not a democrat,' he said, 'but I have enough democratic feeling to refuse to create a Polish government without the Poles being consulted.'[16]

The language used by the three leaders was worryingly opaque. Stalin promised free elections in Poland, but no one thought to define what was meant by a free election. There was a similar lack of precision when they discussed the Kuril Islands, one of the many Far East concessions granted to Stalin in return for his entering the war against Japan. No one thought to define the 700-mile chain of islands, which stretched from Hokkaido in Japan to Kamchatka in Siberia. Stalin would later claim the lot.

Observers of the conference were quick to notice Stalin's obvious skills. Where Roosevelt rambled and Churchill delivered monologues, Stalin remained utterly focused. 'A shrewd and skillful negotiator,' thought Bohlen. 'Always calm and unruffled and almost always courteous in his mood and manner.' This was especially the case with Poland and Eastern Europe. 'He showed himself to be a master of evasive and delaying tactics with no great regard for facts. He had done his homework on the principal issues, but he did not hesitate to cite events and actions which Churchill and Roosevelt, to say nothing of the rest of us, profoundly disbelieved, but could not refute.'[17]

There were some humorous moments, as Kathy recounted in her letters to Pamela. One afternoon, she, Sarah, and Anna were standing outside the conference hall waiting for the afternoon discussions to conclude.

'They did, quickly, and Vyshinsky and Uncle Joe came out in search of a john.' Stalin was led to one, but it was a washroom without a toilet. 'By that time the PM was occupying the next nearest john, so one of the embassy boys took Stalin way-the-hell down a hall to the next nearest toilet.'

In the process, Stalin's NKVD bodyguards got separated. 'Then there was havoc – everyone running around. I think they thought the Americans had pulled a kidnapping stunt or something. A few minutes later, a composed Uncle Joe appeared at the door and order was restored.'

It had been agreed that each of the Big Three would host a conference dinner. Roosevelt and Churchill's soirées were big and formal affairs, whereas Stalin's was to be rather different. Roosevelt persuaded him to hold an intimate 'family party', as he called it, with each of the leaders inviting just ten guests to the Villa Koreis. Roosevelt's ten included Kathy, his daughter, Anna, and Sarah Churchill, which meant that his chiefs of staff, General George Marshall and Admiral Ernest King, had to be struck off the guest list.

'I was horribly embarrassed', wrote Kathy to Pamela, 'and told Anna, for God's sake, to change the list and leave me off.' But Roosevelt insisted that all three young ladies attend.

Averell wrongly assumed that Kathy had pushed herself onto the president's guest list and was extremely annoyed with her. 'He said I'd damn well have to make a speech in Russian.' In the four years of Kathy's correspondence from London and Moscow, these were the only sharp words he ever exchanged with her.

The Villa Koreis was more intimate than the Livadia Palace, an Italianate country house built on a modest scale. Kathy felt increasingly like a gatecrasher as she mingled among guests during the pre-dinner cocktails, for the other delegations had brought their most senior figures. Churchill arrived with the chief of the Imperial General Staff, Sir Alan Brooke, as well as the heads of the Royal Air Force and Royal Navy.

Stalin had also come with his highest-ranking officials. There were raised eyebrows, therefore, when it was discovered that President Roosevelt had brought along Kathy, Sarah, and Anna.

The party soon moved into the dining room, where the long table was set for a feast: caviar, pickled herring, cold pork, duck, salmon in champagne sauce, fried mackerel, grey mullet, lamb, veal, quail, and grouse. There were also copious quantities of wine, champagne, vodka, and brandy. 'In the Soviet fashion,' wrote Kathy, 'Stalin sat in the middle of a long table, with the president on his right and the PM on his left.'

Kathy was watching the Soviet leader attentively. He was convivial, smiling, cracking jokes. 'A splendid host,' she thought, 'and his three speeches were swell.' She would later jot down a short description of him, perhaps as a future reminder – lest it all vanish like a dream – that she had lived through extraordinary times.

'He had a rotund tubby figure with a clumsy gait that really did resemble a bear's. He shook hands in an unassuming way. His face was pock-marked, swarthy, with a big walrus-like mustache. His eyes had a yellowish tinge.'[18]

In one of his speeches, Stalin praised Churchill's steadfastness throughout the long years of war and called him 'the most courageous of all Prime Ministers in the world'. He then raised his glass 'to the health of the man who is born once in a hundred years'. Churchill was no less gracious in his reply, toasting Stalin in the most extravagant language. 'It is no exaggeration or compliment of a florid kind when I say we regard Marshal Stalin's life as most precious to the hopes and hearts of us all.'

Stalin next toasted Roosevelt. 'Even though his country was not directly imperilled,' he said, '[he] had been the chief forger of the instruments which had led to the mobilisation of the world against Hitler.' He spoke specifically of the Lend-Lease programme, calling it 'one of the President's most remarkable and vital achievements in the formation of the Anti-Hitler coalition and in keeping the Allies in the field against Hitler'.[19]

Roosevelt responded by saying that the dinner felt like 'a family meal' (which is exactly what he had proposed), adding that it was 'in those words that he liked to characterize the relations that existed between our three countries'.

While the toasts were being delivered, Kathy was scanning the table to see how many faces she knew. There was one repulsive-looking individual she had never seen before. 'He's little and fat with thick lenses which gave him a sinister look.' She was describing Lavrentiy Beria, the sadistic head of the NKVD.

President Roosevelt had also not recognised Beria. 'Who's that in the pince-nez?' he asked Stalin.

'Ah, that one. That's our Himmler,' replied Stalin.[20]

With all eyes now on Beria, Archie chose this moment to rise to his feet to pay his compliments to Stalin's most revolting commissar. Aware of Beria's reputation as a torturer, murderer, and serial rapist, he offered a highly ironic toast to the man 'who looks after our bodies'. Churchill was not amused by Archie's risqué turn of phrase and wagged an admonishing finger. 'Be careful,' he warned. 'Be careful.'[21]

Archie's interpreter, Arthur Birse, would later record no fewer than forty-five toasts during dinner, each of which had to be instantly translated. 'Both he [Stalin] and Churchill rose to such heights of oratory that Pavlov and I had the greatest difficulty in finding adequate expressions in our respective languages – he in English and I in Russian.'

Churchill was particularly hard to translate. 'He used phrases like, "I propose a toast to the broad sunlight of victorious peace", which had to be translated out of my scribbled notes without hesitation and in a convincing tone to produce the desired effect.'

Stalin was impressed by the skill of both Birse and Pavlov and rose to his feet at one point during the evening to toast the interpreters. 'They have no time to eat or drink,' he said. 'We rely on them to transmit our ideas to each other. I propose a toast to our interpreters.' He then walked round the table clinking glasses.

Churchill also raised his glass and bawled: 'Interpreters of the world unite! You have nothing to lose but your audience!' This parody of the Communist slogan had Stalin shaking with mirth. 'It was some minutes before he could stop laughing,' noted Birse.[22]

The Soviet leader also toasted the three women, Kathy, Sarah, and Anna, walking down to their end of the table and clinking glasses with them. 'He was on top form,' wrote Kathy. 'A charming, gracious, almost benign host, something I never thought he could be. His toasts were sincere and most interesting. More than the usual banalities.'

As the guests tackled their third meat course, Averell leaned across the table and told Kathy it was time for her to make her toast.

'Gee I was scared,' she later recalled. In her faulty but proficient Russian, she was to address the three most powerful leaders in the world. She kept it short, proposing a toast 'to those who had worked so hard in the Crimea for our comfort', adding that 'having seen the destruction wrought by the Germans here, she had fully realised what had been accomplished.'[23]

The Soviet guests were delighted she had made her toast in Russian. Sarah thought she had 'surpassed herself'.[24] Kathy herself was relieved it was over. Charles Bohlen was most impressed with her excellent Russian. In his official account of the evening, written for the State Department, he recorded only eight of the forty-five toasts. Among them was the one given by Kathy.

Kathy makes a speech in Russian; Averell is seated behind her. She was uncharacteristically nervous when she had to make a toast in Russian to Stalin, Roosevelt, and Churchill.

★

The Yalta Conference came to an end on Sunday, 11 February, with a flurry of excitement. There was a widespread feeling that it had exceeded all expectations. Each of the three leaders had made concessions; each of the three had achieved his major goals. There was a genuine belief that America and Britain could continue to cooperate with Stalin in the post-war world.

When they came to sign the final communiqué, they were in the best possible humour. Roosevelt suggested that Stalin sign it first, 'because he has been such a wonderful host'. Churchill joked that he should sign it first, by reason of the alphabet and the fact that he was the eldest of the three. Stalin said if he signed it first, people would say he had controlled the conference from beginning to end. It was eventually signed by Churchill, Roosevelt, and Stalin in that order.

Almost everyone felt a glow of optimism. Harry Hopkins thought they had saved the world. 'We really believed in our hearts that this was the dawn of the new day we had all been praying for and talking about for so many years. We were absolutely certain that we had won the first great victory of the peace – and by "we", I mean all of us, the whole civilized human race.'[25]

But two of those attending the conference were not convinced. Averell and Archie knew Stalin better than anyone else and were familiar with how he operated. They didn't trust him. And they had grave doubts about the future.

39
Averell Goes Rogue

PRESIDENT ROOSEVELT'S HEALTH deteriorated markedly in the weeks that followed the Yalta Conference. The long voyage, the complex negotiations, and the endless banquets had all taken their toll. He was tired, weak, and increasingly unwell.

His relationship with Stalin had also become fraught. The warmth of friendship between the Big Three dissipated with alarming speed. The first crisis occurred in the second week of March, when the SS commander, General Karl Woolf, contacted the Americans about the possible surrender of all German forces in northern Italy. No sooner had Stalin been informed of this than he flew into a rage. His reaction was so paranoid that it caused astonishment in Whitehall and Washington. He openly accused the Western allies of attempting to sign a separate peace with Germany.

Roosevelt assured Stalin that there had been no secret negotiations, but his words fell on deaf ears. The Soviet leader sent a withering reply suggesting that the president was being duped by his own advisers: 'It may be assumed that you have not been fully informed.'

Over the four weeks that followed, Stalin's letters to his Western partners became increasingly unpleasant. Roosevelt was deeply offended, as he said in one of his replies. 'Frankly, I cannot avoid a feeling of bitter resentment toward your informers, whoever they are, for such vile representations of my actions or those of my trusted subordinates.'[1]

Churchill was equally offended, but also confused. In the afterglow of Yalta, he had convinced himself that he had forged a close relationship with Stalin. Yet just a few weeks after their friendly banquets, he was being served up a string of insults. 'What puzzles me is the inconsistency,' he wrote in a letter to his wife, Clementine.[2]

In this moment of instability, Roosevelt wrote a conciliatory letter to Stalin. 'There must not, in any event, be mutual distrust,' he said, before adding that 'minor misunderstandings of this character should not arise in the future.'[3] The president was determined to keep the wartime alliance on track.

His letter was sent to Averell on Wednesday, 11 April, for immediate transmission to Stalin. But Averell prevaricated, convinced that Roosevelt was making a big mistake. Over the weeks since Yalta, he had hardened his opinion about Stalin. He no longer believed in his promise to hold free elections in Poland, nor anywhere else in Central and Eastern Europe. Indeed, he no longer believed a word that the Soviet leader said. 'Stalin wanted weak neighbors,' he wrote, 'because weak neighbors could be dominated.'[4]

The Red Army already controlled most of the territories coveted by the Soviet leader, some 300,000 square miles. Romania, Bulgaria, and large parts of Hungary were now in the grip of Soviet forces, with Budapest having surrendered two months earlier. Soviet troops had also overrun the entirety of Poland and were now approaching the gates of Berlin. Averell thought it inconceivable that Stalin would give up control of these territories. Instead, he would install puppet governments or simply bring them under direct Soviet rule.

He shared his opinions with Bob Meiklejohn, who agreed wholeheartedly with his boss. In one of his less guarded diary entries, he wrote: 'One cannot help but feel that being an ally of these bastards is only one step better than being their enemy.'

Both Meiklejohn and Averell were horrified by Roosevelt's conciliatory approach to Stalin, which they saw as weak, misguided, and naive. 'There is no doubt that we are letting a Frankenstein loose upon Europe,' wrote Meiklejohn, 'and I am convinced that until Frankenstein is disposed of, there will be no peace in the world.'[5]

Adamant that Roosevelt was making a catastrophic mistake, Averell wrote a telegram to the State Department urging an immediate change in policy. 'The President, at great inconvenience and risk to himself, paid the highest possible compliment to the Soviet Union by coming to Yalta. It seems clear that this magnanimous act on his part has been interpreted as a sign of weakness and Stalin and his associates are acting accordingly.'[6]

Averell's telegram came too late. That same day, while sitting for a portrait, Roosevelt collapsed and died of a cerebral haemorrhage.

This devastating news reached Spaso House during a farewell party for one of the embassy regulars. Kathy took the call at a few minutes after one o'clock in the morning and immediately informed her father. 'I noticed Kathleen with a very sober look on her face, drag the ambassador off to the Blue Room,' wrote Meiklejohn. Unsure what had happened, he was surprised to be told to turn off the Victrola [record player] and send everybody home.

'I don't know why we didn't tell our guests,' he later wrote. 'But we're so used to being secret about everything important that I imagine it was instinctive of the ambassador.'[7]

Although late, Averell telephoned Molotov to tell him the news. The foreign commissar rushed over to Spaso House to express his condolences. 'He seemed deeply moved and disturbed,' noted Averell. 'He stayed for some time talking about the part President Roosevelt had played in the war and the plans for peace.' Molotov assured Averell that the Soviet government would place its confidence in the new president, Harry Truman, formerly Roosevelt's vice president.

At eight o'clock the following evening, Averell met Stalin in the Kremlin. It was a curious meeting. The Soviet leader was ashen-faced and held Averell's hand for fully thirty seconds before asking him to sit down. Averell thought Stalin seemed deeply distressed, as if he had lost an old friend. 'President Roosevelt has died,' declared the Soviet leader, 'but his cause lives on. We shall support President Truman with all our forces and all our will.'

Averell took this opportunity to ask Stalin to make a significant gesture. In less than a fortnight, the representatives of forty-six nations were to gather in San Francisco for a conference to create and ratify the United Nations Charter. As relations between the Kremlin and the West had worsened, Stalin had pulled out of the conference. It had been a cruel blow to Roosevelt, who had invested so much in the establishment of this new body.

Averell now seized his moment, asking Stalin to reconsider. If Molotov was sent to San Francisco, he said, it would show to the world that Stalin was serious about the United Nations. But it would mean much more than that. It would make the Soviet Union a formal player in the post-war international order, working from the inside rather than being troublemaking outsiders. This had long been Roosevelt's geopolitical dream. It had motivated him ever since America's entry into the Second World War.

There was a long pause while Stalin considered Averell's request. Then, to Averell's great delight, he 'stated categorically that Mr Molotov's trip to the United States, although difficult at this time, would be arranged'.[8] It was a rare concession from Stalin, and one to be savoured.

'His nibs pulled a real rabbit out of the hat,' wrote Bob Meiklejohn later that night, although both he and Averell remained deeply suspicious of Stalin's motives.

At dawn on Tuesday, 17 April, Averell and Archie set off for San Francisco on an exhausting journey via Italy, Morocco, and the Azores. After a stop-over in Washington, the two ambassadors made their separate ways to San Francisco, with Archie arriving on Monday, 23 April. He soon became a magnet for the world's press, who relished his indiscreet briefings about life in the Soviet Union. 'Moscow's saving grace', wrote one. 'A totally cultivated man.'[9]

But behind the scenes, Archie was as worried as Averell about the future of Europe and the world. Shortly before heading to San Francisco, he wrote a memo to Whitehall warning that the mood in Moscow was rapidly changing. The West needed to sharpen its approach to Stalin – and fast.

'Wherever and whenever we show signs of weakening,' he wrote, 'we may expect to be pounced upon. We must therefore not only *be* strong – we must *look* strong.' The Soviet Union was euphoric in her hour of victory, 'in a state of high buoyancy and utterly confident of her strength'.[10] Swathes of Eastern Europe were now in the hands of the Red Army, and the rapid Sovietisation of the three reoccupied Baltic states – followed by killings and mass deportations – set an alarming precedent for the future. At the Yalta Conference, Stalin had signed up to the Declaration on Liberated Europe, which affirmed 'the right of all peoples to choose the form of government under which they will live'. Now, less than three months later, he was riding roughshod over the territories under his control.

Averell was in complete agreement with Archie's assessment of the Soviet Union, and he was no longer prepared to remain silent. Soon after arriving in San Francisco, he invited a group of America's most influential journalists to what was described as an off-the-cuff press conference. And then he let rip.

What Averell told those reporters was to cause a sensation. They had gathered in San Francisco to witness the late president's vision being put into practice; a vision in which old rivalries were to be forever laid aside. They were not prepared for Averell's stunning message of doom – one that was delivered with the authority of an ambassador who knew Stalin well.

'We must recognize that our objectives and the Kremlin's objectives are irreconcilable,' he began. 'The Kremlin wants to promote Communist dictatorships, controlled from Moscow, whereas we want – as far as possible – to see a world of governments responsive to the will of the people.'

The world, he warned, was splitting into two irreconcilable camps. The Kremlin camp was hell-bent on swallowing as many countries as possible. And Stalin could no longer be trusted. 'Unless we take issue with the present policy, there is every indication the Soviet Union will become a world bully wherever our interests are concerned.'

Averell thought his words would provoke a strong reaction, and they did. The distinguished *New York Herald Tribune* columnist Walter Lippmann stormed out of the press conference in disgust, closely followed by the broadcaster Raymond Gram Swing. The popular radio journalist Johannes Steel was appalled and told his listeners that Averell Harriman 'is obviously not fit to be American ambassador to Moscow and President Truman should remove him forthwith'.

Other reporters stayed to listen but profoundly disapproved of his message. Alexander Uhl declared himself appalled by the 'extraordinary amount of venom in his attitude toward the Russians'. A few were simply puzzled by Averell's criticisms of a country and leader who had played such a major role in winning the war. Journalist Charles van Devender was particularly confused. 'Extraordinary and inexplicable that this rich man could have spent so much time in the Soviet Union and yet somehow failed to see its essential virtues.'

A wave of vitriol now hit Averell, as columnists from around the country sharpened their insults. Some claimed he only feared the Soviet Union because he was a multimillionaire. When Averell later showed up at a cocktail party at the Soviet Embassy in Washington, a senior military official was heard to say, 'It's a wonder Harriman doesn't choke on that vodka. He has had his knife so far into Russia's back it isn't funny.'[11]

The White House and State Department listened to what Averell had to say about Stalin, but the most influential voices in the country were intent on keeping alive the wartime alliance. Chief of Staff General George Marshall spoke for many when he dismissed Averell's fears. 'Discount what he says,' he told one senior official. 'The Russians gave him a hard time and that made him too pessimistic.' General Eisenhower agreed, adding that the United States would have no trouble in containing the Soviet Union and that 'a new era of friendly relations lay ahead'.[12]

Averell found such comments alarmingly naive.

On Monday, 7 May, Bob Meiklejohn recorded a one-line entry in his diary. 'The war in Europe is over, with Germany's surrender.'[13] After five years and eight months of conflict, Hitler's thousand-year Reich had been crushed. The formal surrender took place at Reims, with General Alfred Jodl signing on behalf of the now-defunct Third Reich. Stalin did not accept this capitulation to the Western allies and insisted on a second ceremony in Soviet-occupied Berlin, with Field Marshal Wilhelm Keitel signing for Nazi Germany. Only once this second document had been signed did Stalin announce to his nation that enemy troops had laid down their arms. 'Now we can state with full certainty that there has come the historic day of the final rout of Germany.'[14] Henceforth, Russia and the West would celebrate victory on different days.

Averell was back in Moscow in time for Victory in Europe Day, despite his outspoken comments in San Francisco, and both he and Kathy would remain in the Soviet capital until the following January, when they would leave the Soviet Union for ever. Much would happen in those long and painful months: the Potsdam Conference, the division of both Germany and Berlin, and the steady encroachment of Moscow on the lives of millions of newly liberated people in Eastern and Central Europe.

Kathy kept up her letter writing during these final months in Moscow. One of the most memorable moments was when she joined Stalin for the victory parade in Red Square on Sunday, 26 June.

'Zhukov took the salute mounted on a white charger,' she wrote. 'The soldiers cheered him – their voices echoing back and forth in a way that made shivers run down my back. At the same time, gun salutes went off. Everyone was beautifully trained.' The high point came when the victorious Soviet soldiers flung their captured Nazi banners at Zhukov's feet.

It was around this time that Averell commented to a Soviet guest on a beautiful pedigree horse he had seen on a newsreel; the horse was being ridden by a senior general. As soon as Stalin was told of Averell's comment – and learned that both he and Kathy were experienced riders – he decided to present each of them with a horse. A few days later he sent an official to Spaso House to announce this intention.

Cir. (D 395,201) (Sat. 294,296)

This Clipping From
NEW YORK, N. Y.
WORLD-TELEGRAM

APR 30 1946

From Stalin to Harriman

Miss Kathleen Harriman, daughter of W. Averell Harriman, former Ambassador to the USSR, makes friends with Fact, one of two thoroughbred hunters given her father by Josef Stalin. They arrived in Baltimore yesterday on the Soviet freighter Sukhona.

Acme Telephoto.

A press cutting from Kathy's scrapbook. She and Averell received a number of presents from Stalin, the most valued being two pedigree horses which they eventually shipped to America.

'Ave came upstairs with a document', wrote Kathy, 'beautifully covered in red leather – the picture and pedigrees of two horses, the one which Ave had admired in the movie (English-bred) and the other a Don Basin horse, for me apparently. The first is named Fact, the second Boston. Now we've really got to scurry around and find a dacha with a stable to put them in.'[15]

The horses would eventually be shipped back to the United States and housed in stables at the Arden estate, where they were to live out the rest of their days.

Shortly before Kathy and her father left Moscow for good, Averell paid his final visit to Stalin. The Soviet leader showed no hard feelings about what Averell had said at San Francisco, nor did he reproach him for expressing what was palpably true. It was a wistful final meeting, with a long discussion about the state of the world. As Averell turned to leave, Stalin grasped his hand and shook it warmly. He thanked Averell for everything he had done for the Soviet Union, describing him as 'a friend of many years'.

Averell had performed miracles over the previous four years, keeping the fragile Big Three alliance on track. He had assuaged Stalin's fears of betrayal, fought against the Soviet leader's paranoia, and ensured that the conferences of Teheran and Yalta had not ended in disaster, as could so easily have been the case. Above all, Averell had helped to manage a complex relationship between three leaders with widely different backgrounds, approaches, and goals. Now, in the hour of victory, both he and Stalin knew that this extraordinary relationship was coming to an end.

Yet the Soviet leader remained deeply grateful to Averell. 'When help was needed,' he said, 'he could be counted on.'

That help had come overwhelmingly through the Lend-Lease programme, coordinated with skill and efficiency by Averell and Hopkins. The United States had furnished the Soviet Union with some seventeen million tons of supplies, valued at more than $11 billion. Supplies from Great Britain were smaller but still significant, including 5,600 tanks and over 7,000 aircraft.

This was a fraction of the total produced by the Soviet Union: Stalin said the country had manufactured 100,000 tanks and 120,000 planes during the course of the war. But many of the Lend-Lease deliveries consisted of specialist supplies and raw materials, along with five million tons of vitally needed food necessary to replace crops previously grown on farmland lost to the Nazi invaders.

American raw materials were particularly essential for the Soviet Union's survival, especially aluminium, copper, zinc, and steel. The American steel was a high-quality speciality product, much of it hot-rolled aircraft steel and cold-finished bars, both costly and difficult to produce. Lend-Lease aluminium was also vitally important: the T-34 tank, for example, had an aluminium alloy engine.[16]

The extent to which the West saved the Soviet Union from defeat is much debated. Nikita Khrushchev would later say that Stalin was unequivocal: 'He stated bluntly that if the United States had not helped us, we would not have won the war.'[17] Khrushchev said that Stalin made such comments on several occasions, although always in private. Khrushchev himself, who was often at the battle-front, shared his views. 'Stalin's conclusion was correct,' he wrote. 'When I listened to his remarks, I was fully in agreement with them.'

American trucks certainly aided the mechanised Soviet offensives in 1944, which encircled and trapped huge numbers of German troops. The Soviet Union may have eventually defeated the Wehrmacht on the Eastern Front without them, but it would have taken longer and proved a great deal more costly. Many thousands of lives had been saved by the supplies that Averell had shipped to the Soviet Union in its hours of desperate need. Stalin knew this and was deeply grateful to the American multimillionaire whom he had first met, mistrustfully, in autumn 1941.

Averell left the Kremlin on that January evening with his mind in conflict about the Soviet leader. He had seen him scores of times since his first meeting – at his best and worst. But when he later tried to set down his thoughts about Stalin, he found it difficult to reach any conclusions.

'It is hard for me to reconcile the courtesy and consideration that he showed me personally, with the ghastly cruelty of his wholesale liquidations,' he wrote. 'Others, who did not know him personally, see only the tyrant in Stalin. I saw the other side as well – his high intelligence, that fantastic grasp of detail, his shrewdness and the surprising human sensitivity that he was capable of showing, at least in the war years.

'I found him better informed than Roosevelt, more realistic than Churchill, in some ways the most effective of the war leaders. At the same time, he was, of course, a murderous tyrant. I must confess that for me, Stalin remains the most inscrutable and contradictory character I have ever known – and leave the final judgment to history.'[18]

Archie had also returned to Moscow after the San Francisco conference; he was to have two farewell meetings with Stalin. The first was an intimate dinner at the Kremlin, hosted by the Soviet leader and attended by Molotov, interpreter Pavlov, and a handful of British Embassy staff.

Stalin was in the best possible mood, thanking Archie for his years of friendship. 'You have done a lot for us,' he said. 'We should like to give you something to remember Russia by.'

Archie was quick to respond, doing so in a characteristically eccentric fashion. He told Stalin he was converting to Islam and would like to have four Russian wives. Stalin looked puzzled until the quip had been explained. Archie was referring to the four Russian women who had married members of the British Military Mission but had been refused exit visas to accompany their husbands back to England. He wanted permission for them to leave the country. Stalin promised to look into the matter and would soon prove true to his word. The visas were granted shortly afterwards.

Archie's second farewell meeting with Stalin was on Friday, 25 January, just two days before his departure. It was to prove the strangest meeting ever to take place between an ambassador and the Soviet leader. It was a private audience, with the only other people present being Molotov and Pavlov. No minutes were taken, and there was to be no record of their conversation. This was highly unusual, for all such meetings were reported in detail. Not on this occasion.

Embassy staff could only speculate on what took place. 'There is no knowing why he went alone to this interview,' wrote embassy attaché, Frank Giles. 'He did not speak good enough Russian to sustain a conversation without interpretation; and though Pavlov was there, it is not in diplomacy a usually recommended procedure to put total trust in your interlocutor's interpreter, however proficient.'

Frank Giles was bold enough to question Archie on his return from the Kremlin. The ambassador told him how Stalin had repeated his earlier offer – that he would like to give him something by which he would remember Russia. This time Archie did not joke. 'Would you be willing to part with one Soviet citizen out of two hundred million?' he said.[19]

Stalin asked what he meant.

Archie explained that his most cherished leaving present would be Evgeni Yost, his young masseur. Archie had formed a singular attachment to Yost and was desperate to take him to the West.

Stalin promised nothing at the time, although he asked Molotov to follow it up. Archie assumed nothing would come of his bold request. But at midnight on Saturday, 26 January, the day before his departure, the doorbell of the British Embassy rang unexpectedly. Frank Giles was the on-duty attaché that night and rushed down to the entrance hall, tripping over Archie's trunks and boxes.

He opened the door and saw two men weighed down with gifts for Archie: a panther-skin rug, a huge jar of caviar, two bottles of fine brandy, and a signed photograph of Stalin. But the most unusual present of all was an envelope containing a passport and exit visa for Evgeni Yost. The ambassador would not be leaving Moscow alone.

Archie's thank-you letter to Stalin was written from Indonesia, where he was to spend a few months before heading to Washington to take up his post as Britain's new ambassador to the United States. His letter was written in a characteristically exuberant tone. 'They shot me like a rocket across the sky,' he wrote, 'and I have come to rest here yesterday, happily without exploding.' He explained how he had stopped over in Singapore, where he shared Stalin's caviar with Lord Mountbatten. 'His eyes flashed and he broke into loud praise of you,' wrote Archie, 'as did all his generals. God! The noise they made over that caviar!'

Archie explained that he was honoured to have been given the panther skin and signed photograph, 'lasting souvenirs of a man for whom I have conceived real respect and affection'. But most of all, he was delighted to have been given Evgeni Yost, who was proving such hospitable company. 'He sweats prodigiously, for it is very hot and damp,' he wrote. 'While he flails my back, he asks me ceaseless questions about the magic wonders and tinsel charms of the tropics.'

Archie was deliriously happy for the first time in years. 'For all these things, I should like to thank you very sincerely, for I am really grateful, and still more for the friendliness and consideration which you were good enough to show me through my four years in Moscow. The memory of this will always be, for me, something very solid and precious.'[20]

A rare photo of Kathy, Averell, and Archie. The two ambassadors forged a close personal relationship and were united in their mistrust of Stalin. Kathy was particularly amused by Archie's sparkling wit.

Afterlives

Averell received a number of gifts from the Soviets in recognition of his steadfast support during the war. The most thoughtful and coveted present was a large replica of the Great Seal, the national symbol of the United States. Hand-carved from wood and polished to a sheen, it featured an imposing eagle with outstretched wings.

Averell was deeply touched by the gift and hung it in the ambassador's private library in Spaso House, the room in which he convened many secret meetings. It remained there for the next six years, admired by three successive US ambassadors. But in 1951, a British radio operator in Moscow was fiddling with frequencies when he found himself unexpectedly eavesdropping on a conversation taking place inside that very library. He alerted the Americans, having realised that there must be a bug concealed somewhere in the room. There was. It was inside the Great Seal – a state-of-the-art Soviet listening device that required no power source, which gave it an unlimited lifespan.

The Americans kept the discovery a secret for seven years, making it public only in 1960 when the Soviets shot down an American U-2 spy plane over their air space. Feigning outrage, the USSR lodged a formal complaint against American espionage at the UN Security Council. The Americans responded by producing the Soviets' gift to Averell Harriman and revealing to the world the listening device concealed inside. It was a moment of high tension in the Cold War and one with long-term consequences. In the aftermath of the debacle, all dialogue between the opposing sides ended abruptly and the arms race escalated dangerously. The world inched closer to conflict.

Averell's return to the United States from Moscow in 1946 marked the beginning of a long and distinguished political career. His first years in Washington were spent warning of the dangers posed by the Soviet Union, a warning fully borne out by Stalin's 1948 blockade of the Western-occupied sectors of Berlin. Thereafter, Averell would serve as secretary of commerce and governor of New York, as well as being appointed a roving ambassador at large. In the late 1960s, he was an outspoken critic of the Vietnam War.

In all these years he did not see his wartime amour, Pamela Churchill, who had forged her own path in life and had a string of lovers since her divorce from Randolph Churchill in 1945.

Although she had often written to Averell during his years in Moscow, her eye wandered far and wide. The wealthy banker Elie de Rothschild had been one of her lovers; next came the Italian playboy (and car manufacturer) Giovanni Agnelli. Finally, in 1961, she married the film producer Leland Hayward, whose many hits included *The Sound of Music*. When Hayward died in spring 1971, Pamela found herself single and lonely.

At that very moment she was invited to a Washington dinner party hosted by an old friend. She had already arrived when in walked an unexpected guest: Averell Harriman. Like her, he had recently lost his spouse. And like her, he was lonely. Their old friendship was re-ignited in a flash. 'Since we were both suddenly free and alone,' said Pamela, 'it just seemed the most natural thing in the world to kind of get together again.'

This time their relationship was on more solid ground. That September, they were married in New York, with Kathy acting as a witness. 'It was either the beginning or the end of an era,' wrote wedding guest Truman Capote, who knew all about their long-standing relationship.[1] The couple would remain together until Averell's death in 1986. They had always wondered whether Winston and Clementine Churchill had known of their secret affair back in 1941. In the wake of their engagement, Pamela wrote to her former mother-in-law to tell her the news.

'My, my,' was Clementine's response, 'an old flame rekindled.'[2]

Archie's appointment as ambassador to Washington was the post he had always coveted and a richly deserved reward for those arduous years in Moscow and Chungking. He was even more delighted when told that the posting came with an elevation to the peerage.

He chose as his title Lord Inverchapel of Loch Eck in the County of Argyll. This had been his boyhood fantasy, and now it had come true. He was lord of the place he loved more than anywhere else in the world.

He raised more than a few eyebrows when choosing his coat of arms. The heraldic shield was conventional enough, but the two figures supporting it were decidedly unconventional: two male athletes, both naked, with their genitalia generously exposed. The motto he chose was similarly risqué: *Concussus surgo*, 'Having been shaken, I rise'. When his arms came to be published in *Burke's Peerage*, the abashed editors provided the two figures with underpants.

Archie's ambassadorship to the United States was not a success. Although he oversaw a cementing of post-war relations between America and Great Britain, he was widely perceived as being tired, old, and out of touch. His past did not help. He was best known for having been an intimate of the West's wartime ally, Joseph Stalin. But Stalin was now trampling roughshod over the peoples of Eastern Europe, making Archie yesterday's man.

He had also shocked many in Washington with his outlandish humour. 'I have a Russian slave at the embassy, given to me by Stalin,' he would tell them.[3] It was a joke that did not play well in the United States.

After two years in the post, Archie was informed that he was being stood down. He was almost relieved, for he was now sixty-five and in need of rest. 'I should be packed away in the museum among the mothballs, whose fragrance becomes more and more alluring to me,' he wrote.[4] He was saddened that the dreams of a happier post-war era had not come to pass. 'The hopes for a new world of harmony, brotherhood and peace, which were high in our hearts, have been sadly pushed about and jostled.'[5] As he well knew, they had been jostled by his old friend, Joseph Stalin.

There was another reason why Archie was happy to quit his post in Washington. In summer 1947, Tita had suddenly reappeared in his life. The circumstances of their reconciliation are unclear, but it happened rapidly and dramatically. Within weeks, while on holiday in Edinburgh, the two of them were remarried. The wedding was supposed to have been secret, but the press got wind of it and ended up chasing their car through the streets.

After a brief return to Washington, the newlyweds left the United States for the last time in the spring of 1948, travelling to Loch Eck with the bemused Evgeni Yost in tow. Tita did not enjoy her first winter in such a remote part of Scotland and subsequently spent much of her time in the United States, leaving Archie in the company of his masseur.

Tita would return sporadically, but she got bored in the wilds of Scotland. Yost himself loved the countryside; he worked at the Inverchapel farm for two years before Archie lent him enough money to pursue his dream – running a fish and chip shop in Rothesay, on the remote island of Bute. He would later marry a Scottish woman and father nine children.

Archie was to live only a few more years after his retirement. He had been suffering from recurrent heart problems and these grew increasingly acute in summer 1951. In the first week of July, he was rushed to hospital in severe pain. It proved too late to save him. On the afternoon of Thursday, 5 July, he died of heart failure. Aged just sixty-nine, he was buried at the southern end of his beloved Loch Eck. His grave, these days half-obscured by fallen branches and leaf mulch, makes no mention of his remarkable wartime experiences, nor of his intimacy with Stalin, Churchill, and Roosevelt. It merely records his name and title: First Baron Inverchapel of Loch Eck.

A year and a half before his death, the BBC had commissioned Archie to write a profile of Stalin. The tone of his piece was widely held to be unwarranted, for it imagined a future in which Stalin's murderous crimes would be forgotten and he would be remembered as a triumphant war hero who had saved his country from disaster.

'I do not propose to follow him through the long and sordid story of his rise to power,' he wrote, 'the sickening annals of his tyranny and his vicious regime. The memory of all this will be lost to his own people in the golden haze of his glory. The saviour of his country, the mastermind of the strategy of victory that lifted the nation out of its slough of the Middle Ages and made it the leading industrial country in Europe.' Stalin, he said, would not be viewed as George Orwell's

Big Brother. Rather, his would be seen as a name 'to kindle the pride and the love of multitudes of Russians'.

Such a sentiment seemed totally misplaced in the early 1950s, when Stalin was a pariah in the West and denounced even by those who had formerly served under him. A similar piece by Archie, commissioned by the *New York Times*, was unceremoniously spiked. 'Something of a relief,' he scrawled on their rejection letter.[6]

In recent years, the current regime in Russia has been overseeing the steady rehabilitation of the Soviet Union's tyrannical wartime leader. In summer 2023, a newly fashioned statue of Stalin was erected in the Pskov region and blessed by the local Orthodox priest. It may not be long before the city of Volgograd reverts to its wartime name, Stalingrad. If that comes to pass, Archie's words will have been proved to be chillingly prophetic.

Kathy settled down within a year of returning from Moscow, marrying Stanley Mortimer, a wealthy American advertising executive, and having three children. She never spoke about her wartime years in the Soviet Union, but she must have been quietly proud of what she had achieved, for she carefully pasted all her press cuttings into bound scrapbooks.

Clementine Churchill had read a number of Kathy's wartime letters to Pamela and found them thoroughly entertaining. 'I think your letters will make a wonderful book one day – not, however, to be published just now!'[7] But Kathy scorned those who cashed in on their wartime experiences. 'As peace returned many underlings of the war leaders sprang into print. I felt they abused their wartime privilege (& luck) of being on hand as history was made & swore I'd not do likewise.'[8]

She wrapped her letters into neat little bundles, tied them up with ribbon, and stored them in a cupboard. They remained there for decades, and it was not until her son, David, was sorting through her paperwork, just a few weeks before she died, that he noticed a box containing two large brown scrapbooks. Inside was a collection of photographs and scores of newspaper cuttings with her name on them, the products of a career that her family knew next to nothing about. There were also several hundred letters sent from both London and Moscow.

Kathy kept copies of her wartime letters and glued her photos and newspaper cuttings into a scrapbook. Yet she rarely spoke about her four years in London and Moscow.

'Hey, Mom, what is this about?' asked David on discovering the papers.[9] 'Oh, that,' said Kathy, before changing the subject. Since her mind was beginning to fade, David let the matter drop. But when he looked through the letters and read the press cuttings, he discovered an unknown chapter of his mother's life.

In 2023 David gave the originals of Kathy's letters to the Manuscript Division of the Library of Congress, so that a wider public may henceforth read and enjoy them.

And what of the other important players in *The Stalin Affair*? Bob Meiklejohn spent a great deal of time writing up the notes he had made about his years in London and Moscow, all of which were eventually given to the Library of Congress. He was already married when he first headed to London in 1941. Now he had a family and pursued a successful post-war business career, becoming a vice president of the Allied Chemical and Dye Corporation.

Archie Clark Kerr's interpreter, Arthur Birse, also became a successful businessman, but he continued to assist the British government with high-level interpreting. When Anthony Eden was prime minister, he asked Birse to be his interpreter at the Berlin Conference of 1954.

Stalin's interpreter, Vladmir Pavlov, worked as head of the British desk at the Soviet Foreign Ministry in the years that followed the end of the Second World War. But he fell out of favour after Stalin's death and lived the rest of his life in quiet seclusion. He died in 1993, leaving neither letters nor a memoir about his remarkable wartime service.

The 'half-man', Harry Hopkins, died in January 1946, just nine months after President Roosevelt. He was fifty-five years old. It was a miracle that he had lived so long, for his body was broken by cancer, massive blood transfusions, and huge doses of iron supplements. He had proved a true friend to all of the Big Three, organising the American end of the vast Lend-Lease programme.

A great deal of that Lend-Lease equipment was still in Britain at the end of the war. This was sold at a knock-down price to the near-bankrupt government, with payments stretched out over six decades. The last instalment was paid on 26 December 2006.

America found it rather harder to negotiate a deal with the Soviet Union. As Roosevelt had always made clear, the United States sought no compensation for equipment destroyed in the war, nor for weaponry that was still usable. It asked for payment only for civilian supplies such as lorries, machine tools, and industrial equipment. These were valued at $2.6 billion.

The Soviet government was indignant. 'It is like asking us to pay for saving your life, after we have been severely wounded in the process,' commented one Soviet writer. 'What are a few thousand trucks and planes compared with the blood of seven million Russians.'[10]

After years of wrangling, the two sides reached a compromise in 1972, with the Soviet Union agreeing to pay $722 million.

The last word in this saga must go to Winston Churchill, whose relationship with Stalin was to undergo one final permutation. In spring 1946, less than a year after Averell's explosive press conference in San Francisco, Churchill was to cause even more of a stir when President Truman invited him to make a speech in Fulton, Missouri, his home state. Surrounded by pressmen and speaking on a world stage, the former prime minister forcefully turned on his wartime partner, Joseph Stalin, accusing him of posing a grave threat to global peace and stability. Deploying a phrase filled with Churchillian resonance, he urged the world to wake up to the fact that Stalin and the Soviet Union had gone from ally to foe: 'From Stettin in the Baltic to Trieste in the Adriatic, an Iron Curtain has descended across the continent.'[11]

Churchill's thinking about the Soviet Union had come full circle. Back in 1919, when secretary of state for war, he had done more than anyone else to try to strangle the new regime at birth, despatching weaponry and troops to fight the Red Army. Then came his spectacular volte-face in 1941 when he displayed great political courage by declaring his support for Stalin in the fight against Hitler.

In the years that followed, he had seen the Soviet leader face to face on five occasions, and the two leaders had also exchanged hundreds of letters and telegrams.* Churchill had witnessed Stalin at his gregarious best and his duplicitous worst.

Now, just thirteen months after their most successful meeting, at Yalta, Churchill was declaring to the world that Stalin could no longer be trusted. He was brutally imposing his will on the countries and peoples of Eastern Europe and the world needed to wake up to his tyrannical rule of terror.

The Soviet leader's response to Winston Churchill's 'Iron Curtain' speech was bellicose. In an article in *Pravda*, he denounced it as 'a call to war with the Soviet Union'. He also took the opportunity to launch a vitriolic personal attack on Churchill, saying his ideas about race were very similar to those of Adolf Hitler. It was a uniquely offensive comment.

The *New York Times* was outraged by the viciousness of Stalin's language and noted that relations between the Soviet Union and the

* They had met for a final time at the Potsdam Conference in Berlin in summer 1945. This conference is described in the author's book *Checkmate in Berlin*.

West had sunk to their lowest point in years. This was an understatement. The remarkable wartime partnership had come to an abrupt and definitive end.

There were to be many ups and downs in the years that followed, but Churchill's outspoken speech – and Stalin's chilling response – fired the opening salvo of the Cold War.

Over the previous five years, the Big Three leaders had built the most unlikely coalition in history. They had set aside their profound personal and political differences to defeat a common enemy. Archie and Averell had played a central role in keeping the alliance on track, advising President Roosevelt throughout those difficult years and skilfully handling the deep-seated aversion between Churchill and Stalin.

But the Big Three alliance was always fragile, and it was destined not to endure. Against all the odds, it had won the war for the Allies. But it was unable to survive the peace.

Acknowledgements

In spring 2019 I learned of a cache of curious wartime letters held in private hands in New York. The letters were written by Kathy Harriman, whose life was to take an unexpected twist in spring 1941.

I contacted Kathy's son, David Mortimer, who graciously invited me to his Manhattan apartment where he kept his late mother's letters, scrapbooks, press cuttings, and photographs. There were more than two hundred letters, tied together in bundles and roughly sorted by date. Some were handwritten in fountain pen or ballpoint; others had been typed on Kathy's Underwood portable typewriter. As is revealed in *The Stalin Affair*, they are observant and endlessly fascinating.

I am deeply grateful to David for allowing me unlimited access to this private family archive, and for his generous hospitality during my time in New York. A warm thank-you, also, to Catherine Grace Katz, who first put me in contact with him.

Kathy's letters set me off on an international paper trail, with much of my research taking place in the Manuscript Division of the Library of Congress. This houses the vast Averell Harriman archive. This research took place in the immediate aftermath of the last Covid-19 lockdown, when Washington was hesitantly reopening, and research spaces were restricted. I am deeply grateful to the Manuscript Division archivists for being both accommodating and knowledgeable, and also to a local researcher who anonymously relinquished her pre-booked slots so that I (a long-distance visitor) could have extra time in the archive. I also wish to thank Penguin Random House for allowing me to quote from Averell Harriman's memoir, *Special Envoy.*

On the west coast of America, thank you to Kira Elyse Conte who photographed the entirety of George Hill's typescript diary, *Reminiscences of Four Years with N.K.V.D.*

I would like to thank the film/TV duo, Tom and Kit Mangan, for putting me up during my stay in New York. In Washington, I was generously looked after by Jill and Flo Dauchy (and Abigail and Harrison), whose Georgetown home provided a welcome respite after long days in the archives.

In England, I am grateful to the staff of The National Archives, which holds so many of Archibald Clark Kerr's official papers. I am no less grateful to the ever-helpful staff of the Weston Library (Bodleian) in Oxford, which holds Clark Kerr's private jottings and office diaries, along with an impressive array of newspaper cuttings. The research notes of Donald Gillies, compiled for his excellent biography of Clark Kerr, *Radical Diplomat*, also proved invaluable, as did the information he shared in his correspondence with me.

Thank you to Professor Geoffrey Roberts for providing me with useful information about Kathy Harriman's letters; Professor Roberts is the author of the article, 'The Correspondence of Kathleen Harriman', cited in the Notes and Bibliography.

Thank you also to Richard Davenport-Hines and Roland Philipps for sharing colourful discoveries about Clark Kerr.

In London, I am grateful to the team at the Parliamentary Archives, repository of the Beaverbrook papers (along with much other material on the September 1941 mission to Moscow).

I am, as ever, grateful to the brilliant staff at the London Library, where much of this book was written.

In Cambridge, I am most thankful, once again, to the director of the Churchill Archives Centre, Allen Packwood, for allowing me access to all the material from this period, including the handwritten diaries of Mary Churchill. I am equally grateful to Mary's daughter, Emma Soames, for allowing me to quote from her mother's diary.

With thanks to Yale University Press for allowing me to reproduce short extracts from the Maisky diaries.

A great deal of work goes into the production of a book. At my British publishers, John Murray, I owe a debt of gratitude to my brilliant editors, the managing director Nick Davies and publishing director Joe Zigmond. Their advice and suggestions proved invaluable. The book has been steered towards production by an impressive team: Caroline Westmore, Siam Hatzaw, Juliet Brightmore, Chris

Bell, designer Sara Marafini, Diana Talyanina (production), publicist Charlotte Hutchinson, and marketeer Ellie Bailey. Equal thanks to my American publishers: my editor Caroline Zancan, and the marvellous team at Henry Holt: editorial assistant Leela Gebo, designer Meryl Levavi, managing editor Janel Brown, production editor Chris O'Connell, and production manager Eve Diaz.

Warmest thanks to my long-standing literary agent Georgia Garrett, and her team at Rogers, Coleridge & White, who do such a wonderful job selling the foreign rights; also, to my TV and film agent, Rob Kraitt, at Casarotto Ramsay & Associates.

Lastly, my most heartfelt thanks are due to my brilliantly talented wife Alexandra, and our three daughters, Madeleine, Héloïse, and Aurélia. They showed admirable patience and understanding as *The Stalin Affair* steadily took over my life.

La Muscade, Magny, Burgundy, spring 2024

Picture Credits

Alamy Stock Photo: p. 5/Everett Collection, p. 15/Chronicle, p. 51/ Associated Press, p. 89/World History Archive, p. 134/Granger Historical Picture Archive, p. 140/Trinity Mirror/Mirrorpix, p. 168/ World of Triss, p. 206/Geopix, p. 288/Fremantle, p. 290/Everett Collection, p. 314/Associated Press. Margaret Bourke-White: p. 70/ The LIFE Picture Collection/Shutterstock. Getty Images: p. 57/ Bettmann, p. 73/Picture Post, p. 158/Hulton Deutsch. Courtesy of Donald Gillies: p. 145/photographer unknown, from *Radical Diplomat: The Life of Archibald Clark Kerr, Lord Inverchapel, 1882–1951* (I. B. Tauris, 1999). Library of Congress, Manuscript Division: p. 202/diary of Robert P. Meiklejohn in the W. Averell Harriman papers. David Low, 'Coming Down to Earth': p. 91/Evening Standard Ltd. Courtesy of David Mortimer: pp. 28, 49, 52, 54, 102, 190, 197, 219, 243, 246, 262, 295, 303, 308. The National Archives, UK: p. 84/HO 216/29, p. 125/FO 800/300 pages 44/45, p. 164/FO 800/300/2, p. 193/FO 800/301/215FF, p. 270/FO 800/302/96. George Skadding: p. 253/ The LIFE Picture Collection/Shutterstock. Courtesy of Emma Soames: p. 39. TopFoto: p.113.

The Kathleen Lanier Harriman Mortimer papers have recently been donated to the Library of Congress, Manuscript Division.

Notes

Abbreviations

BNW:	Bodleian Library, Weston Special Collections, Oxford
CAC:	Churchill Archives Centre, Cambridge
IWM:	Imperial War Museum, London
MDLoC:	Manuscript Division, Library of Congress, Washington
PA:	Parliamentary Archives, London
TNA:	The National Archives, Kew, London
WAH:	W. Averell Harriman Papers, Manuscript Division, Library of Congress, Washington

Prelude

1. Cited in Beevor, *Second World War*, p. 228.
2. Cited in *New York Times*, 21 June 1981.
3. Cited in Dimbleby, *Barbarossa*, p. 128.
4. Cited in Sebag Montefiore, *Stalin*, p. 316.
5. Ibid., p. 317.
6. Ibid.
7. Shirer, *Third Reich*, p. 822.
8. Overy, *Russia's War*, p. 73.
9. Winston Churchill, *Second World* War, vol. 3, pp. 327ff. See also Gorodetsky, *Grand Delusion*, pp. 311ff.

Chapter 1: Winston's Broadcast

1. Colville, *Fringes of Power*, p. 405.
2. Ibid. See also Gilbert, *Winston S. Churchill*, vol. 6, p. 1119, and Winston Churchill, *Second World War*, vol. 3, p. 330.

3. *Weekly Despatch*, 22 June 1919, cited in Ponting, *Churchill*, p. 229.
4. Colville, *Fringes of Power*, p. 404.
5. Quoted in *American Mercury*, 1 July 1942. See Beaverbrook Papers, especially 'Mission to Moscow', PA, BBK/D/90–1. See also Alexander Werth, *Russia at War*, p. 270, and Cripps's letter to his wife, 26 August 1940, BNW, MS 9661/120.
6. Winston Churchill, *Second World War*, vol. 3, p. 330.
7. All from 'Minister Winston Churchill's Broadcast on the Soviet-German War', London, 22 June 1941, British Library of Information, http://www.ibiblio.org/pha/policy/1941/410622d.html. See also Winston Churchill, *Second World War*, vol. 3, pp. 331–3.
8. Colville, *Fringes of Power*, p. 405.
9. Mary Churchill, Diaries, Sunday, 22 June 1941, CAC, MCHL 1/1/3.

Chapter 2: Roosevelt Meets the Press

1. *New York Times*, 23 June 1941.
2. Ibid.
3. Henry Stimson's policy was nuanced. He was opposed to the United States being drawn into the war, which led him to vigorously support Lend-Lease aid to the United Kingdom (see Stimson, *On Active Service*, pp. 173–81). But his diary makes clear that he had serious reservations about also supplying the Soviet Union with weaponry (see Eyck, 'Secretary Stimson and the European War', pp. 46–7). The subject of American support for both the UK and Soviet Union is covered in Herring, *Aid to Russia*, pp. 2–11.
4. Cited in Herring, *Aid to Russia*, p. 6.
5. Both from *New York Times*, 24 June 1941.
6. A transcript of the press conference is available at http://www.fdrlibrary.marist.edu/_resources/images/pc/pc0118.pdf

Chapter 3: Stalin's Crisis

1. Alexander Werth, *Russia at War*, p. 123.
2. Cited in Overy, *Russia's War*, p. 74.
3. Sebag Montefiore, *Stalin*, p. 324.
4. Ibid., p. 325.

5. Alexander Werth, *Russia at War*, pp. 159–60. See also Cassidy, *Moscow Dateline*, p. 36.
6. Sebag Montefiore, *Stalin*, p. 325.
7. Ibid., p. 148.
8. Overy, *Russia's War*, 78.
9. As recorded by Bourke-White, *Taste of War*, pp. 40ff.

Chapter 4: A Man Named Averell

1. Marie Brenner, 'To War in Silk Stockings', *Vanity Fair*, 18 April 2018, https://www.vanityfair.com/style/2018/04/to-war-in-silk-stockings-kathleen-mortimer
2. All from 'Memorandum of Conversation with the President', WAH, Box 863.
3. 'Franklin Roosevelt's Press Conference', 17 December 1940, Franklin Delano Roosevelt Presidential Library and Museum, http://docs.fdrlibrary.marist.edu/odllpc2.html
4. All from 'Memorandum of Conversation with the President', WAH, Box 863.
5. Meiklejohn, 'World War II Diary at London and Moscow, March 10, 1941–February 14, 1946', WAH, Box 211.
6. Harriman and Abel, *Special Envoy*, p. 17.
7. Ibid., pp. 19–22. For the early months of the Harriman Mission, see Meiklejohn, 'Report on the Harriman Mission, March 1941–October 1943', WAH, Box 165.

Chapter 5: Meeting Winston

1. Soames (ed.), *Speaking for Themselves*, p. 225.
2. 'War Reminiscences', WAH, Box 872. See also Box 159 for a wealth of papers about Harriman's early days in England.
3. Harriman and Abel, *Special Envoy*, p. 21.
4. Mary Churchill, Diaries, Sunday, 15 March 1941, CAC, MCHL 1/1/3.
5. Harriman and Abel, *Special Envoy*, p. 21.
6. Ibid., p. 22. See also WAH, Box 872, 'War Reminiscences'.
7. All from Harriman and Abel, *Special Envoy*, pp. 22–3, and 'War Reminiscences', WAH, Box 872.

8. Mary Churchill, Diaries, Monday, 17–Tuesday, 18 March 1941, CAC, MCHL 1/1/3.
9. Meiklejohn, Diary, 19 April 1942.

Chapter 6: A Deepening Friendship

1. Mary Churchill, Diaries, Sunday, 20 April 1941, CAC, MCHL 1/1/3.
2. Harriman and Abel, *Special Envoy*, p. 23. But see also 'War Reminiscences', WAH, Box 872.
3. 'War Reminiscences', WAH, Box 872.
4. Harriman and Abel, *Special Envoy*, p. 31.
5. Ibid., pp. 32–3.
6. Ibid., p. 33.
7. Beaton, *The Years Between*, p. 52.
8. Letter, Meiklejohn to Knight Woolley, WAH.
9. All from 'First Trip with Prime Minister: Swansea, Bristol and Cardiff', WAH, Box 159. See also Harriman and Abel, *Special Envoy*, p. 28.
10. Harriman and Abel, *Special Envoy*, p. 28.
11. All from 'First Trip with Prime Minister: Swansea, Bristol and Cardiff', WAH, Box 159. See also Harriman and Abel, *Special Envoy*, p. 28.
12. Cowles, *Looking for Trouble*, p. 113.
13. As cited in Bedell Smith, *Reflected Glory*, p. 97.
14. Ibid., p. 85.
15. Ibid., pp. 83–5.
16. Ibid., p. 85.

Chapter 7: Kathy and Churchill

1. All from WAH, Box 11. This box contains all the paperwork surrounding Kathy Harriman's visit to London.
2. Kathleen Harriman, Letters, 17 May 1941.
3. *New York Daily Mirror*, 9 May 1941.
4. Kathleen Harriman, Letters, 17 May 1941.
5. Ibid., May 1941 (date unclear).
6. Ibid., 17 May 1941.
7. Ibid.
8. Ibid., n.d., probably May 1941.
9. INS report by Kathleen Harriman, *New York Journal*, 4 June 1941.

10. All from Kathleen Harriman, Letters, May 1941 (date unclear).
11. Letter from Herbert Swope to Averell Harriman, 7 August 1941, WAH, Box 11.
12. Kathleen Harriman, Letters, n.d., probably May 1941. But see also 7 July 1941.
13. Ibid., 14 June 1941 and 15 June 1941.
14. Ibid., n.d., probably May or June 1941.
15. All from ibid.
16. From Kathleen Harriman, Letters, 12 July 1941.
17. Bedell Smith, *Reflected Glory*, p. 88.
18. Cited in Marie Brenner, 'To War in Silk Stockings', *Vanity Fair*, 18 April 2018,https://www.vanityfair.com/style/2018/04/to-war-in-silk-stockings-kathleen-mortimer
19. Kathleen Harriman, Letters, 27 June 1941.
20. Ibid., 8 August 1941.

Chapter 8: Unwelcome Guests

1. All from Bourne and Watt (eds), *British Documents on Foreign Affairs*, pp. 398ff.
2. See Cripps, unpublished letter to his wife, 28 June 1941, BNW, MSS 9661/122.
3. For a full catalogue of Cripps's miseries, see Gorodetsky, *Stafford Cripps' Mission*, pp. 83–6.
4. Cripps, Diary, 8 July 1941.
5. Cassidy, *Moscow Dateline*, p. 46.
6. Sebag Montefiore, *Stalin*, p. 331.
7. Ibid., pp. 332–3; Overy, *Russia's War*, pp. 78–9; Service, *Stalin*, pp. 414–16.
8. Bourke-White, *Taste of War*, pp. 40–1.
9. Cripps, Diary, 12 July 1941.
10. Cassidy, *Moscow Dateline*, p. 52.
11. Cripps, Diary, 12 July 1941.
12. Butler, *Mason Mac*, p. 136.

Chapter 9: Moscow Aflame

1. Alexander Werth, *Russia at War*, p. 164.
2. Elvin, *Cockney in Moscow*, p. 98.

3. Ibid.
4. Cripps, Diary, 21 July 1941.
5. Cassidy, *Moscow Dateline*, p. 64.
6. Elvin, *Cockney in Moscow*, p. 100.
7. Cassidy, *Moscow Dateline*, p. 68.
8. Cripps, Diary, 22 July 1941.
9. Cited in Beevor, *Second World War*, p. 241.

Chapter 10: The Big Two

1. Colville, *Fringes of Power*, p. 415.
2. All quotes from Maisky, *Diaries*, vol. 3, pp. 1120–2.
3. Sherwood, *Roosevelt and Hopkins*, p. 2.
4. Gilbert, *Churchill Documents*, vol. 16, p. 58.
5. Maisky, *Diaries*, vol. 3, p. 1124.
6. Meiklejohn, Diary, 30 July 1941.
7. Harriman and Abel, *Special Envoy*, p. 75.
8. Roll, *Hopkins Touch*, p. 137.
9. Ibid., p. 138.
10. Ibid., p. 140. A good account of the conference can be found in Theodore Wilson, *The First Summit* (University of Kansas Press, 1991).
11. Averell Harriman, letter to Kathy and Pamela Churchill, August 1941, WAH, Box 159.
12. Chisholm and Davie, *Beaverbrook*, p. 394.
13. Ibid.
14. Williams, *Beaverbrook*, p. 403.
15. Cited in Bedell Smith, *Reflected Glory*, p. 66.
16. Cited in Purnell, *First Lady*, p. 266.
17. Williams, *Beaverbrook*, p. 116.
18. Gourlay, *The Beaverbrook I Knew*, p. 103.
19. 'Beaverbrook Admits He'd Like to See US in War', INS article in Kathleen Harriman's scrapbook, n.d.
20. Kathleen Harriman, Letters, 14 October 1941.

Chapter 11: Meeting Stalin

1. This account of the Moscow trip is derived from several sources, published and unpublished. The former include Harriman and Abel, *Special Envoy*,

chapter IV. The latter include Harriman, 'Memorandum of a Trip to Moscow', WAH, Box 159; 'Report on the Harriman Mission', WAH, Box 165; and many unsorted papers. See also Meiklejohn, Diary; 'Moscow Diary' by Harold Balfour, PA, BAL/1, and the vast collection of Lord Beaverbrook material, especially PA, BBK/D/89.
2. Meiklejohn, Diary, 23 September 1941.
3. 'Memorandum of a Trip to Moscow', WAH, Box 159.
4. Balfour, 'Moscow Diary', p. 23.
5. Chisholm and Davie, *Beaverbrook*, p. 413.
6. Bohlen and Phelps, *Witness to History*, p. 131.
7. Harriman and Abel, *Special Envoy*, p. 87.
8. Chisholm and Davie, *Beaverbrook*, p. 414.
9. Harriman and Abel, *Special Envoy*, p. 89.
10. Meiklejohn, Diary, 29 September 1941.
11. Meiklejohn, Diary, 1 October 1941, and following entries.
12. WAH, Box 159, various untitled files.
13. Ibid.
14. Ibid.
15. Meiklejohn, Diary, various entries, especially 1 September 1941.
16. Balfour, 'Moscow Diary', p. 42.
17. Quentin Reynolds, *Only the Stars*, p. 85.
18. Meiklejohn, Diary, 1 October 1941.
19. Chisholm and Davie, *Beaverbrook*, p. 418.
20. Quentin Reynolds, *Only the Stars*, p. 79.
21. Cripps, Diary, 29 September, 1 October and 4 October 1941.
22. Harriman and Abel, *Special Envoy*, p. 105.

Chapter 12: Taking Flight

1. Quentin Reynolds, *Only the Stars*, pp. 135–6.
2. Haldane, *Russian Newsreel*, p. 168.
3. All from Elvin, *Cockney in Moscow*, p. 195.
4. Cited in Beevor, *Second World War*, p. 278.
5. Toland, *Hitler*, p. 685; Overy, *Russia's War*, p. 94.
6. All from Cripps, Diary, 16 October 1941.
7. Haldane, *Russian Newsreel*, p. 169.
8. Alice-Leone Moats's account of the evacuation is in her book *Blind Date with Mars*, pp. 406ff.

9. Haldane, *Russian Newsreel*, p. 172.
10. The story of the diplomats' exodus from Moscow is compiled from the following: Cripps, Diary; Quentin Reynolds, *Only the Stars*, pp. 133–43; Cassidy, *Moscow Dateline*, pp. 111–19; Haldane, *Russian Newsreel*, pp. 160–73; Moats, *Blind Date*, pp. 406–16; Jordan, *Russian Glory*, pp. 93–105; and Admiral Miles, 'Personal Diaries', 15–20 October 1941.
11. Cripps, Diary, various entries, October 1941.
12. Miles, 'Personal Diaries', 20 October 1941.
13. Cassidy, *Moscow Dateline*, p. 114.

Chapter 13: At Chequers

1. Harriman and Abel, *Special Envoy*, p. 111.
2. Gilbert, *Winston S. Churchill*, vol. 6, p. 1265.
3. Martin, *Downing Street Years*, p. 67. There are various accounts of how that evening unfolded: by Churchill, Harriman, and Kathy. All differ slightly. I have presented the most likely narrative.
4. All from Harriman and Abel, *Special Envoy*, pp. 111–12.
5. Gilbert, *Winston S. Churchill*, vol. 6, p. 1268.
6. Martin, *Downing Street Years*, p. 67.
7. Gilbert, *Winston S. Churchill*, vol. 6, p. 1268.
8. Harriman and Abel, *Special Envoy*, p. 112.
9. Both quotations from Gilbert, *Churchill Documents*, vol. 16, p. 1577.
10. Harriman and Abel, *Special Envoy*, p. 112.
11. Kathleen Harriman, Letters, undated but clearly written on 7 December 1941.
12. Gilbert, *Winston S. Churchill*, vol. 6, p. 1629.
13. Kathleen Harriman, Letters, undated but clearly written on 7 December 1941.
14. Harriman and Abel, *Special Envoy*, p. 114.
15. Churchill's account of his time in America is recounted in chapters 35–7 of *Second World War*, vol. 3, pp. 587–629.
16. Chisholm and Davie, *Beaverbrook*, p. 427.
17. Berezhkov, *At Stalin's Side*, p. 202.
18. Cripps, Diary, 4 November 1941.
19. Ibid., 25 November 1941.
20. Ibid.

21. For Cripps's final days in Kuibyshev and Moscow, see Diary, 29 December 1941 to 13 January 1942.
22. Cripps, Diary, 29 July 1941.
23. Unpublished typescript by Geoffrey Wilson, 20 December 1941, IWM, 63/125/1. See also letter, Cripps to Clark Kerr, 12 June 1942, TNA, FO 800/300 29.

Chapter 14: Call Me Archie

1. Bertram, *Shadow of a War*, p. 87.
2. Frank Giles, 'From Russia with Love', *Sunday Times*, 6 January 1980.
3. *Evening Standard*, 25 March 1965.
4. Tom Driberg, *Leader*, 3 February 1945.
5. *The Times*, 20 January 1942.
6. Both from Gillies, *Radical Diplomat*, pp. 78–9.
7. Ibid., p. 39.
8. Letter, Walter Bell to Donald Gillies, 25 July 1991, BNW, MS Eng. c. 6727.
9. Letter, Harold Nicolson to Archibald Clark Kerr, 4 January 1912, Clark Kerr archive, BNW, MS 12101/5.
10. Letter, Harold Nicolson to Archibald Clark Kerr, 3 August 1910, ibid., 12101/4.
11. Harrison Salisbury article, *Collier's*, 25 May 1946.
12. *The Times*, 17 January 1942.
13. *The Times*, 5 February 1942.

Chapter 15: In Stalin's Bunker

1. Clark Kerr archive, BNW, MS 12101/28.
2. Ibid.
3. Elvin, *Cockney in Moscow*, p. 49.
4. Moats, *Blind Date with Mars*, p. 241.
5. Barman, *Diplomatic Correspondent*, p. 139.
6. Letter, Clark Kerr to Cripps, TNA, FO 800/300.
7. Tolley, *Caviar and Commissars*, p. 61.
8. Birse, *Memoirs of an Interpreter*, p. 83.
9. Letter, Clark Kerr to Eden, TNA, FO 800/300.

10. This section is drawn from three principal sources: Clark Kerr's diaries, TNA, FO 800/300; records of the Prime Minister's Office, TNA, PREM 3/395/18, and Clark Kerr archive, BNW, MS 12101/114. This last file contains two long unpublished articles by Clark Kerr: 'Stalin as I Knew Him' and 'Generalissimo Stalin'.

Chapter 16: Spring Thaw

1. As recounted in Taubman, *Khrushchev*, p. 168.
2. Larry LeSueur, *Twelve Months*, p. 161.
3. TNA, FO 371/32878.
4. Clark Kerr archive, BNW, MS 12101/28 2.
5. BNW, MS Eng.c.6727.
6. Ibid.
7. Frank Costigliola, 'Archibald Clark Kerr, Averell Harriman and the Fate of the Wartime Alliance', p. 88.
8. Birse, *Memoirs*, p. 135.
9. BNW, MS Eng.c.6727.
10. Costello, *Mask of Treachery*, p. 191.
11. BNW, MS Eng.c.6727.
12. TNA, FO 800/300.
13. Kathleen Harriman, Letters, 10 May 1942.
14. Ibid.
15. Ibid., 9 September 1942.
16. Sir Stafford Cripps, interview with A. J. Cummins, 1942, https://www.britishpathe.com/ass et/173881/

Chapter 17: Old Bootface

1. Winston Churchill, *Second World War*, vol. 4, p. 301.
2. Maisky, *Diaries*, vol. 3, p. 1266.
3. Dilks (ed.), *Diaries*, p. 454.
4. Maisky, *Memoirs*, p. 266.
5. Roosevelt, *This I Remember*, p. 199.
6. 'Memorandum of Conference Held at the White House, by Mr Samuel H. Cross, Interpreter', 29 May 1942, *Foreign Relations of the United States: Diplomatic Papers, 1942, Europe*, vol. 3, https://history.state.gov/historicaldocuments/frus1942v03/d468

7. 'Memorandum of Conference Held at the White House, by Mr Harry L. Hopkins, Special Assistant to President Roosevelt', 29 May 1942, *Foreign Relations of the United States: Diplomatic Papers, 1942, Europe*, vol. 3, https://history.state.gov/historicaldocuments/frus1942v03/d469; see also Maisky, *Diaries*, vol. 3.
8. 'Memorandum of Conference Held at the White House, by Mr Samuel H. Cross, Interpreter', 30 May 1942, *Foreign Relations of the United States: Diplomatic Papers, 1942, Europe*, vol. 3, https://history.state.gov/historicaldocuments/frus1942v03/d471
9. All from Harriman and Abel, *Special Envoy*, pp. 133–4.
10. Aide-memoire in Winston Churchill, *Second World War*, vol. 4, p. 305.
11. Dilks (ed.), *Diaries*, p. 457.

Chapter 18: Troubled Waters

1. All from Meiklejohn, Diary, 20 February 1943.
2. Ibid., 14 March 1942.
3. Harriman and Abel, *Special Envoy*, p. 142.
4. Ibid., p. 241.
5. All from Maisky, *Diaries*, vol. 3, p. 1307.
6. Gilbert, *Churchill Documents*, vol. 17, p. 964.
7. Harriman and Abel, *Special Envoy*, p. 134.
8. Winston Churchill, *Second World War*, vol. 4, p. 428.
9. Cited in Folly, 'Seeking Comradeship in the "Ogre's Den"'.
10. Winston Churchill, *Second World War*, vol. 4, p. 425.
11. Kathleen Harriman, Letters, n.d., 1942.

Chapter 19: Mission from Hell

1. Harriman and Abel, *Special Envoy*, p. 152.
2. Winston Churchill, *Second World War*, vol. 4, p. 428.
3. All from TNA, FO 800/300.
4. LeSueur, *Twelve Months*, p. 243.
5. Moran, *Churchill*, p. 57.
6. Thompson, *Churchill's Shadow*, p. 96.
7. There are many papers about the Moscow mission in the Averell Harriman archives. Most useful are those in boxes 161 and 165.

8. TNA, FO 800/300/2.
9. All from TNA, FO 800/300.
10. Thompson, *Churchill's Shadow*, p. 97.
11. Berezhkov, *At Stalin's Side*, p. 295.
12. Ibid.
13. TNA, FO 800/300.
14. Bryant, *Turn of the Tide*, p. 460.
15. See WAH, Boxes 161 and 165. See also Harriman and Abel, *Special Envoy*, pp. 149–67.
16. Dilks (ed.), *Diaries*, p. 471.
17. TNA, FO 800/300.
18. Ibid.
19. Cited in Gillies, *Radical Diplomat*, p. 132.
20. TNA, FO 800/300.
21. Bryant, *Turn of the Tide*, p. 466.
22. Tolley, *Caviar and Commissars*, p. 91.
23. Ibid.
24. TNA, FO 800/300.

Chapter 20: A Battle of Wills

1. TNA, FO 800/300/2.
2. This and the following excerpt from ibid.
3. Birse, *Memoirs*, p. 97.
4. TNA, FO 800/300.
5. Ibid.
6. Ibid.
7. Birse, *Memoirs*, pp. 100–1.
8. Berezhkov, *At Stalin's Side*, p. 298.
9. All from Birse, *Memoirs*, p. 102.
10. All from Svetlana Alliluyeva, *Twenty Letters*, pp. 183–4.
11. All from Birse, *Memoirs*, p. 103.
12. Ibid., p. 104.
13. TNA, FO 800/300.
14. Moran, *Churchill*, p. 64.

Chapter 21: Stalin's Lifeline

1. See Alexander Werth, *Russia at War*, pp. 619–29, for a detailed account of Russian industry and its wartime losses. See also Herring, *Aid to Russia*, pp. 30off.
2. Harriman and Abel, *Special Envoy*, p. 165.
3. Ibid., p. 166.
4. Rudy Abramson, *Spanning the Century*, p. 342.
5. 'U. P. Snowplow', *Time*, vol. 40, 1942.
6. Quentin Reynolds, 'Yanks in Iran'.
7. *New York Times*, 27 May 1942.
8. Ibid.
9. Harriman and Abel, *Special Envoy*, p. 167.
10. Ibid., p. 171.
11. Sherwood, *Roosevelt and Hopkins*, p. 626.

Chapter 22: Uncle Joe

1. As cited in Carlton, *Churchill and the Soviet Union*, p. 102.
2. Maisky, *Memoirs*, p. 342.
3. Ibid.
4. Clark Kerr archive, BNW, MS 12101/114.
5. TNA, FO 800/301.
6. Ibid.
7. Geoffrey Roberts, *Stalin's Library*, p. 99.
8. Clark Kerr archive, BNW, MS 12101/114.
9. TNA, CAB 79/87/16.
10. Cited in Gillies, *Radical Diplomat*, p. 141.

Chapter 23: Uncertain Allies

1. Harriman and Abel, *Special Envoy*, p. 177.
2. Ibid., p. 216.
3. David Reynolds and Pechatnov, *Kremlin Letters*, pp. 269–70.
4. Ibid., p. 272.
5. TNA, PREM 3/333/5.

6. David Reynolds and Pechatnov, *Kremlin Letters*, p. 226.
7. All from Maisky, *Diaries*, vol. 3, pp. 1408–10.
8. Ibid., p. 1410.
9. Ibid., pp. 1406 and 1408.
10. TNA, PREM 3 354/8.
11. Maisky, *Diaries*, vol. 3, p. 1423.
12. Ibid., p. 1424.
13. Ibid., p. 1428.
14. TNA, FO 181/966/4.

Chapter 24: Ambassador Averell

1. Harriman and Abel, *Special Envoy*, p. 221.
2. Kathleen Harriman, Letters, September 1943 (no specific date).
3. Winston Churchill, *Second World War*, vol. 5, p. 63.
4. Bryant, *Turn of the Tide*, p. 567.
5. Mary Churchill, *Mary Churchill's War*, p. 219.
6. Gilbert, *Churchill Documents*, vol. 18, pp. 2183–71. Most of the papers covering Harriman and Churchill's visit to Quebec are in WAH, Box 165.
7. Cited in Gilbert, *Churchill Documents*, vol. 18, p. 2200.
8. Harriman and Abel, *Special Envoy*, p. 227.
9. Kathleen Harriman, Letters, October 1943.

Chapter 25: The Deep End

1. Meiklejohn, Diary, 14 October 1943.
2. James Reston, 'War's Casey Jones Gets Aid to Soviets', *New York Times*, 29 April 1943.
3. Meiklejohn, Diary, 'Teheran', October 1943.
4. Meiklejohn, Diary, 14 October 1943.
5. Harriman and Abel, *Special Envoy*, p. 240.
6. Meiklejohn, Diary, 4 November 1943.
7. Alexander Werth, *Russia at War*, p. 748.
8. Harvey, *War Diaries*, pp. 312–18.
9. Ibid., p. 315.
10. Alexander Werth, *Russia at War*, p. 747.

11. Harriman and Abel, *Special Envoy*, p. 244.
12. TNA, FO 800/301.
13. *Full Text of United Nations Documents, 1941–1945*, Royal United Services Institute, 1946, https://archive.org/stream/unitednationsdoc031889mbp/unitednationsdoc031889mbp_djvu.txt
14. Ibid.
15. Meiklejohn, Diary, 21 October 1943.
16. Ibid., 26 October 1943.
17. Alexander Werth, *Russia at War*, pp. 437–8.
18. Ibid., p. 740.
19. Kathleen Harriman, Letters, 9 November 1943.
20. TNA, FO 800/301.
21. Tolley, *Caviar and Commissars*, p. 186.
22. Ibid.
23. Gillies, *Radical Diplomat*, p. 151.
24. TNA, FO 800/301.

Chapter 26: The Real Moscow

1. Kathleen Harriman, Letters, 26 October 1943.
2. Ibid., November 1943.
3. Ibid.
4. Ibid.
5. Ibid., 28 December 1943.
6. Ibid., mid-October 1943.
7. Kathleen Harriman, 'Do the Crows Still Roost in the Spasopeckovskaya Trees?', unpublished typescript.
8. Kathleen Harriman, Letters, 21 January 1944.
9. Ibid., 28 October 1943.
10. Tolley, *Caviar and Commissars*, p. 184.

Chapter 27: In the Ruins of Stalingrad

1. Birse, *Memoirs*, p. 148.
2. Deane, *Strange Alliance*, p. 36.
3. Meiklejohn, Diary, 19–20 November 1943.
4. Birse, *Memoirs*, pp. 149–50.

5. Ibid., p. 150.
6. Meiklejohn, Diary, 19–20 November 1943.
7. Harriman and Abel, *Special Envoy*, p. 257.
8. Meiklejohn, Diary, 19–20 November 1943.
9. Birse, *Memoirs*, p. 151.
10. Harriman and Abel, *Special Envoy*, p. 257.
11. Deane, *Strange Alliance*, p. 38.
12. Birse, *Memoirs*, p. 150.
13. Kathleen Harriman, Letters, 17 November 1943.
14. Ibid., 24 December 1943.
15. Ibid., 26 November 1943.
16. Ibid., 8 March 1944.
17. Martel, *Outspoken Soldier*, p. 257. For more on Martel's work in the Soviet Union, see Lieutenant General Sir Giffard Martel, IWM, GQM 4/1–4/4.

Chapter 28: The Big Three

1. Meiklejohn, Diary, 27 November–2 December 1943.
2. Moran, *Churchill*, p. 133.
3. Meiklejohn, Diary, 27 November–2 December 1943.
4. Bohlen and Phelps, *Witness to History*, p. 135.
5. Harriman and Abel, *Special Envoy*, p. 264.
6. Bohlen and Phelps, *Witness to History*, p. 139.
7. Harriman and Abel, *Special Envoy*, p. 266.
8. Meiklejohn, Diary, 27 November–2 December 1943.
9. Bohlen and Phelps, *Witness to History*, p. 142.
10. Berezhkov, *At Stalin's Side*, p. 237.
11. Birse, *Memoirs*, p. 155.
12. Bohlen and Phelps, *Witness to History*, p. 143.
13. Moran, *Churchill*, p. 135.
14. Bohlen and Phelps, *Witness to History*, p. 146.
15. Harriman and Abel, *Special Envoy*, p. 271.
16. Bohlen and Phelps, *Witness to History*, p. 145.
17. Ibid., p. 148.
18. Moran, *Churchill*, p. 142.
19. Cited in Dilks (ed.), *Diaries*, p. 582.
20. Bohlen and Phelps, *Witness to History*, p. 143.

21. Clark Kerr, unpublished Teheran Diary, BNW, MS 12101/43.
22. Dilks (ed.), *Diaries*, p. 582.
23. Moran, *Churchill*, p. 141.
24. Winston Churchill, *Second World War*, vol. 5, p. 330.
25. Moran, *Churchill*, p. 141.
26. Both quotations are from Bohlen and Phelps, *Witness to History*, p. 146.
27. Birse, *Memoirs*, p. 157.
28. Moran, *Churchill*, p. 136.
29. Cited in Harriman and Abel, *Special Envoy*, p. 265.
30. Winston Churchill, *Second World War*, vol. 5, p. 339.
31. Birse, *Memoirs*, p. 160.
32. Ibid.
33. Harriman and Abel, *Special Envoy*, p. 276.
34. WAH, Box 170. This contains a wealth of material pertaining to the Teheran Conference.
35. Bohlen and Phelps, *Witness to History*, p. 150.
36. Ibid.
37. Ismay, *Memoirs*, p. 341.
38. Harriman and Abel, *Special Envoy*, p. 282.
39. Ibid., p. 279.
40. Bohlen and Phelps, *Witness to History*, pp. 151–2.
41. Sherwood, *Roosevelt and Hopkins*, p. 789.
42. 'Memorandum by the First Secretary of Embassy in the Soviet Union (Bohlen)', 15 December 1943, *Foreign Relations of the United States: Diplomatic Papers, The Conferences at Cairo and Tehran, 1943*, vol. 5, p. 846.

Chapter 29: Christmas in Moscow

1. Clark Kerr archive, BNW, MS 12101/91, Folder 2.
2. Ibid., Folder 3.
3. As cited in K. Young (ed.), *Diaries*, p. 394.
4. Kathleen Harriman, Letters, n.d., probably December 1943.

Chapter 30: Into the Forest

1. This chapter is based on three principal sources: Kathleen Harriman, Letters (various, all dated January/February 1944); memoranda written

by Kathleen Harriman and John Melby, interspersed with the letters and press cuttings; WAH, Box 187.

2. *New York Times*, 27 January 1944.
3. Ibid.

Chapter 31: Behind the Soviet Curtain

1. Kathleen Harriman, Letters, 12 April 1944.
2. The account of lunch with Tolstoy is from Kathleen Harriman, Letters, 22 March 1944.
3. Harriman and Abel, *Special Envoy*, p. 299.
4. Lyons, *Assignment in Utopia*, p. 587.
5. Birse, *Memoirs*, p. 99.
6. Ibid., p. 100.
7. Kathleen Harriman, Letters, 4 June 1945.
8. Barman, *Diplomatic Correspondent*, p. 156.
9. Hill, 'Reminiscences', p. 148.
10. Ibid., p. 155.

Chapter 32: Sunshine in Moscow

1. Harriman and Abel, *Special Envoy*, p. 306.
2. Ibid., pp. 296ff.
3. Meiklejohn, Diary, 31 January–6 February 1944.
4. WAH, Box 188. This contains a great deal of information about the US air bases in the Soviet Union.
5. Harriman and Abel, *Special Envoy*, p. 311. See also WAH, Box 872.
6. Harriman and Abel, *Special Envoy*, p. 311.
7. Kathleen Harriman, Letters, 3 June 1944.
8. Deane, *Strange Alliance*, p. 119.
9. Kathleen Harriman, Letters, 4 June 1944.
10. TNA, FO 800/300, part 1.

Chapter 33: D-Day

1. Kathleen Harriman, Letters, 9 June 1944.
2. Meiklejohn, Diary, 6 June 1944.

3. Kathleen Harriman, Letters, 9 June 1944.
4. Harriman and Abel, *Special Envoy*, pp. 314 and 350.
5. Deane, *Strange Alliance*, p. 151.

Chapter 34: Poles Apart

1. Kathleen Harriman, Letters, 12 April 1944.
2. Ibid., 14 June 1944.
3. Kathleen Harriman, Letters, 6 July 1944.
4. Ibid.
5. Meiklejohn, Diary, 12 July 1944.
6. Harriman and Abel, *Special Envoy*, p. 324.
7. See ibid., chapter 14, for a detailed overview of Stalin's views on Poland.
8. Birse, *Memoirs*, p. 169.
9. Harriman and Abel, *Special Envoy*, p. 333.
10. See Bór-Komorowski, *Secret Army*, p. 213.
11. Harriman and Abel, *Special Envoy*, p. 338.
12. Ibid., p. 340.
13. Ibid., p. 349.
14. Ibid., p. 337.
15. Clark Kerr archive, BNW, MS 12101/114.
16. Cited in Gillies, *Radical Diplomat*, p. 160.
17. Harriman and Abel, *Special Envoy*, p. 344.

Chapter 35: The Face of War

1. Kathleen Harriman, Letters, 19 June 1944.
2. Various Kathleen Harriman Letters, August 1944.
3. Birse, *Memoirs*, p. 167, and Meiklejohn, Diary, 17 July 1944.
4. Meiklejohn, Diary, 1 September 1944.
5. Kathleen Harriman, Letters, 20 August 1944.

Chapter 36: Churchill's Naughty Document

1. Nel, *Mr. Churchill's Secretary*, p. 141.
2. Moran, *Churchill*, p. 191.

3. Harriman and Abel, *Special Envoy*, p. 352.
4. Ibid., p. 354.
5. TNA, FO 800/300/3.
6. Ibid.
7. Churchill, *Second World War*, vol. 6, p. 198.
8. Ibid.
9. Harriman and Abel, *Special Envoy*, p. 358.
10. Moran, *Churchill*, p. 200.
11. All from Birse, *Memoirs*, pp. 169ff.
12. Jacob, *Window in Moscow*, p. 247.
13. Birse, *Memoirs*, p. 174.
14. Ibid.
15. Kathleen Harriman, Letters, 16 October 1944.
16. Meiklejohn, Diary, 14 October 1944.
17. 'Memorandum of Conversation', 14 October 1944. WAH, Box 174.
18. Kathleen Harriman, Letters, 16 October 1944.
19. Churchill, *Second World War*, vol. 6, p. 200.
20. Nel, *Mr. Churchill's Secretary*, pp. 148–9.
21. Moran, *Churchill*, p. 204.
22. Jacob, *Window in Moscow*, p. 259.
23. Churchill, *Second World War*, vol. 6, p. 212.

Chapter 37: Archie's Moscow Masseur

1. TNA, FO 371/47941.
2. *Sunday Dispatch*, 24 December 1944.
3. *Sunday Times Weekly Review*, 6 January 1980.

Chapter 38: The Future of the World

1. Meiklejohn, Diary, pp. 611ff.
2. Birse, *Memoirs*, p. 178.
3. Ibid., p. 617.
4. Sarah Churchill, *Keep on Dancing*, p. 74.
5. Bohlen and Phelps, *Witness to History*, p. 173.
6. Harriman and Abel, *Special Envoy*, p. 388.
7. Birse, *Memoirs*, p. 183.

8. Dilks (ed.), *Diaries*, p. 707.
9. Kathleen Harriman Letters and Pamela Churchill Harriman Archive, Kathy to Pamela, 4 February 1945.
10. Birse, *Memoirs*, p. 182.
11. Bohlen and Phelps, *Witness to History*, p. 180.
12. Harriman and Abel, *Special Envoy*, p. 391.
13. Bohlen and Phelps, *Witness to History*, p. 178.
14. Harriman and Abel, *Special Envoy*, p. 395.
15. Pamela Churchill Harriman Archive, see letters dated 30 January and 13 February 1944.
16. Bohlen and Phelps, *Witness to History*, p. 188.
17. Ibid., p. 178.
18. Untitled and undated handwritten note, Kathleen Harriman, Letters, February 1944.
19. Telegram, 'The Secretary of State to the Acting Secretary of State (Grew)', 8 February 1945, *Foreign Relations of the United States: Diplomatic Papers, Conferences at Malta and Yalta, 1945*, Doc. 402.
20. Cited in Sebag Montefiore, *Stalin*, p. 483.
21. Harriman and Abel, *Special Envoy*, p. 416.
22. Birse, *Memoirs*, pp. 184–5.
23. 'Bohlen Minutes', 8 February 1945, *Foreign Relations of the United States: Diplomatic Papers, Conferences at Malta and Yalta*, Doc. 403.
24. Cited in Katz, *Daughters of Yalta*, p. 233.
25. Cited in Sherwood, *Roosevelt and Hopkins*, p. 870.

Chapter 39: Averell Goes Rogue

1. The relevant correspondence is in David Reynolds and Pechatnov, *Kremlin Letters*, p. 570ff.
2. Gilbert, *Winston S. Churchill*, vol. 7, p. 1283.
3. David Reynolds and Pechatnov, *Kremlin Letters*, p. 582.
4. Harriman and Abel, *Special Envoy*, p. 405.
5. Meiklejohn, Diary, 12 April 1945.
6. David Reynolds and Pechatnov, *Kremlin Letters*, p. 582.
7. Meiklejohn, Diary, 12 April 1945.
8. All from Harriman and Abel, *Special Envoy*, pp. 440ff.
9. Thomas, *Armed Truce*, p. 301.
10. TNA, FO 371/47941.

11. All from WAH, Box 11.
12. Both from Harriman and Abel, *Special Envoy*, pp. 502–3.
13. Meiklejohn, Diary, 7 May 1945.
14. Harriman and Abel, *Special Envoy*, p. 459.
15. The story of the horses is also in ibid., p. 475.
16. A comprehensive breakdown of Lend-Lease deliveries, including an analysis of costs and benefits, can be found in Jones, *Roads to Russia*, pp. 215–39.
17. Khrushchev, *Memoirs*, vol. 1, p. 639.
18. Harriman and Abel, *Special Envoy*, pp. 535–6.
19. All from *Sunday Times Weekly Review*, 8 January 1980.
20. FO 800/300/2, letter dated 2 February 1946.

Afterlives

1. All from Bedell Smith, *Reflected Glory*, pp. 264ff.
2. Cited in Abramson, *Spanning the Century*, p. 685.
3. *Sunday Times Weekly Review*, 8 January 1980.
4. TNA, FO 800/514/119.
5. Cited in Gillies, *Radical Diplomat*, p. 213.
6. All in Clark Kerr archive, BNW, MS 12101/114.
7. Cited in Geoffrey Roberts, 'Correspondence'.
8. Ibid.
9. Ibid., and author interview with Kathy's son, David Mortimer.
10. *New York Times*, 26 December 1946. See also Herring, *Aid to Russia*, Appendix: 'Lend-Lease Settlement Negotiations'; Winston Churchill, speech at Westminster College, Fulton, Missouri, 5 March 1946, https://www.nationalchurchillmuseum.org/sinews-of-peace-iron-curtain-speech.html
11. *New York Times*, 14 March 1946. See also David Reynolds and Pechatnov, *Kremlin Letters*, p. 592.

Bibliography

Primary Sources, Unpublished

Balfour, Captain Harold, 'Moscow Diary', typescript, PA BAL 1–BAL 2

Beaverbrook, Lord, 'Mission to Moscow' and assorted papers, PA BBK/D, especially BBK/D/90–1 and BBK/D/99

Cadbury, L. J., 'Letters from Moscow', privately printed booklet, 1941, IWM Docs 17085

Churchill, Mary, Diaries, 1941 and 1945, manuscript, CAC, MCHL 1/1/3–4 (1941) and MCHL 1/1/14–15 (1945)

Clark Kerr, Sir Archibald, Diaries, letters, memoranda, and official and unofficial papers, TNA, FO 800/300/1–FO 800/303/2

——, Office diaries, letters, memoranda, and assorted papers including two typescripts, 'Stalin as I Knew Him' and 'Generalissimo Stalin', BNW, MS 12101–12101/141

Cripps, Sir Stafford, Diary, BNW, MS 9661/7–10

Drax, Admiral Sir Reginald Plunkett-Ernle-Erle, 'Mission to Moscow', typescript, CAC, GBR/0014/DRAX 6/5

Exham, Colonel Kenneth, 'Colonel Exham's Papers', TNA, WO 178/92

Gillies, Donald, Working papers of Donald Gillies, biographer of Archibald Clark Kerr, BNW, MS Eng.c.6721–6725

Harriman, Kathleen, Letters, assorted private papers and press cuttings, including short typescript, 'Do the Crows Still Roost in the Spasopeckovskaya Trees?', private collection at time of research, now in MDLoC (as yet uncatalogued)

Harriman, Pamela Digby Churchill, Letters to Kathleen and Averell Harriman, MDLoC, https://catalog.loc.gov/vwebv/search?searchCode=LCCN&searchArg=mm%2098084292&searchType=1&permalink=y

Harriman, W. Averell, Papers, MDLoC, https://catalog.loc.gov/vwebv/search?searchCode=LCCN&searchArg=mm%2085061911&searchType=1&permalink=y

——, Interview, https://wayback.archive-it.org/org-419/20230105143654/ https://livinghistory.sanford.duke.edu/interview/averell-harriman/

——, Oral interview, https://digitalarchive.wilsoncenter.org/document/209788.pdf?v=d41d8cd98f00b204e9800998ecf8427e

——, Oral interview, IWM 2884

Hill, George, 'Reminiscences of Four Years with NKVD', typescript, 1945, Hoover Institution Library and Archives, George Alexander Hill Papers, 68002

Lunghi, Hugh, Papers, CAC, GBR/0014/LUNG especially LUNG 1/1–3 and 1/6

——, Interview, https://nsarchive2.gwu.edu/coldwar/interviews/episode-1/lunghi7.html

Meiklejohn, Robert, 'Robert Pickens Meiklejohn World War Two Diary at London and Moscow, March 10, 1941–February 14, 1946', WAH, Box 211 https://catalog.loc.gov/vwebv/search?searchCode=LCCN&searchArg=mm%2085061911&searchType=1&permalink=y

Miles, Admiral Sir Geoffrey, 'Personal Diaries, 1937–1947', handwritten manuscript, Royal Museums Greenwich, London, MLS/9 and MLS/13

Roberts, Frank, Interview, https://nsarchive2.gwu.edu/coldwar/interviews/episode-1/roberts1.html

——, and George Urban, 'A Diplomat Remembers Stalin', *The World Today*, vol. 46, no. 11, 1990, 208–13, http://www.jstor.org/stable/40396160

Symonds, Colonel Guy, 'Report on Col. Symonds' Visit to Moscow, 3 July to 16 August 1941', typescript, TNA, HO 216/29

Primary Sources, Published

Alliluyeva, Svetlana, *Twenty Letters to a Friend*, HarperCollins, 2016

Balfour, John, *Not Too Correct an Aureole*, Michael Russell, 1983

Barman, Thomas, *Diplomatic Correspondent*, Hamish Hamilton, 1969

Beaton, Cecil, *The Years Between: Diaries 1939–44*, Sapere Books, 2018

Berezhkov, Valentin Mikhailovich, *At Stalin's Side*, Carol Publishing, 1994

Birse, Arthur Herbert, *Memoirs of an Interpreter*, Michael Joseph, 1967

Bohlen, Charles E., and Robert Howard Phelps, *Witness to History, 1929–1969*, Weidenfeld & Nicolson, 1973

Bór-Komorowski, Tadeusz, *The Secret Army: The Memoirs of General Bór-Komorowski*, Frontline, 2010

Bourke-White, Margaret, *Shooting the Russian War: Written and Photographed by M. Bourke-White*, Simon & Schuster, 1943

——, *The Taste of War*, Trafalgar Square, 1985

Brown, James E., *Russia Fights*, Charles Scribner's Sons, 1943

Bryant, Sir Arthur, *Turn of the Tide: A History of the War Years Based on the Diaries of Field-Marshal Lord Alanbrooke, Chief of the Imperial General Staff*, Doubleday, 1957

Cassidy, Henry Clarence, *Moscow Dateline 1941–1943*, Cassell, 1943

Churchill, Mary (ed. Emma Soames), *Mary Churchill's War*, Simon & Schuster, 2022

Churchill, Sarah, *Keep on Dancing: An Autobiography*, Weidenfeld & Nicolson, 1981

Colville, John, *The Fringes of Power: Downing Street Diaries 1939–1955*, Hodder & Stoughton, 1986

Cowles, Virginia, *Looking for Trouble*, Hamish Hamilton, 1941

Davies, Joseph Edward, *Mission to Moscow*, Victor Gollancz, 1944

Deane, John, *The Strange Alliance*, John Murray, 1946

Dilks, David (ed.), *The Diaries of Sir Alexander Cadogan, O.M., 1938–1945*, Cassell, 1972

Djilas, Milovan, *Conversations with Stalin*, Penguin, 2014

Eden, Anthony, *The Eden Memoirs*, vol. 2, *The Reckoning: 1938–1945*, Cassell, 1965

Elvin, Harold, *A Cockney in Moscow*, Cresset Press, 1958

Gilbert, Martin, *The Churchill Documents*, 21 vols, Heinemann, 1993–2018

Gilmore, Eddy, *Me and My Russian Wife*, Country Life Press, 1968

Haldane, Charlotte, *Russian Newsreel*, Secker & Warburg, 1943

Harriman, William Averell, and Elie Abel, *Special Envoy to Churchill and Stalin, 1941–1946*, Random House, 1975

Harvey, Oliver (ed. John Harvey), *The War Diaries of Oliver Harvey 1941–1945*, Collins, 1978

Heffer, Simon (ed.), *Henry 'Chips' Channon: The Diaries*, vol. 1, *1918–38*, Hutchinson, 2021

Hindus, Maurice Gerschon, *Mother Russia*, Doubleday, Doran, 1943

Ismay, Lionel, *The Memoirs of General the Lord Ismay K.G., P.C., G.C.B., C.H., D.S.O.*, Heinemann, 1960

Jacob, Alaric, *A Window in Moscow, 1944–45*, Collins, 1946

Johnstone, Archie, *In the Name of Peace*, Foreign Languages Publishing House, 1952

Jordan, Philip Furneaux, *Russian Glory*, Cresset Press, 1942

Kerr, Walter, *The Russian Army*, Victor Gollancz, 1944

——, *The Secret of Stalingrad*, Doubleday, 1978

Khrushchev, Nikita (trans. Serge Khrushchev), *Memoirs of Nikita Khrushchev*, vol. 1, *Commissar, 1918–1945*, Pennsylvania State University Press, 2004
Lauterbach, Richard Edward, *These Are the Russians*, Harper & Brothers, 1945
Lawrence, John, *Life in Russia*, George Allen & Unwin, 1947
Lehmann, John, *I Am My Brother*, Longmans, 1960
LeSueur, Larry, *Twelve Months That Changed the World*, Harrap, 1943
Lyons, Eugene, *Assignment in Utopia*, Harcourt, Brace, 1937
Maclean, Fitzroy, *Eastern Approaches*, Penguin, 2009
Maisky, I. M., et al., *Memoirs of a Soviet Ambassador*, Scribner, 1968
——, *The Complete Maisky Diaries: Vols 1–3*, Yale University Press, 2018
Martel, Sir Giffard, *An Outspoken Soldier*, Sifton Praed, 1949
Martin, Sir John, *Downing Street: The War Years*, Bloomsbury, 1991
Moats, Alice-Leone, *Blind Date with Mars*, Doubleday, Doran, 1943
Molotov, V. M., and Feliz Chuev, *Molotov Remembers*, Ivan R. Dee, 2007
Moran, Charles McMoran Wilson, *Churchill: Taken from the Diaries of Lord Moran: The Struggle for Survival, 1940–1965*, Constable, 1966
Nel, Elizabeth, *Mr. Churchill's Secretary*, Coward McCann, 1958
Read-Jahn, Shirley, *Hidden in Plain Sight: A British Military Agent's Story*, privately published, 2019
Reynolds, Quentin, *Only the Stars Are Neutral*, Cassell, 1942
——, *The Curtain Rises*, Random House, 1944
Roosevelt, Eleanor, *This I Remember*, Praeger, 1975
Shirer, William L., *The Rise and Fall of the Third Reich: A History of Nazi Germany*, Simon & Schuster, 2011
Soames, Mary (ed.), *Speaking for Themselves: The Personal Letters of Winston and Clementine Churchill*, Doubleday, 1998
Standley, William Harrison, and Arthur Ainsley Ageton, *Admiral Ambassador to Russia*, Henry Regnery, 1955
Stimson, Henry, *On Active Service in Peace and War*, Hutchinson, 1949
Thayer, Charles Wheeler, *Bears in the Caviar*, Michael Joseph, 1951
Thompson, William Henry, *I Was Churchill's Shadow*, C. Johnson, 1959
Tolley, Kemp, *Caviar and Commissars*, US Naval Institute Press, 1983
Werth, Alexander, *Moscow '41*, Hamish Hamilton, 1942
——, *Russia at War 1941–1945: A History*, Skyhorse, 2017
Wilgress, Dana, *Memoirs*, Ryerson Press, 1967
Winterton, Paul, *Report on Russia*, Cresset Press, 1945
Young, K. (ed.), *The Diaries of Sir Robert Bruce Lockhart 1939–1965*, Macmillan, 1980

Secondary Sources

Periodical articles

Barcella, Ernest, 'The American Who Knows Stalin Best', *Collier's*, 3 May 1952

Brenner, Marie, 'To War in Silk Stockings', *Vanity Fair*, 18 April 2018, https://www.vanityfair.com/style/2018/04/to-war-in-silk-stockings-kathleen-mortimer

Clemens, Diane S., 'Averell Harriman, John Deane, the Joint Chiefs of Staff, and the "Reversal of Co-Operation" with the Soviet Union in April 1945', *International History Review* 14, no. 2, 1992, 277–306, http://www.jstor.org/stable/40792748

Cockett, R. B., '"In Wartime Every Objective Reporter Should Be Shot": The Experience of British Press Correspondents in Moscow, 1941–5', *Journal of Contemporary History* 23, no. 4, 1988, 15–30, http://www.jstor.org/stable/260832

Costigliola, Frank, 'After Roosevelt's Death: Dangerous Emotions, Divisive Discourses, and the Abandoned Alliance', *Diplomatic History* 34, no. 1, 2010, 1–23, http://www.jstor.org/stable/24916031

——, 'Archibald Clark Kerr, Averell Harriman and the Fate of the Wartime Alliance', *Journal of Transatlantic Studies* 9, no. 2, 2011, 83–97

——, 'Pamela Churchill, Wartime London, and the Making of the Special Relationship', *Diplomatic History* 36, no. 4, 2012, 753–62, http://www.jstor.org/stable/44376171

'Day in the Forest', *Time*, 7 February 1944

Eyck, Gunther, 'Secretary Stimson and the European War', *US Army War College Quarterly: Parameters* 2, no. 1, 1972

Folly, Martin H., 'Seeking Comradeship in the "Ogre's Den": Winston Churchill's Quest for a Warrior Alliance and His Mission to Stalin, August 1942', Brunel University, 2007, https://bura.brunel.ac.uk/bitstream/2438/5738/2/Fulltext.pdf

——, 'British Attempts to Forge a Political Partnership with the Kremlin, 1942–3', *Journal of Contemporary History* 53, no. 1, 2018, 185–211, https://www.jstor.org/stable/26416683

Giles, Frank, 'From Russia with Love', *Sunday Times*, 8 January 1980

Hanak, H., 'Sir Stafford Cripps as British Ambassador in Moscow May 1940 to June 1941', *English Historical Review* 94, no. 370, 1979, 48–70, http://www.jstor.org/stable/567157

Hess, Rae Richard, 'Convoy to Murmansk', *Collier's*, 31 October 1942

Jelavich, Barbara, 'British Observers of Soviet Affairs, 1917–1939', *Russian Review* 51, no. 3, 1992, 408–17, https://doi.org/10.2307/131120

'Lend-Lease to Russia', *Life*, 29 March 1943

Lukes, Igor, 'Ambassador Laurence Steinhardt: From New York to Prague', *Diplomacy and Statecraft* 17, no. 3, 523–45, https://doi.org/10.1080/09592290600867610

Mastny, Vojtech, 'Stalin and the Prospects of a Separate Peace in World War II', *American Historical Review* 77, no. 5, 1972, 1365–88, https://doi.org/10.2307/1861311

Mayers, David, 'Soviet War Aims and the Grand Alliance: George Kennan's Views, 1944–1946', *Journal of Contemporary History* 21, no. 1, 1986, 57–79, http://www.jstor.org/stable/260472

——, 'The Great Patriotic War, FDR's Embassy Moscow, and Soviet-US Relations', *International History Review* 33, no. 2, 2011, 299–333, http://www.jstor.org/stable/23032806

Moats, Alice-Leone, 'The Legend of Sir Stafford Cripps', *American Mercury*, July 1942

Pechatnov, Vladimir O., 'The Rise and Fall of Britansky Soyuznik: A Case Study in Soviet Response to British Propaganda of the Mid-1940s', *Historical Journal* 41, no. 1, 1998, 293–301, http://www.jstor.org/stable/2640154

Reynolds, Quentin, 'Russians Learn Fast', *Collier's*, 4 September 1941

——, 'City of Courage', *Collier's*, 8 November 1941

——, 'Voice of Russia', *Collier's*, 13 December 1941

——, 'I Don't Like to Travel', *Collier's*, 7 March 1942

——, 'Russia Uncensored', *Collier's*, 25 April 1942

——, 'The Road to Vyazma', *National Weekly*, 19 June 1943

——, 'Diplomat on the Spot', *Collier's*, 24 July 1943

——, 'Yanks in Iran', *Collier's*, 15 January 1944

Roberts, Geoffrey, 'The Correspondence of Kathleen Harriman', *Harriman Magazine*, winter 2015, http://www.columbia.edu/cu/creative/epub/harriman/2015/winter/kathleen_harriman.pdf

Ross, Graham, 'Foreign Office Attitudes to the Soviet Union 1941–45', *Journal of Contemporary History* 16, no. 3, 1981, 521–40, http://www.jstor.org/stable/260319

'Russia: Willkie and the Bear', *Time*, 5 October 1942

Salisbury, Harrison E., 'Britain's Hot-Spot Man', *Collier's*, 25 May 1946

Searle, Alaric, *Uneasy Intelligence Collaboration, Genuine Ill Will, with an Admixture of Ideology: The British Military Mission to the Soviet Union, 1941–1945*, University of Salford, 2007

Skariatuna, Irina, 'I Heard Russia Sighing', *Collier's*, 31 October 1942

Strauss, Patricia, 'Red Squire', *Collier's*, 15 November 1941

Sunseri, Alvin R., 'Patrick J. Hurley at the Battle of Stalingrad: An Oral History Interview', *Military Affairs* 50, no. 2, 1986, 88–92, https://doi.org/10.2307/1987792

Watson, Derek, 'Molotov and the Moscow Conference, October 1943', Centre for Russian and East European Studies, University of Birmingham, n.d.

Willkie, Wendell, 'Stalin: "Glad to See You, Mr. Willkie"', *Life*, 5 October 1942

Books and monographs

Abramson, Rudy, *Spanning the Century*, William Morrow, 1992

Bedell Smith, Sally, *Reflected Glory*, Simon & Schuster, 2013

Beevor, Antony, *The Second World War*, Weidenfeld & Nicolson, 2014

Bertram, James, *The Shadow of a War*, Victor Gollancz, 1947

Bourne, Kenneth, and D. Cameron Watt (eds), *British Documents on Foreign Affairs*, Part II, series A, vol. 15, *The Soviet Union 1917–1939*, Appendix II, 'Leading Personalities in the Soviet Union', 1939

Braithwaite, Roderick, *Moscow 1941: A City and Its People at War*, Profile, 2006

Brendon, Piers, *The Dark Valley: A Panorama of the 1930s*, Vintage, 2000

Butler, Ewan, *Mason Mac: The Life of Lieutenant-General Sir Noel Mason-Macfarlane*, Macmillan, 1972

Carlton, David, *Churchill and the Soviet Union*, Manchester University Press, 2000

Chisholm, Anne, and Michael Davie, *Beaverbrook: A Life*, Pimlico, 1993

Churchill, Winston Spencer, *The Second World War*, 6 vols, Cassell, 1948–53

Costello, John, *Mask of Treachery*, William Morrow, 1988

Cumins, Keith, *Cataclysm: The War on the Eastern Front 1941–45*, Helion, 2011

Dimbleby, Jonathan, *Barbarossa: How Hitler Lost the War*, Viking, 2021

Foreign Relations of the United States: Diplomatic Papers, Europe: Union of Soviet Socialist Republics, assorted volumes, US Government Printing Office, 1941–5

——, *Diplomatic Papers: The Conferences at Malta and Yalta, 1945*, US Government Printing Office, 1955

——, *Diplomatic Papers: The Conferences at Cairo and Tehran, 1943*, US Government Printing Office, 1961

Gilbert, Martin, *Winston S. Churchill*, 8 vols, Heinemann, 1966–88

Gillies, Donald, *Radical Diplomat*, I. B. Tauris, 1999

Glantz, David, *Barbarossa: Hitler's Invasion of Russia 1941*, Tempus, 2001

Glees, Anthony, *The Secrets of the Service*, Jonathan Cape, 1987

Gorodetsky, Gabriel, *Grand Delusion: Stalin and the German Invasion of Russia*, Yale University Press, 1999

——, *Stafford Cripps' Mission to Moscow, 1940–42*, Cambridge University Press, 2002

Gourlay, Logan, *The Beaverbrook I Knew*, Quartet, 1984

Herring, George C., Jr, *Aid to Russia, 1941–1946*, Columbia University Press, 1973

Holmes, Richard, *The World at War: The Landmark Oral History from the Classic TV Series*, Ebury, 2011

Jones, Robert H., *The Roads to Russia: United States Lend-Lease to the Soviet Union*, University of Oklahoma Press, 1969

Katz, Catherine Grace, *The Daughters of Yalta: The Churchills, Roosevelts, and Harrimans: A Story of Love and War*, Houghton Mifflin, 2020

Kotkin, Stephen, *Stalin*, vol. 2, *Waiting for Hitler, 1928–1941*, Allen Lane, 2018

Lindsay, Michael, *The Unknown War*, Foreign Languages Press, 1975

McMeekin, Sean, *Stalin's War: A New History of World War II*, Basic Books, 2021

Mayers, David, *The Ambassadors and America's Soviet Policy*, Oxford University Press, 1997

Moorhouse, Roger, *The Devils' Alliance: Hitler's Pact with Stalin, 1939–41*, Bodley Head, 2014

Motter, T. H., *United States Army in World War II: The Middle East Theater: The Persian Corridor and Aid to Russia*, US Army Center of Military History, Washington, DC, 1952, https://history.army.mil/books/wwii/persian/index.htm#contents

Overy, R. J., *Russia's War*, Penguin, 2010

Plokhy, Serhii, *Forgotten Bastards of the Eastern Front: American Airmen Behind the Soviet Lines and the Collapse of the Grand Alliance*, Oxford University Press, 2019

Ponting, Clive, *Churchill*, Sinclair-Stevenson, 1994

Preston, Diana, *Eight Days at Yalta*, Atlantic, 2020

Purnell, Sonia, *First Lady: The Life and Wars of Clementine Churchill*, Aurum, 2015

Reynolds, David, Warren Kimball, and A. O. Chubarian (eds), *Allies at War: The Soviet, American, and British Experience, 1939–1945*, Macmillan, 1994

Reynolds, David, and Vladimir Pechatnov, *The Kremlin Letters: Stalin's Wartime Correspondence with Churchill and Roosevelt*, Yale University Press, 2018

Roberts, Andrew, *Churchill: Walking with Destiny*, Viking, 2019

Roberts, Geoffrey, *Stalin's Library: A Dictator and His Books*, Yale University Press, 2022

Roll, David L., *The Hopkins Touch: Harry Hopkins and the Forging of the Alliance to Defeat Hitler*, Oxford University Press, 2013

Ross, Graham, *The Foreign Office and the Kremlin*, Cambridge University Press, 1984

Sebag Montefiore, Simon, *Stalin: The Court of the Red Tsar*, Weidenfeld & Nicolson, 2004

Service, Robert, *Stalin: A Biography*, Macmillan, 2004

Sherwood, Robert E., *Roosevelt and Hopkins*, Harper, 1950

Stettinius, Edward Reilly, *Lend-Lease*, Penguin, 1944

Taubman, William, *Khrushchev: The Man and His Era*, W. W. Norton, 2003

Thomas, Hugh, *Armed Truce*, Atheneum, 1987

Thompson, Sherry, and Jenny Thompson, *The Kremlinologist: America's Man in Cold War Moscow*, Johns Hopkins University Press, 2018

Toland, John, *Adolf Hitler*, Doubleday, 1976

Watt, Donald Cameron, and Kenneth Bourne, *British Documents on Foreign Affairs – Reports and Papers from the Foreign Office Confidential Print, Part II, Series A, the Soviet Union 1917–1939, Vol. 15, Jan–Sept 1939*, University Publications of America, 1984

Werth, Nicholas, et al., *The Black Book of Communism: Crimes, Terror, Repression*, Harvard University Press, 1999

Williams, Charles, *Beaverbrook: Not Quite a Gentleman*, Biteback, 2019

Index

Page numbers in italic denote illustrations.